Learning Flex 3

Learning Flex™ 3

Getting up to Speed with Rich Internet Applications

Alaric Cole

Beijing · Cambridge · Farnham · Köln · Sebastopol · Taipei · Tokyo

Learning Flex 3
Getting up to Speed with Rich Internet Applications
by Alaric Cole

Published by O'Reilly Media, Inc., 1005 Gravenstein Highway North, Sebastopol, CA 95472.

O'Reilly Media books may be purchased for educational, business, or sales promotional use. Online editions are also available for most titles (*safari.oreilly.com*). For more information, contact our corporate/institutional sales department: 800-998-9938 or *corporate@oreilly.com*.

Editor: Robyn G. Thomas

Production Editor: Michele Filshie

Copy Editor: Kim Wimpsett

Technical Reviewer: Allen Rabinovich

Proofreader: Nancy Bell

Interior Designer: Ron Bilodeau

Composition: David Van Ness

Cover Designer: Matthew Woodruff and Karen Montgomery, based on a series design by Mark Paglietti

Indexer: Ted Laux

Print History:

June 2008:   First edition.

 This book uses RepKover™, a durable and flexible lay-flat binding.

ISBN: 978-0-596-51732-8
[F]

Adobe Developer Library, a copublishing partnership between O'Reilly Media Inc. and Adobe Systems, Inc., is the authoritative resource for developers using Adobe technologies. These comprehensive resources offer learning solutions to help developers create cutting-edge interactive web applications that can reach virtually anyone on any platform.

With top-quality books and innovative online resources covering the latest tools for rich-Internet application development, the *Adobe Developer Library* delivers expert training, straight from the source. Topics include ActionScript, Adobe Flex®, Adobe Flash®, and Adobe Acrobat® software.

Get the latest news about books, online resources, and more at *adobedeveloper-library.com*.

CONTENTS

Chapter 4
Using Source Mode 37

Chapter 5
Learning the Basics of Scripting 47

Chapter 6
Adding Interactivity with ActionScript 63

Chapter 10

Gathering and Displaying Data

Chapter 11

Controlling Flow and Visibility

Chapter 12

Working with View States

Chapter 13

Applying Behaviors, Transitions, and Filters

Chapter 14
Styling Applications 219

Chapter 15
Deploying Your Application 239

Index 265

PREFACE

A lot of software developers cut their teeth on learning COBOL, Pascal, or one of those other programming languages that have stuck around for years. I didn't learn programming that way. I didn't take computer science courses in school. I studied anthropology.

Being a developer was not something I imagined I would ever do for a living. I did enjoy creating graphics and building websites, though, and I supported myself through school doing just that. I found that I wanted to create some fancy animated content for a website, so I decided to spend a weekend and learn the Flash IDE. I was too cheap to buy a good book, so I spent a lot of time perusing the included documentation. Hours later, I figured out how to animate a line drawing I had made. Ecstatic, I dove through the documentation, learning more and more. What started as a weekend experiment turned into a weekly passion, as I slowly progressed from simple timeline animations into scripting.

Flash was cool. I could take text and render it as a graphic, something I couldn't do with regular old HTML and JavaScript (DHTML). It also empowered me to build applications on the Web that were not possible at the time with DHTML. I could get data from a remote computer such as the weather forecast and display it right in my Flash content, with complete control over the look and feel. I could have a user send an email through Flash without having to refresh the web page. I could display a photo gallery on my site, rotating the photos, adding borders, and making it look like a real photo album. I was hooked.

As the language of Flash, ActionScript, matured, I grew along with it. I found that as my imagination led me to create richer experiences, the code I was required to write became more and more complex. No longer just scripting one-offs, I was learning real programming. I was pushing Flash beyond its limits and had to continually find ways of making my code more readable and maintainable. I found myself longing for a better way.

Then along came Flex. It was far from perfect in its first iteration, but I knew it was going to stick. For once, I could create my applications with simple, structured XML, which felt comfortably like the HTML I had been using all along. Flex made sense, and it helped me to build complex applications more quickly and easily than ever before.

I wasn't the only one who felt this way. As Flex got better with each new version, more developers began adopting it. Flex grew into a powerful framework that can hold its own with the more traditional means of software development. And it still hasn't lost its fun.

Who This Book Is For

I wrote this book as a way for anyone to get started using Flex, even those completely new to software development. This means those with no experience with the Flash IDE, web design, or programming in general can feel comfortable jumping right in and tinkering with examples. While I attempt to explain some basic concepts of programming to help the reader along, this is not exactly a how-to book for programming or software design. My aim is to get you going quickly and at a fun pace, learning Flex from the inside out. My hope is at the end of each chapter you will be itching with questions, and the following chapter will scratch that itch.

Flex is a powerful programming environment, and I'm not claiming to cover everything about it. If you find that you enjoy this technology and want to learn more, there are many great ways to continue your studies, including taking a course, studying the code of others, or finding a suitable book for advanced Flex or programming techniques. I'll give you some fun, real-world examples to play with that you should feel free to extend.

How This Book Is Organized

This book is meant to be read cover-to-cover. Skills are taught progressively, so each chapter builds on the one preceding it. This is done using a hands-on approach, allowing you to apply key concepts by building applications progressively. You can feel comfortable being away from the computer and reading each chapter, peeking at the code and seeing how it affects the applications through extensive screenshots. Later, you can skim that chapter and add the code to your examples, practicing each concept by applying it directly. If there's a topic you're not interested in, feel free to skip that chapter. Just make sure you grab the necessary code from the companion website at *www.greenlike.com/flex/learning*, which contains the code for each chapter, so your applications will work.

What This Book Covers

My aim is to give you a step-by-step tutorial through all aspects of Flex development, from familiarizing yourself with the right tools to learning basic features of ActionScript and MXML to sharing your completed work with others. I chose topics based on what I felt empowered you to begin development without overwhelming you.

The book therefore begins with the first step, setting up your computer for Flex development. I chose to cover the most popular and (in my opinion) best option for working in Flex: Flex Builder. While it is true that you can develop Flex applications with just a text editor and a command-line interpreter, this option doesn't provide the optimum experience for a new developer. The visual tools in Flex Builder make writing and understanding Flex code much more natural and fun.

I supply you with simple, visual examples to get you started creating Flex applications right away. I then discuss the basics of MXML and ActionScript so that you'll have a deeper understanding of the languages and how they work together in Flex. After this introduction, I have you start building a few real-world applications that you'll continue with throughout the book. I explain the standard set of skills for Flex, including the ability to move data around and structure your applications. I talk in depth about different ways of making a dynamic user interface and accepting user input. Once these basic skills are in place, I give you plenty of time to have fun with your applications, going over the "flashy" stuff like animations and styles.

This is a beginner's book, and Flex is a very powerful and fully featured development tool, so there are some advanced subjects that I chose not to cover. When I think it will help, I refer you to learn more about such related topics.

Companion Website

All the exercises included in this book are available for download from the book's companion website, *www.greenlike.com/flex/learning*. While I will frequently show sections of code in the book, you may find it easier to download the Flex projects and copy and paste the appropriate code into your examples. This will prevent typos from ruining your fun. However, I do hope that you follow along with the examples, because I've tried to create examples that you'll build upon from chapter to chapter.

Typographical Conventions Used in This Book

The following typographical conventions are used in this book:

Plain text

> Indicates menu titles, menu options, menu buttons, and keyboard modifiers (such as Alt and Command).

Italic

> Indicates new terms, URLs, email addresses, filenames, file extensions, and pathnames.

`Constant width`

> Indicates ActionScript code, text output from executing scripts, XML tags, HTML tags, and the contents of files.

`Constant width bold`

> Shows commands or other text that should be typed by the user.

`Constant width italic`

> Shows text that should be replaced with user-supplied values.

Using the Code Examples

This book is here to help you get your job done. In general, you can use the code in this book in your programs and documentation. You do not need to contact us for permission unless you're reproducing a significant portion of the code. For example, writing a program that uses several chunks of code from this book does not require permission. Selling or distributing a CD-ROM of examples from O'Reilly books does require permission. Answering a question by citing this book and quoting example code does not require permission. Incorporating a significant amount of example code from this book into your product's documentation does require permission.

We appreciate, but do not require, attribution. An attribution usually includes the title, author, publisher, and ISBN. For example: *Learning Flex 3* by Alaric Cole. Copyright 2008 O'Reilly Media, Inc., 978-0-596-51732-8.

If you think your use of code examples falls outside fair use or the permission given here, feel free to contact us at *permissions@oreilly.com*.

We'd Like to Hear from You

Please address comments and questions concerning this book to the publisher:

O'Reilly Media, Inc.
1005 Gravenstein Highway North
Sebastopol, CA 95472
(800) 998-9938 (in the United States or Canada)
(707) 829-0515 (international or local)
(707) 829-0104 (fax)

We have a web page for this book, where we list errata, examples, and any additional information. You can access this page at:

www.oreilly.com/catalog/9780596517328

To comment or ask technical questions about this book, send email to:

bookquestions@oreilly.com

For more information about our books, conferences, Resource Centers, and the O'Reilly Network, see our website at:

www.oreilly.com

Acknowledgments

Like a good film, a good technical book is a product of the combined efforts of lots of dedicated people. While I'm the only author for this book, I couldn't have done it alone.

I would like to personally thank the following:

Micah Laaker for the initial push and for all the insider tips.

Eli Robison for continued encouragement and for being a real friend.

Sharif Zawaideh at *http://globalimagesllc.com* for his stunning photos that make the book shine.

Hepp Maccoy for the helpful feedback early on.

Justin Kelly for his reality checks (even though one of them bounced).

Michael Hoch for his un-boss-like understanding and patience when I came to work dreary from all-night writing marathons.

Allen Rabinovich for going above and beyond the title of tech editor.

Lydia Schembri for her ornery motivation, positive energy, and grace.

Mom and Dad for being a true mother and father, respectively.

Robyn Thomas, Steve Weiss, Michele Filshie, Dennis Fitzgerald, David Van Ness, and the rest of the O'Reilly team for their continued support. The quality of this book is a direct result of their guidance and hard work.

The Adobe Flex team for another solid release.

CHAPTER 1

GETTING UP TO SPEED

The future is already here. It's just not evenly distributed.

—William Gibson

Welcome to the future. Adobe Flex 3 is the hot new technology for creating rich experiences both for the web and for the desktop (with Adobe AIR). Bridging the gap between the expressiveness and ubiquity of Adobe Flash and the power of desktop-class development, Flex is in a league of its own.

I have been working with Flex since its inception, and I can say with confidence that there's no better time to be learning Flex. With Flex 3, it's easier and faster than ever to create beautiful and powerful applications. Flex has been around for just a few years, but it's been growing exponentially. Not only is there a solid market for those proficient in Flex, but the product has matured into such a robust and open platform that current developers would be wise to add it to their skill set and anyone just starting out can rest assured they've chosen a great technology.

What Is Flex?

Flex is the way to make rich Internet applications (RIAs) quickly and easily. At its basic level, it's a framework for creating RIAs based on Flash Player. Along with being a framework, Flex is also a new language. At its heart is MXML, a markup language based on Extensible Markup Language (XML) that makes it really easy and efficient to create applications. Unlike developing for some desktop platforms requiring a proprietary binary file format, MXML is just text, so it's easy to read and modify using just a text editor. Therefore, sharing code is as easy as sharing a simple text file.

Flex Is a Modern, Hybrid Language

This XML-based system of creating applications will be familiar to traditional web programmers, because it uses a markup language and a JavaScript-like scripting language. For web developers and designers who are used to Hypertext Markup Language (HTML) and JavaScript, Flex will feel pretty natural. While quite different architecturally, the similarities at the surface makes it easy to get started. It was created using the best parts of desktop programming languages combined with the modern standards and practices of the web.

What Does Flex Look Like?

You may have seen a few Flex applications on the web, or perhaps you've used an Adobe AIR application. Maybe you've seen only those that have the default theme, called Aero, which creates a bluish, translucent look. More than likely, you've witnessed a Flex application that looked nothing like this (and you might not have realized it). That's because the entire look and feel of a Flex application is not set in stone. It doesn't have to look like Windows or Mac or anything else. Because Flex is fully *skinnable*, meaning you can change the entire look just by plugging in a new theme file. Even easier than that, a lot of free themes are available that let you change the look dramatically with one simple switch. You can even let the users of your application use their own themes!

Flex Is Flash

When Flex first came out, a friend of mine who enjoyed the expressiveness of Flash asked me about Flex. She had glanced at a few applications built in Flex and commented that they looked comparatively boring. "It's all buttons and panels," she remarked. "Where's the fun?"

So, I hacked a couple of examples to show her. One was a "flashy" little visualization, and another was a typical application full of "buttons and panels," to which I quickly added a few effects and transitions. When I showed her the beauty of Flex, she understood why I was so excited about the technology.

Flex applications, just like other Flash content, are deployed as *.swf* files (usually pronounced "swiff"). SWF files are very compact files that Flash Player reads and renders onscreen, often in a browser. This means you can create full-fledged applications that are small enough to download very quickly and that will (with few exceptions) look and act the same on any computer or operating system.

What's the Flash Platform?

The Flash Platform is the overall term for the development platform based on Flash Player, the little plug-in that could. Chances are, even if you've never thought about it, you already have Flash Player installed on your system and have witnessed the rich content it enables. If not, you're in a small group of Internet users—less than 1 percent of all Internet users, that is. That makes Flash Player one of the most widely distributed pieces of software today. If you're developing on the Flash Platform, you can rest assured that you're targeting a platform with huge presence as shown in Figure 1-1. More people can use Flash applications than nearly any other platform— even developing for Windows has less reach!

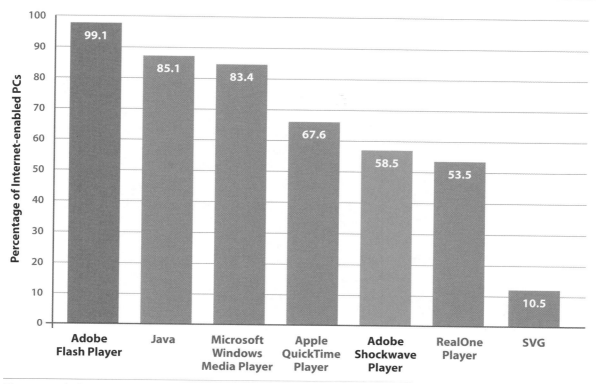

Figure 1-1. Flash Player reach

Flex Is the Flex SDK

Flex is a set of user interface and other components that help developers perform the tasks they need to create applications. This is all available in the Flex Software Development Kit (SDK). The Flex SDK consists of a compiler, documentation tools, and an extensive library of UI components and utilities that greatly facilitate development. Now, instead of writing line upon line of low-level code to draw a button programmatically or deal with timeline animation, a Flex developer can simply type `<mx:Button/>` or drag and drop a button where they want it.

Flex developers can use the SDK with just a text editor or via Flex Builder, the powerful development environment from Adobe. Although it's not necessary to have a copy of Flex Builder to build Flex applications, it can really help. If you don't already have a favorite development environment, Flex Builder can really speed up the development of Flex applications.

What about AIR?

Adobe Integrated Runtime (AIR) is the solution for bringing Flash and other web-based content to the desktop. With all the benefits of the web-based model these days, why would anyone want to do this? The main reason is that the browser is a bit limiting. Browsers don't have any built-in support for drag-and-drop from the desktop, they have security limitations, and users can't access web applications when they don't have an Internet connection. Also, many users enjoy having an application in their Dock or Start menu that they can quickly access by clicking an icon.

Another reason AIR shines is that it's great for developers. With the prevalence of the web, a lot of developers are focusing on web technologies such as HTML, JavaScript, and Flash in lieu of traditional desktop development environments. And it's a lucky day for those who are interested in Flex, because Flex is a fantastic way to create AIR applications.

With Adobe AIR, there's no need to learn C# or Java just to create a stand-alone application—you can take your existing skills with Flex, Flash, or JavaScript and start creating desktop applications; if you decide to make web applications as well, there's no learning curve. In fact—and this is perhaps the most compelling reason for AIR—you don't need to be chained to a particular operating system to develop for the desktop, because AIR applications are operating system agnostic. In other words, you don't need to decide whether to develop for Windows, Mac, or Linux—you just write it once in the language of your choice, and anyone can use it with Adobe AIR (see Figure 1-2).

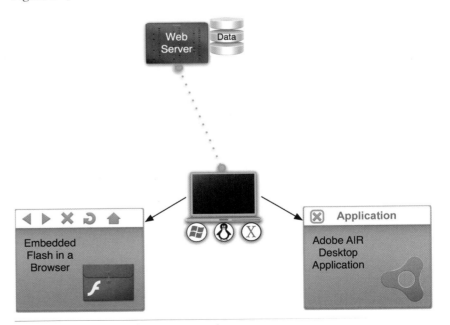

Figure 1-2. How Flex applications are used

Where Flex Fits

Flex is the next step in the development of RIAs. The phrase *rich Internet applications* was coined by Macromedia (now Adobe) in 2002 to account for the trend in more expressive applications on the web. In the beginning, HTML documents on the web were just that, documents. They were text and, later, images and multimedia. This client-server paradigm meant a user, by typing a URL in their browser, would request a document. The web being so far-reaching, savvy folks quickly learned to create server-based applications, programs, which a user could access online. Think of all those forms you've filled out, where you type your name and address and hit the submit button. After a few moments, you're greeted with an entirely new page telling you your form was submitted (or that you had some errors you have to fix first). This was a client-server model, where a "thin" client (a browser) requested content and sent it back to a server for processing. To create dynamic HTML pages, a server had to create the HTML and send it to the client, which would read it like any other page. This took time.

Then, with the advent of JavaScript came the power to offload some application workload onto the client. For instance, when configuring an item in an online store, it used to be necessary send all calculations like shipping or sales tax back to the server. With scripting, it was possible to calculate that information right on the client machine and update the layout of the page based on user interaction. Dubbed a "thick" client in contrast to the thin client, a user's computer needed to be a bit more powerful in order to run the scripts and re-render the page.

However, this was still quite limiting to some developers, myself included. Folks like me wanted to do much more. We wanted animation, transitions, a rich experience. We wanted to be able to load data without refreshing the page. Before Ajax was created, the answer for many was Flash.

The Flash IDE began as a solution for creating animations and multimedia on the web. However, as it matured, more and more interactive elements were added, and people began discovering ways to create things like games in this new platform. Because Flash was quick, lightweight, and by nature rich, others developed complex applications that could load and visualize data, product catalogs, and photo viewers. But because the Flash IDE was an animation tool, creating complex interactions was often difficult and, for traditional developers, a bit messy. With the advent of Flash Professional in 2003, a number of time saving features were added, such as reusable components and data connectors; however, that version left a lot to be desired, especially for enterprise projects or projects with large teams.

Enter Flex. Building upon the power of Flash Player, Flex made it easy to develop rich interfaces in a highly extensible way. With a more developer-centric model, it was easier for Java programmers and others to jump on board and start developing without the "What is this timeline?" confusion.

Even better, the new markup-based language made it easy to read and share code, which has definitely contributed to its growing success.

Why Use Flex?

This is the question you may be asking yourself when you picked up this book. Why use Flex? What are the pros and cons of using it? Flex was created for the purpose of making rich experiences on the web much easier, but it has quickly grown into a solid platform for even desktop development (coupled with AIR).

Flex Is for Applications

Flex was built to speed up the development of richly interactive applications built on Flash Player. It includes a number of robust, customizable components that make configuring an application quick and comparatively simple. These programs can be run in a web browser or deployed as an AIR application, so Flex is the perfect solution for writing an application once and giving it to anyone, on the web and beyond.

Web Applications Defined

You're probably familiar with a *desktop application*; it's simply a piece of software that you use, such as your web browser or your word processor. A *web application* is an application you access through a web browser. You might even use the same application in a desktop version and a web counterpart—an email program is a common one that people use on their desktop as well as on the web. The desktop email program makes it easy to access your mail any time, even when you're offline; the web version can be useful because it's available anywhere there's an Internet connection, such as when you're traveling and don't have your home computer with you. Now imagine that this same program existed both online and on the desktop, with the same look and feel—and the same code base. Flex makes that possible.

For Easy Interactivity

Flex makes it easy to create a high level of interactivity. It comes with support for data binding, an excellent event architecture, and a set of components with great user feedback. Add to this the ability to quickly create beautiful effects and transitions, and it's easy to see why Flex is a great tool for developers.

For Development Speed

There is no faster way to create such compelling applications. In comparison to development in the Flash IDE, Flex speeds up application development exponentially. Although everything you can do in Flex can be done in the Flash IDE, development in Flex will take just a fraction of the time. With Flex Builder, development is faster still.

For Speed All Around

Flex components are built in ActionScript 3.0, the newest incarnation of the programming language for Flash Player. Flash Player was totally rewritten with performance in mind, and it shows. Although with any program you should make an effort to optimize, you can feel confident that even with loads of data and animations, your application will be responsive and not hog the user's resources.

Because It's Clean

Flex is a developer's dream. By design, it encourages good coding practices such as code organization and class-based applications. Inheriting the idea from web design, Flex supports the separation of content and design by allowing the external styling of your applications. Because of this, you can easily change your application's skins, and you can drop in one of the many freely-available themes to totally restyle your application on the fly. Along with this, proponents of the Model-View-Controller (MVC) design pattern will find that Flex supports this as well. Free sets of libraries are available, such as the Cairngorm framework, which make implementing MVC easy.

Because It's Free

Although you'll have to pay for a copy of Flex Builder, the de facto visual editor for Flex, the Flex framework is completely free. Therefore, if you so choose, you can edit your application in your favorite text editor and compile it on the command line without paying a dime. The scope of this book is for beginners, and because a great way to get started quickly and easily is by using Flex Builder, I'll be referring to that most of the time. Luckily, Adobe offers a fully functional free 30-day trial, so there's no reason not to check it out: *www.adobe.com/products/flex*.

> ### Try Flex Without Installing
>
> If you want to see Flex in action but don't feel like downloading anything just yet, feel free to try the Flex Online Compiler at *http://try.flex.org*. You can paste any code or choose from the introductory pieces and see the results immediately in your browser.

Because It's Open

Flex is also open source. This means all the component code is yours for the looking (and using and reusing in most cases). This helps you as a new developer learn, because you can study the code for the Flex framework. And this also means that Flex is yours. That's right, you can modify and improve the code and submit it for inclusion in future versions. Not only this, but the compiler is open as well, meaning every aspect of Flex is open source.

Being open source, a community has grown around extending and improving Flex. Loads of great high-level components are available that build upon the base set, so you're sure to find what you need to get the job done. And if you want to contribute to making Flex better, you're welcome to do so. Flex is yours.

For Data (and Fast)

In Flash Player, data transmission over the wire has less overhead, and the result is a much faster experience for your users. Flex offers built-in support for XML and Java objects as a way to exchange data and also has support for Action Message Format (AMF). With Java and ColdFusion servers, you can transmit compressed, binary data over the wire to your Flex application, making data submission and retrieval much faster than is possible with typical applications. And for you PHP folks, there's AMFPHP, an open source alternative for use with PHP.

Along with this, connecting your data to Flex has never been easier. With some great new data wizards in Flex Builder, you'll be able to easily connect to a database—in many cases, most of your code will be generated for you. With ColdFusion and Flex, you supply the database, and Flex Builder will build out the application and server components for you.

Because It's Beautiful

Although Flex comes with a default theme that might suit you well, its look and feel is limited only by your imagination. You're not required to make it look like software made for a specific operating system or anything you've seen before. Because of the way styles and skins are implemented in Flex, you'll be able to quickly and easily change the way your programs look, all with a single line of code.

With the robust set of user interface controls that are available right out of the box and with a wide variety of open source controls, you can create any interface you like. With Flex Charting, you have a great set of charting and data visualization tools at your disposal. You can use bar charts, pie charts, or high-low-open-close charts. You name it. Because of the power and expressiveness of Flash and the ease of development in Flex, the number of third-party data visualization components is growing every day.

How Flex Compares to Other Technologies

Flex is a hybrid technology of sorts, taking the best bits from modern programming languages while adhering to standards such as XML and Cascading Style Sheets (CSS). In this way, it resembles some technologies a great deal, and it differs from others.

Flash IDE

Like the Flash integrated development environment (IDE) in Flash and Flash Professional, Flex creates applications that are run by Flash Player. However, besides sharing a common scripting language, Flex is quite different from using Flash. Flash is at its core an animation and drawing editor, and development features were added later. Flex was designed from the ground up to build applications. Although some users of Flash who have dealt only with simple scripting may find using Flex a bit overwhelming, Java or C developers will feel more at home.

A Note about the Term *Flash*

I might as well get this out of the way early. I'll often mention the term *Flash* in the book, a term that for many is tough to define. That's because *Flash* can refer to a few things. One is the Flash IDE, the animation and development tool that started it all. Another is the content you actually see on the web, like animations, advertisements, or applications, which are *.swf* files that run inside the browser. Yet another is the umbrella term for the technology that's built upon Flash Player, the little plug-in that makes it possible to view all this stuff on your computer. Out in the wild, you'll hear the word thrown around in different ways, but in this book, I'll try to keep things a bit solid. When I say "Flash," I'm referring to the technology or the actual content. When I want to talk about the development software, I'll say the "Flash IDE" or the "Flash authoring tool."

There's nothing you can't do in Flash that you can do in Flex—technically, that is. It would be possible to build a great application using just the Flash IDE, and in fact that's what I've done successfully for a large part of my career (and that's what many developers still do). However, there's always a right tool for any job, and Flex was built from the ground up to help you create applications. It has support for easily moving data around, built-in support for styling and skinning your applications, advanced controls for interactivity, and a ton of other features to help you. (As you'll see very soon, adding rich animations and graphical effects to your programs is intuitive and easy with Flex.) By the same token, Flex is not a drawing program or animation tool, so if you're looking to create movies or animated cartoons, the Flash authoring environment is the best tool for the job.

C Languages

Though based on a language different from C++, Objective-C, and so on, Flex is a developer's dream. Using Flex Builder, which is an IDE similar to Visual Studio and XCode, you can lay out, code, and deploy your application from one solid piece of software. However, one of the great benefits of Flex's MXML markup language is that you can easily modify it without an IDE, or even lay out an entire application with just a text editor. Because markup language is much more readable than a scripting language, it's easier to edit, share, and maintain.

Being a class-based, object-oriented language and framework, developers in C++ and other languages will be able to quickly get going with Flex. However, C# developers may find the easiest transition, because the language shares a number of commonalities.

Java/Java FX

Flex is similar to Java and the Java Swing platform. The way the scripting language, ActionScript, is used and structured is similar. It inherits the concept of packages, and its syntax is nearly identical. MXML will be the biggest difference, but as you'll discover, that's an easy change as well. Because Flex Builder is built on Eclipse, many Java programmers will already be comfortable using the IDE.

Java, like Flex, allows an application to be built that can be deployed either on the web or to the desktop. However, the ubiquity and small size of Flash Player compared to the Java SDK makes Flex applications available to a wider audience. A lot of Java developers are learning Flex, and a lot of projects that might have been built in Java are moving to Flex.

HTML/JavaScript/Ajax

Flex was built after the web explosion, and incorporated into its design are a number of similarities to traditional web development. Most notably is a tag-based language (MXML) coupled with an ECMA-compliant language (ActionScript). Because JavaScript syntax is so similar, web programmers proficient in this language will find working in ActionScript easy. Web programmers with knowledge of XML or HTML will quickly understand how MXML works. While, behind the scenes, MXML and ActionScript have a different relationship to one another as compared with HTML and JavaScript, on the surface the interaction will make sense to most traditional web developers.

Ajax (asynchronous JavaScript and XML) and Flex can do a lot of the same things, and developers in either technology like to use what they know; in fact, many can be downright religious. If you're new to both, then you'll have more of a chance to make an objective opinion—but if you've made it this far, I can assume you've found something about Flex you like. Flex can do a lot of the same things as Ajax, letting a developer create web applications that don't rely so heavily on a page metaphor. Ajax libraries have really grown recently, and with the right environment, working in Ajax isn't too bad. But MXML/ActionScript code is still easier to write and easier to maintain, and there's much less "hackery" than writing in Ajax.

Silverlight/XAML

Silverlight is Microsoft's solution for rich web content; it shares the XML-based markup paradigm coupled with a choice of programming languages. In this way, knowing Silverlight will definitely help in learning Flex, and vice versa. Silverlight is also an attempt at offering true cross-platform compatibility. With Flex, whatever you build will work pretty much the same everywhere because of the Flash plug-in, which is extremely small and already installed on most computers. The Silverlight plug-in is larger, but its presence is growing. Out-of-the-box, Silverlight offers a good number of advanced controls and layout containers, although with the open-source initiative, the number of third-party Flex components are increasing quickly.

OpenLaszlo

OpenLaszlo is a popular open source framework using Scalable Vector Graphics (SVG) and XML/JavaScript to build RIAs. As such, developers in this framework will make an easy adjustment to MXML and ActionScript and will find a number of new, powerful features. Flex is open source, too!

How Do I Know It's a Flex Application?

With the explosion of Web 2.0 and the rich interfaces that have become mainstream, the lines have blurred between what's possible in HTML and what's reserved for Flash. Just a few years ago, if you saw a fancy transition or animation, you could be sure it was Flash. Nowadays, it's tough to tell just by looking.

One trick to check whether a section of a website was done in Flex is to right-click (Control-click on a Mac) the area in your browser. If the content is Flash or Flex, a context menu will appear with the About Adobe Flash Player item at the bottom. This will always tell you whether something is being shown with Flash Player—but that doesn't necessarily mean it was built using Flex. For that, there's no sure method, because folks have built some pretty sophisticated applications using just the Flash IDE. However, once you get a feel for a few Flex applications and become familiar with the most common components, you'll often be able to tell by interacting with the application a bit.

When Not to Use Flex

Flex is a great technology, and many will find it solves issues that have plagued past development. However, it's not for everyone. If you're looking to do simple animations and don't want to write any code, a timeline-based animation utility like Flash might be the best choice for you. Because it uses a framework of components, Flex applications will often result in a larger file size than custom Flash or ActionScript-only applications (however, this can mostly be overcome with framework caching, which I'll discuss near the end of the book). In most cases, a slight increase in size is well worth the reduced development time and functionality of the Flex framework. However, you may not want simple widgets or small applications with minimal functionality to be weighed down by the framework. Luckily, it's not necessary to use the Flex components (or even MXML) to use Flex. It's completely possible to do an ActionScript-only project that you can compile with the free Flex compiler. And the default Flex IDE, Flex Builder, is a great tool for such projects.

If you need lots of functionality that deals with rich text, or need only simple user interaction, you might be better off using HTML/Ajax. Although Flex has great support for HTML, it may not be enough for some projects, and may suffer a bit of a performance lag if there is a lot of text. However, if you plan to deploy to AIR, Flex might be a great choice. AIR has native support for the full gamut of HTML. But if you're just looking for a website with loads of text, use HTML. If you want animations or bits of interactivity, a great solution is to use Flash or Flex in chunks within your HTML page.

Evaluating Flex

For more information on Flex as a choice for you or your business, check out the O'Reilly Short Cut *Flex Early Evaluation: Assessing Flex and Your Project Needs.* You can purchase a copy from O'Reilly by going to *www.oreilly.com/catalog/evaluator1/.*

Summary

Hopefully, you have a better idea of what Flex is all about. Created as a means of developing applications based on the Flash Player, it has become a key player in the world of rich applications for the web and the desktop. With a robust set of components to make development easier, and a new markup language for easy coding, Flex is a great choice for many developers. You've seen how it compares to the Flash IDE and other languages, and learned what it's good for and when it's not the best choice. If Flex is the tool you're looking to learn, the following chapters will get you started quickly. The next chapter jumps right in to the basics of using Flex and Flex Builder.

CHAPTER 2

SETTING UP YOUR ENVIRONMENT

Adobe Flex 3 is free, and you can use any editor you like to develop with it. Your code is going to be just some text files that you can edit in any text editor, and you'll be able to compile the files with the free Flex compiler. That said, when getting to know Flex, Adobe's Flex Builder is indispensable. Not only is it the premier editor for Flex code, making it easy to get accustomed to what's available, but it will also seamlessly compile and organize your code for you. I've been developing in Flex since the technology was introduced, and although I've used other editors in the past, I continue to use Flex Builder in my daily work. So, the goal of this book will be introducing you to developing in Flex with Flex Builder.

If you don't have Flex yet, it's easy to download from Adobe at *www.adobe. com/products/flex*. If you prefer to use your own editor and compile via the command line or other alternatives, you can download just the Flex SDK. I recommend you grab a copy of Flex Builder, because Adobe will give you 30 days to try it with no limits. (Well, they'll put a watermark in any chart you create, but besides that, no features are taken away.) You have a couple of options when buying or downloading Flex Builder, which I'll discuss in the later section "Flex Flavors."

Using Alternatives to Flex Builder

If your copy of Flex Builder has expired, if you can't install it, or if you're just being stubborn, any text editor will work in its stead. However, since you'll be working primarily in an XML-based language, you'll be best off with an editor that knows how to work with XML, because you'll benefit from nice features such as syntax highlighting (color-coded text). Here are a few popular editors:

Eclipse

This is the open source and free editor that, coupled with an XML-editing plug-in, makes a great editor. Because it's an IDE and not just a text editor, it's possible to set it up to compile your applications. *www.eclipse.org*

FlashDevelop (Windows only)

This has been a popular open source IDE for ActionScript developers. Now it has the ability to edit and compile Flex as well. *http://osflash.org/flashdevelop*

TextMate (Macintosh only)

This is a great text editor with built-in support for ActionScript, but be sure to look for a "bundle" for Flex, which makes working with MXML second-nature. *http://macromates.com*

TextPad (Windows only)

Touted as a powerful editor that's easy to get up and running, TextPad is a good choice for coding MXML by hand in Windows. *www.textpad.com*

NOTE

For more information about using the command-line Flex compiler to compile Flex code, check out Adobe's LiveDocs at http://livedocs.adobe.com/flex/3/html/compilers_01.html.

Your editor will take care of the writing part, but you'll still need to compile your code. Because this is an open platform, new options for compiling Flex are available every day, so a quick search might help you find just what you need. All of these third-party solutions are going to be built around the free Flex command-line compiler, which you can use with just a few keystrokes in your computer's terminal or command prompt.

Introducing Flex Builder and Eclipse

Once you have a copy of Flex Builder, go through the program to familiarize yourself with the most important features. Flex Builder is built on the popular and open source Eclipse IDE. Eclipse is powerful, but it might not be the most beautiful or user-friendly program ever developed, so I'll be here to hold your hand through the process of discovering what's what.

More about the IDE

IDE stands for *integrated development environment*, which is a piece of software made just for making other software. That is to say, an IDE is a programmer's tool for writing code, organizing projects, debugging them, and deploying them—an all-in-one solution for development. Other popular IDEs are Microsoft Visual Studio and XCode.

You'll be seeing mentions of the Eclipse IDE more than a few times in this book in regard to Flex Builder. I'll often refer to Eclipse when I'm talking about a feature that isn't specific to Flex Builder but is part of the default Eclipse IDE, which it's built on.

What's the deal with Eclipse? By default it comes packaged as a Java editor, but it can handle anything you throw at it via a plug-in architecture. A lot of Java programmers use Eclipse as their main development environment, but it's also great for JavaScript, HTML, C, Python, and tons of other languages. It also works with source control when you're developing as part of a team and want to easily share and maintain your code.

Adobe chose to build upon Eclipse because of the IDE's popularity with Java programmers and because it offered a number of tried-and-true features out of the box. This way Adobe could concentrate less on building an entire IDE and more on great new features. It was also cross-platform already, so they didn't need to create separate code bases for Mac, Windows, and Linux.

Eclipse is most useful if you develop in multiple languages, because you can use the same software for everything at once. Many Flex developers might be writing HTML, PHP, or ColdFusion along with their Flex applications, and they can open all their files in one program.

Eclipse is built in Java and was inherited from an IBM project, becoming fully open sourced in 2001.

Flex Flavors

Flex Builder comes in two flavors: stand-alone (or standard) and an Eclipse plug-in. What's the difference, you ask? Well, branding. If you're used to your setup in Eclipse and tend to use it for more than just Flex, feel free to download and use just the plug-in. However, if Flex is your primary interest, be good to yourself and get the stand-alone version. It will come with great features like a Flex icon for your Dock/Start menu, a Flex splash screen, and—well, you get the idea. Seriously, though, because it's integrated, it'll be easier for you to get to the features you need. I'll be using the stand-alone version in my examples, so if you're using the plug-in, there might be a few instances where the screen looks different or menu items aren't in the same place. You can always install a copy of the stand-alone in a separate location from your other Eclipse install, and later you can install the plug-in.

Flex Builder Installation

Once you have a copy of Flex Builder, open the installer, and follow the onscreen instructions. It may ask you a few questions about where you'd like to put your project files and things of that nature; unless you're picky, just trust the defaults. When everything's finished, open Flex Builder, and you should be greeted with a screen that looks like Figure 2-1.

Figure 2-1. The Flex Start Page

This is the Flex Start Page, essentially a browser window running in Eclipse (yes, it has its own browser). This page has a few tutorials and sample projects for you to get your hands dirty in Flex, and it's a great introduction. It's not necessary since you have this book, but you might enjoy playing around with it. If you click the "Full Tutorial" link on the Create a Simple RIA tab, you'll see another browser window with an introduction to Flex, complete with a table of contents on the left. In the "Get oriented with Flex" section is an animated overview of the technology you might find useful.

Your Editor at a Glance

Eclipse and Flex Builder are built on the concept of panels, and you'll see a few open in your fresh install. The *Flex Navigator* will be the place you work with your files and projects, the *Outline* panel will show you a tree view of your application, and the *Problems* panel will show you all your problems (like bugs and warnings). Luckily, because you're starting fresh, you don't have any problems yet! I'll go into more detail about the interface later, but for now have some fun and run an application.

Running Your First Application

Note that everything is a project in Eclipse/Flex Builder. This means you'll never have just one stand-alone file; instead, you'll have a group of files that work together to make everything happen. So to create a new Flex application, you'll need to create a project.

Importing a Project Archive

To get your first project, you're going to import an existing one into Flex Builder. I've provided one on my site that you can download and import. Point your browser to *www.greenlike.com/flex/learning/projects/simple.zip*, and save it to your desktop or wherever you like.

Once you've downloaded the *.zip* file, go to Flex Builder, and choose File→Import→Flex Project. The Import Flex Project dialog box appears, as shown in Figure 2-2. This dialog box can take a zipped project archive and import it into the Flex Builder workspace. Simply choose Archive file from the "Import project from" section. Then click Browse, choose the *.zip* file you just downloaded, and accept the default location to store it. Click Finish to finalize the import.

NOTE

To view this book's companion website, go to www.greenlike.com/flex/learning. There you'll find the source code for the projects you'll build as you read through the book.

WARNING

If your browser unzips the archive when you download the file or if you've unzipped it yourself, the Import Flex Project Archive command won't work. Instead, you'll want to use the Import Existing Projects into Workspace dialog box, which I'll explain later in the section "Importing an Existing Project."

Figure 2-2. Importing a Flex project archive (.zip)

After a few moments, you'll see your project in the Flex Navigator. Click the arrow next to the project name in the Flex Navigator to expose the contents of the folder. You'll see even more folders, but one of them contains the main application. Which one is it? Well, it's a common practice among programmers to include the source code in a folder called source or src. So, expand the src folder as shown in Figure 2-3, and you'll see the application file *SimpleFlexExample.mxml*.

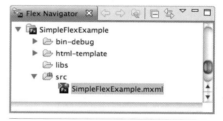

Figure 2-3. Your first project

Opening a Sample Application

You've downloaded a project and imported it into your workspace, and now you're ready to look at the code. Double-click the *SimpleFlexExample.mxml* file, and it opens in Flex Builder's Design mode. This renders the application in Design mode, giving you a pixel-perfect preview of how the application's structured. To see the underlying code, switch to Source mode by clicking Source on the Source/Design mode tab, as shown in Figure 2-4. I'll go into detail later; for now, let's get running!

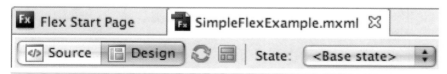

Figure 2-4. Switching between Source and Design mode

The Little Green Button: Running the Application

Now that the *SimpleFlexExample.mxml* file is open in Flex Builder, you can run the application in a browser by selecting Run→Run SimpleFlexExample or by clicking the green arrow button in your toolbar (shown in Figure 2-5 to the left of the green bug icon). This will launch a browser window after a few moments, and you'll see your first Flex application running in an HTML page.

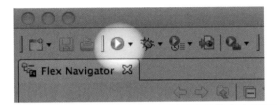

Figure 2-5. The Run button

Everything Is a Project

So now that you've imported your first project and run it, delete it. Yes, all that hard work, and you're going to throw it all away! Not to worry, though—you can always bring it back. That's because of the way projects are used in Flex Builder: Deleting a project from your workspace doesn't mean you have to delete the actual source code, and just because source code exists on your hard drive doesn't mean it's available to Flex Builder. I'll show you how this works; just follow along.

NOTE

I'll usually tell you how to access commands using the menu bar, but many of the most common commands are available as context menus in Flex Builder. For example, to delete the project, you could also right-click the project folder (Control-click on OS X) and choose Delete from the context menu.

First, select the project in the Flex Navigator (select the top folder titled SimpleFlexExample, not just one of the files or folders under the top folder). Then choose Edit→Delete. You'll be prompted with a dialog box asking whether you'd like to delete the contents of the project (see Figure 2-6). Be sure to select "Do not delete contents" (which should already be selected), because this will keep the project files on your machine.

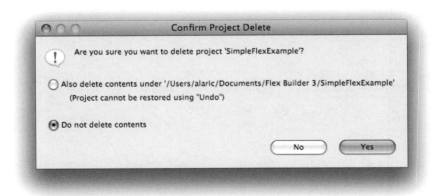

Figure 2-6. Deleting a project

Now you can check your filesystem for the project folder (usually your documents folder→Flex Builder 3 folder or wherever you originally placed the project). The project should still be there, and you should see a directory structure similar to what was displayed in the Flex Navigator.

So, what's the point? Well, it shows you that a project in Flex Builder is a specific thing. Just because you have some Flex code lying around doesn't mean Flex Builder can use it—not until you turn it into a project. You can try this by going to the src folder and double-clicking the *SimpleFlexExample.mxml* file on your machine. It might open in a text editor, or your computer may not even know what to do with the file. You might expect it to open in Flex Builder, but unfortunately that's not the case. If you want to use it, you have to make it into a project so that Flex Builder can understand how to work with it. To do that now, you'll import the project again.

Importing an Existing Project

Sorry for the busywork, but importing projects is one of those tasks you'll be doing a lot of in Flex, so it's best to get accustomed to how to do it. You might think you already know how to import a project, but this is a little different. Previously, you imported a project archive, which is a zipped-up version of what you're working with now. To import this "expanded" set of files, you'll use a slightly different command.

In Flex Builder, select File→Import→Flex Project just as before. However, this time choose the Project folder option from the "Import project from" section (as seen in Figure 2-7). This will allow you to import an expanded folder of files instead of an archived project.

Click Browse, and choose the SimpleFlexExample folder you just looked at, which holds the project and supporting files. Click Finish, and Flex Builder will import the project.

Your Workspace

I'll often mention *workspaces* in Flex Builder. A workspace is any folder on your system that you choose to keep projects in, and it also contains preference settings. You can actually have more than one workspace, but the one you set up when you install Flex is the main one, and by default it's located in your documents folder→Flex Builder 3 folder. If you'd like another, you can select File→Switch Workspace→Other and create a new one.

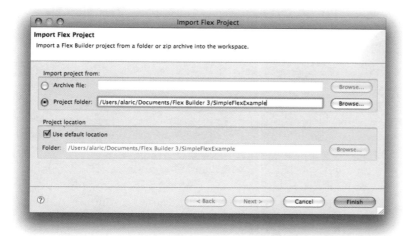

Figure 2-7. Importing a project from a folder

Cooking from Scratch:
Creating a New Flex Project

Of course, when you're creating Flex applications, you'll usually be creating new projects. So, I'll go over how to set one up from scratch, which you'll then use to get your hands dirty with Flex.

To create a new project, go to the File menu, and choose New→Flex Project. A dialog box will pop up, giving you options for your project. Give the project a name in the "Project name" field. In this case, I'll call the project **HelloWorld**.

This dialog box has three sections: Project location, Application type, and Server technology. "Project location" lets you modify where the project folder and files will be stored on your machine. It defaults to your workspace folder, but you can change this if you'd like by deselecting "Use default location" and entering your own.

WARNING

You can't use spaces or funky characters in your project name—only letters, numbers, the dollar sign ($) character, and the underscore (_) character are allowed. Eclipse is very good about warning you in its dialog boxes, so rest assured you won't be able to get away with anything.

The second section is "Application type." This is where you get to choose between developing for the web and developing for the desktop with Adobe AIR. In this example, you want your application to run in a web browser, so leave the default as a web application.

Adobe AIR

Adobe AIR is getting a lot of recognition lately, and it's for good reason. Using AIR, you can turn your web applications into full-fledged desktop applications, with a Dock/Start menu icon, drag-and-drop support, and everything you'd expect from a native application. Flex not only is a solid platform for creating programs that run in a browser but it's also the premier solution for creating applications deployed as AIR applications. With Flex Builder, deploying a project on the web or the desktop is as simple as flipping a switch. I'll talk about AIR occasionally throughout the book.

The third section, "Server technology," refers to server technologies you might want to use. This helps you get started connecting your Flex application to data on a server, such as a remote XML file or database. For this simple example, just leave the default server type as None, because you're not going to use any remote data. Later, if you want to connect your application to ColdFusion or PHP or use LiveCycle Data Services, this is the place to start. I'll talk more about different data services and how to connect to them in Chapter 10. You'll notice the Next, Cancel, and Finish buttons at the bottom of the dialog box. We're in the mode of keeping it simple, so just click Finish to accept the defaults for this project.

NOTE

You might have noticed the "Copy projects into workspace" check box. This is useful for when you have a project in another location (such as one you've downloaded and is sitting on your desktop or other folder where you download files) and you want to import the project and place it in your workspace in one step. It's nice to keep your projects together so you don't accidentally delete something (like when cleaning up your desktop).

NOTE

Each project has its own folder, which typically has the same name as the project's name, but this isn't necessary. If you want your **HelloWorld** *project to be in the folder Hello World Project, that's perfectly fine; if you want it outside your workspace, like in a folder on your desktop, that's cool, too. For me, I like to keep it simple and organized and leave the defaults.*

NOTE

You can always change project settings later, and this dialog box is just to help you get started. Select your project, and then select Project→Properties if you want to change something.

The Structure of a Flex Project

Now that you've created a few projects, it's a good time to go over what all these folders mean. (I promise you'll get to bin-debug something in just a moment.) Every Flex project has, by tradition, a bin folder, an html-template folder, a libs folder, and a src folder. Table 2-1 describes the purpose of each of these folders, and Figure 2-8 shows the structure in the Flex Navigator panel.

Table 2-1. Project folder structure

Name	Short for	Purpose
bin-debug	binary debugging	Holds the compiled code (the SWF file). For Flex web applications, this also contains an HTML container and supplemental files. For AIR applications, it holds the Application Descriptor File as well.
html-template	html-template	Holds the template HTML file that generates the container HTML file (web applications only).
libs	libraries	Holds files for additional compiled libraries.
src	source	Holds the source code. This can be *.mxml* files, *.as* files, and an Application Descriptor File (AIR only).

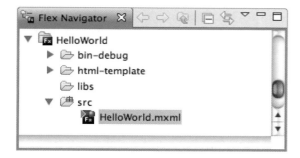

Figure 2-8. The new project

Summary

Now that I've covered all the necessary stuff for getting started, you're ready to have some fun and build something. You've learned the basics of using projects in Flex Builder, you know how to open and run an application, and you understand the basic structure of a typical Flex application. Now you'll take what you know and build your own!

NOTE

It's not necessary to keep these folder names as is. If you'd like to call the source folder source instead of src, or if you'd like to omit it altogether and keep your main MXML file in the top level of the project, that's fine, too. You can set this up when creating a new project by clicking Next instead of Finish in the New Project dialog box, or you can change the settings later by right-clicking the project and choosing Properties. You can modify these default folders by going to the Flex Build Path section and changing the Main source folder and the Output folder.

CHAPTER 3

USING DESIGN MODE

Design mode is your what-you-see-is-what-you-get (WYSIWYG) editor for Adobe Flex 3. It's a great place to start, whether you're an experienced coder or a designer. Available at your disposal is a nice list of visual components you can simply drag and drop to build your interface. You can modify every option for these components visually, with the most common ones you'll need readily available. In this chapter, you'll get acquainted with Design mode and will begin to build an application visually.

A Blank Slate: Your Canvas

Let's head back to the **HelloWorld** project and open the main application (the main *.mxml* file) in Design mode. You'll see a blank, bluish background, the default style for all Flex applications. When you're in Design mode, the Components panel should be visible by default and appear on the lower left next to the Outline panel and under the Flex Navigator. If the Components panel is not visible, you can get it back by going to the Window menu, which has the most common panels for Flex right at its top. Note that the Components panel isn't available when you switch to Source mode, because in Source mode you'll use MXML code to create components.

You can display the Components panel via Window→Components. This panel holds all your user interface (UI) components that will help you build everything.

Adding Components to the Application

To place components in your application, you can drag them from the Components panel and drop them anywhere you like on your canvas, as shown in Figure 3-1. They'll then be on the canvas, and you can move them around and set their properties visually. Let's try dropping a button component, which you'll find near the top of the Components panel, under the heading Controls.

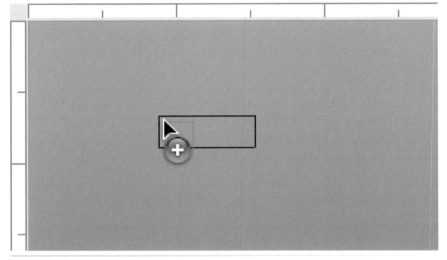

Figure 3-1. Dragging a component onto the stage

Canvas ≈ Stage ≈ Application

I'll be using the terms *canvas*, *stage*, and *application container* interchangeably. The blue background you see in Design mode is actually a visual container component called Application, which is the root of every Flex application. It's also a canvas of sorts, if you think in terms of design, because it's a blank slate on which you place your visual assets. Specifically, a Canvas (uppercase) is a separate type of container component, which is different from the more generic term *canvas*. I might also refer to the canvas as the *stage*, which is an older Flash term. This is in contrast to the uppercase Stage object, which is actually a class that all Flash/Flex applications have at their root. The term *stage* makes more sense when referring to creating animations and movies with the Flash IDE, but old habits die hard.

Moving Components Around

Now that you have a button component on the stage, you can move it around by dragging it to different parts of the stage. You might notice that if you drag it toward the edges of the stage, some reference lines appear to help you line the component up. These are known as *guides* or *smart guides* in the design world, and you might have encountered them in Photoshop or your favorite design program. These guides are a visual representation of what is called snapping, which forces the component to align with adjacent edges or other components. When dragging a component to an edge of the stage, snapping will typically cause the component to snap 10 pixels from that edge. When dragging near other components, the guides may appear and cause what you're dragging to snap 10 or 20 pixels from the other component. They may also appear when dragging farther from another component, allowing you to easily align what you're dragging to other components on the stage. This can be helpful to quickly line up your components and make your application symmetrical and sleek.

TIP

If you don't want snapping to occur when moving components around, hold down the Alt (Option) key while dragging. This will remove snapping and reference lines and give you pixel-perfect control over your placement. If you want to turn snapping off, you can toggle the menu item at Design→Enable Snapping.

Exploring Common Components

A component is simply any reusable piece of code which can be used as a tool to build your application. The term component implies that it will be used as a piece of a system, and you'll tend to use more than a few of them in any application. One of the more useful parts of Flex is the great set of components it offers. And while they can be huge timesavers and require very little know-how to get up and running, mastering them can take a while. Getting to know them well and being able to customize them a great deal will take some time, but once you've done that, you're on your way to becoming a Flex guru! Luckily, a few simple bits of information can get you up and running; you'll learn the intricacies as you gain experience.

Following are some of the more common components you're likely to use.

Controls

Controls are visual components that are a basic part of a UI, such as buttons and text. They're called *controls* because they control the use of an application. Think of a remote control, which has buttons to manipulate a television, or a volume control, which can change the volume on your stereo.

Here are some of the more common controls you're likely to use:

 Button

This is pretty simple: a clickable control that looks and acts like a physical button. It also has the ability to toggle via the **toggle** property, and its state can be accessed by the **selected** property.

 CheckBox

This is much like a button, but with toggling as a default behavior.

 ComboBox

This component combines a list component with a button component, allowing a compact, drop-down/pop-up list of items for selection. The **selectedItem** (object) or **selectedIndex** (integer) property lets you get or set the selection.

▣ *Image*

This component lets you load external assets. Possible types are GIF, JPEG, PNG, and other SWFs. Use the **source** property to set a reference to an image.

A *Label*

This is a good solution for a simple, single-line label identifier.

▤ *List*

This component takes a list of items and displays them, allowing selection and adding scroll bars if there are too many items for its size.

ProgressBar

This component is great for showing progress of things like downloads. Pair this up with an Image component by setting the ProgressBar's **source** property to an Image control, and you'll see the download progress.

RadioButton

This CheckBox-like control is useful when grouped, so that selecting one deselects the others. The easiest way to use this control is by dragging a RadioButtonGroup to the stage, which will pop up a dialog box that lets you build your set of buttons visually.

Text

Use the Text component when you want to display chunks of text that you don't want to have scroll bars. It will set its size to a square that fits the text.

TextArea

Use a TextArea when you want a piece of text that may be larger than the available space. It will add scroll bars as needed.

TextInput

This is a common component for single-line input. With it, you can get or set the value of the text via the **text** property (this applies to all text components such as Text, TextArea, and RichTextEditor).

Layout Containers

Layout containers, or simply *containers*, are visual components used to manage the way an application is aligned or how controls are placed in relationship to one another. Sometimes, they will have an explicit visual representation, such as a Panel's title bar, but often they will only *show* themselves by the way they arrange other controls (or even other containers).

Application

You don't even have to think about this one. All Flex applications have an instance of the Application component as their root. It's a type of container with some special mojo that makes it work well as the base for everything else. By default, it lets you place components anywhere you like, but you can also make it line your components up vertically or horizontally. It's more than a container though, and provides support for a start-up progress bar (which you may have witnessed while loading a Flex application in your browser), and it has a few special options which help with customizing your application.

Canvas

This is a container that doesn't do any special layout. Set the **x** and **y** of any component that you place inside to have them show up where you want.

 Form

This container makes creating an HTML-like form layout easy. Pair it up with some FormItem components (explained next), and it will stack them up vertically, with the form fields being left-aligned.

 FormItem

This container takes a control such as a TextInput and gives it the option of having a label. Just set the **label** property on the FormItem container itself. When you place a few of these inside a Form container, everything will line up like those HTML forms you're used to using.

 HBox

This takes components and lines them up horizontally.

 Panel

This component is a container that has a window-like look, complete with a title bar. When you drop these on the stage in Design mode, the default layout will be "absolute," meaning components placed inside it should give x and y coordinates, much like a Canvas. But you can change the layout to "horizontal" or "vertical" as well, which means you can line up child controls in any way you like.

 VBox

This takes components and lines them up vertically.

Navigators

Navigators are a hybrid type of visual component that's like a layout container and a control mixed together. Its job is to take a set of containers, making only one visible at a time. Navigators make designing a modular interface easy.

 Accordion

This is similar to a TabNavigator (explained next), except it stacks containers vertically and animates when different sections are selected. A common usage scenario is with a group of Form containers, separating into sections what would instead be a large, scrolling form.

TabNavigator

It takes a set of containers, like HBoxes and Panels, and makes it so only one is visible at a time. File folder-like tabs are created with labels corresponding to the **label** properties of the individual containers within, and depending on which tab is selected by the user, that specific container will be made visible, hiding the rest.

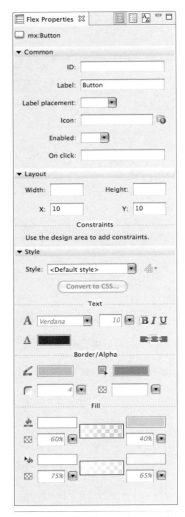

Figure 3-2. Flex Properties panel (Standard view)

There are also components called non-visual components, which provide functionality that isn't inherently visual. Think of a data component that could make connecting to remote data very easy—this would be one example of a component that doesn't have a face, so to speak. This means that for non-visual components, you won't be able to use Design mode to add them or modify them, but will need to code them in directly. In the next chapter we'll discuss coding in Source mode, and later in Chapter 8 we'll use our first non-visual component.

Modifying Properties Directly

You can modify your button component directly in Design mode, such as change its label and set up its size. For now, you can try changing the label of your button by double-clicking the button on your stage. A text input will pop up and let you change the label. You can also drag one of the handles that appear around your component to change its size. As for the blue dots that surround your component, those are constraint handles that let you easily set up a constraints-based layout, which I'll discuss a little later in Chapter 8.

Everything at Your Fingertips: The Properties Panel

To modify a component's properties, however, we'll need to learn about one more panel, the Flex Properties panel. You'll probably see it over on the right unless you've moved the panel or closed it. If you don't see it, you can show it by selecting Window→Flex Properties. Note that this panel doesn't appear in Source mode, because it's assumed you don't need it—you're coding by hand anyway, right? But in Design mode it can be your best friend.

It changes its options when you select different items on the stage, so if you select a button component by clicking it on the stage, you'll notice that the Flex Properties panel ("properties panel" for short) changes to show `mx:Button` in its heading and displays a custom set of properties for the button.

Standard View

Standard view is the default view of the Flex Properties panel (Figure 3-2), and it includes a custom layout for each component. It's really useful for modifying the most common properties of a component, such as its label, ID, width, and height. It's extremely useful for modifying styles of your component such as the font, text decoration (bold, italic, underline, and so on), and transparency.

Category View

Category view (Figure 3-3) is another view of the Properties panel. This view organizes all of a component's properties into a hierarchical tree view. This is much like how Standard view is organized into a few groups like Common, Layout, and Style. However, in Category view you have every possible property available. It's useful for getting to a particular kind of property quickly.

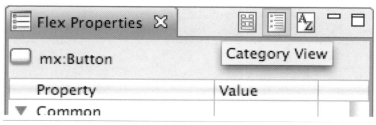

Figure 3-3. Flex Properties panel (Category view)

Alphabetical View

The third and final view available in the properties panel is Alphabetical view. This, like Category view, has all the possible properties available. However, unlike Category and Standard view, none of the properties are organized in Alphabetical View. It's just a flat list organized from A to Z. This view is great when you know the name or at least the first few letters of the property you want to modify. It's also useful for seeing at a glance what properties have been set on a particular component.

Feel free to drag a few components onto the stage and move them around. Modify some properties such as **label**, **width**, and **color** to get a feel for how this panel works.

NOTE

Flex Builder for Windows offers a quick way to get to a property when using Alphabetical view. Simply start typing the first few letters of the property, and the selection will scroll to the first match. This also works for other panels in Flex Builder that have a large list of items. Unfortunately, this functionality doesn't exist in the Mac version.

Common Properties

All Flex visual components (the ones you can manipulate in Design mode) inherit from a base component called UIComponent. This component has several properties related to visibility, mouse and keyboard interaction, focus, sizing, and all the goodies you'd expect for visual manipulation. Because buttons, text inputs, and containers *extend* this base component, meaning they inherit all of its functionality and add their own, they get all that stuff for free. This means that once you learn the usage of a property for one common component, you'll be able to take what you know and apply it to other components.

Take the **width** property of a button control, for example. You can likely guess that this property changes the width of this component. Because **width** is one of those properties that is shared among visual components, understanding how to use it with a button will help you to use it with other components as well.

What's an API? Or an SDK?

API stands for *application programming interface*, and it's a catch-all term for program functionality that's exposed to developers. You might have heard the term in the context of web services like the Yahoo! Search API, which allows you to query the Yahoo! search database. But *API* applies equally to any way you can access or modify some program or language. So for Flex, you'll often hear the term referring to how to use components.

You may also hear the term SDK, which is short for *software development kit*. This typically refers to a set of components or tools to aid (or enable) development for a particular platform. When downloading Flex Builder, you are downloading the development environment along with the Flex SDK, which is the library of components, the compilation tool, and a few other tools that make development in Flex possible.

Here's a fun sentence for you: "I built a Flex API for the Yahoo! Search API, and it's included in the Yahoo! Search SDK." This means, "I built a better way to connect to Yahoo! Search results via Flex, and this is part of a family of tools for using Yahoo! Search." You can get this Flex API by downloading the Yahoo! Search SDK (which includes APIs for other languages like Java and ColdFusion), available at *http://developer.yahoo.com/download*.

Following is a list of the most commonly used properties for the most common components, along with an example of each:

id

> id (short for *identifier*) is a very important property, because it's the name you give to a specific instance of a component. If you've placed two buttons on the stage, calling them button1 and button2 allows you to distinguish them later in code. Even better is when you give them descriptive names based on what they do in the application (for example, submitButton and refreshButton). It's not always necessary to type an id yourself, because Flex assigns one as necessary. But it's helpful to do so.

```
<mx:Button id="submitButton"/>
```

x

> This is a number that gets or sets the number of pixels a component should display to the right of its parent. This means, when a component is placed within a container, and that button's x value is set to 20, the button will display 20 pixels to the right of that container's left-most edge.

```
<mx:Button x="20"/>
```

y

> This is a number that gets or sets the number of pixels a component should display from the top of its parent. Similar to x, except this property controls vertical position instead of horizontal position. See the Sidebar "X and Why?: A Note about Coordinates" in Chapter 4 for more information on how the x and y properties work.

```
<mx:Button y="10"/>
```

visible

This property controls whether an item is visible on stage. Setting **visible** to **false** will make an item disappear from view, but it will still take up space. For instance, if I have four buttons inside an HBox container, aligning all four horizontally, and I make the second button invisible, the two buttons to its right and the one to its left will remain in the same place, because the invisible button still makes room for itself (see Figure 3-4).

```
<mx:HBox>
    <mx:Button label="One"/>
    <mx:Button label="Two" visible="false"/>
    <mx:Button label="Three"/>
    <mx:Button label="Four"/>
</mx:HBox>
```

Figure 3-4. Button "Two" is invisible, in case you didn't notice.

includeInLayout

Setting this to **false** on a component will cause a container to ignore that component when calculating layout. If you don't want something to take up space, you set this to **false**. It's useful when wanting to make a component invisible along with not affecting your layout (see Figure 3-5).

```
<mx:HBox>
    <mx:Button label="One"/>
    <mx:Button label="Two" visible="false" includeInLayout="false"/>
    <mx:Button label="Three"/>
    <mx:Button label="Four"/>
</mx:HBox>
```

Figure 3-5. Button "Two" still exists, though it's invisible and doesn't take up space.

toolTip

A *toolTip* is a little pop-up message that displays when you hover your mouse over a component for a moment, as shown in Figure 3-6. It can help describe the item's purpose. All Flex UI components support the **toolTip** property, so it's easy to implement.

```
<mx:Button toolTip="Click Me!"/>
```

Figure 3-6. A button with a toolTip

label

Not all components use labels, but many do. For a button, a label is a no-brainer—it's the text that displays on the button. CheckBox components use them in a similar way. Containers use them as well. For instance, the FormItem container will display a label, and can be used as a description of a field when paired with another control, such as a TextInput, in a Form (see Figure 3-7). For other layout containers, the label will display when paired with navigation components. That is to say, when using a navigation component such as a TabNavigator, a container's label will display as the label of the tab that selects it.

```
<mx:CheckBox label="I have read the terms and conditions"/>
<mx:Button label="Submit"/>
```

> **NOTE**
>
> *Note that there is also a control called* **Label** *which is used to place single lines of text throughout your application. As such, it doesn't take a property called* **label** *to change the words it displays. Rather, it uses a property called* **text**.

I have read the terms and conditions

Submit

Figure 3-7. A checkbox and button with their own labels

text

This property changes the text displayed in text controls such as TextInput, TextArea, and Label (see Figure 3-8).

```
<mx:Label text="Enter Your Name:"/>
<mx:TextInput text="Alaric"/>
```

Enter Your Name: Alaric

Figure 3-8. Two controls that both use the text *property*

alpha

alpha is short for *alpha channel*, and it is a number from 0 to 1 that controls how transparent an item is. If you want what is behind a component to show through, you set an alpha value to less than 1. It's percentage-based, so .9 means 90 percent opaque, .45 means 45 percent opaque, and so on. In the case of a list control, setting its alpha to .5 would allow the colored background of your application to show through (see Figure 3-9), making the list halfway transparent. (Or is it halfway opaque?)

```
<mx:TextArea alpha="0.5" text="The alpha of this TextArea control is
    set to .5"/>
```

> The alpha of this TextArea control is set to .5, or 50%. This doesn't affect the text itself, but it does affect the background, which is by default white.

Figure 3-9. A TextArea control with an alpha *set to 50%*

enabled

Setting **enabled** to **false** makes a component unavailable. Typically, this will cause the component to gray out and to not respond to mouse actions as shown in Figure 3-10. This is useful if you'd like to disable a button that shouldn't be used yet, but it also works with containers and their children. You can set an entire Panel's **enabled** property to **false**, and everything inside will be disabled as well.

```
<mx:Panel title="Enabled Panel" enabled="true">
    <mx:ColorPicker/>
    <mx:NumericStepper/>
    <mx:Button label="Button"/>
    <mx:CheckBox label="Checkbox"/>
    <mx:DateField/>
    <mx:ComboBox/>
</mx:Panel>

<mx:Panel title="Disabled Panel" enabled="false">
    <mx:ColorPicker/>
    <mx:NumericStepper/>
    <mx:Button label="Button"/>
    <mx:CheckBox label="Checkbox"/>
    <mx:DateField/>
    <mx:ComboBox/>
</mx:Panel>
```

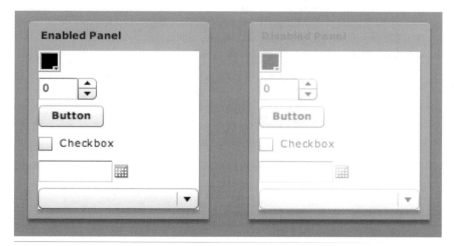

Figure 3-10. Two Panels with the same contents; one is enabled, the other disabled

source

You can use this property for Image controls and other controls that point to an external file. You can also use it with the ProgressBar control to determine the progress of that Image control. For instance, two usages of this property would be for what an Image control should display, and for what a ProgressBar should watch.

```
<mx:ProgressBar source="{photo}"/>
<mx:Image id="photo" source="http://greenlike.com/photos/lydia.jpg" />
```

Figure 3-11. An Image and a ProgressBar working together beautifully

Let's face it, some of these properties will take rote memorization, but when using Design mode, the most common options are right at your fingertips. Plus, because these components were designed well and with a lot of commonalities, most of the properties will seem natural.

Building a User Interface

Now that you're familiar with some basics of Design mode, you can begin to plan your `HelloWorld` application. If you've added some components to the stage, remove them so you have a blank slate again. You can select each one individually and press the Delete key, or you can click and drag on the stage to select components and press the Delete key. Alternatively, select Edit→Select All or press Ctrl+A (⌘+A in OS X) to select everything, and then press Delete.

Let's build a simple example using some common components:

1. Drag a Panel to the stage. A Panel is a type of container, so you'll find it in the Components panel in the Layout section.

2. Give the Panel a title by double-clicking it or entering it in the properties panel. I'll use `Howdy Ya'll`, but feel free to say "hi" any way you like.

3. Drag a Label component into the Panel. Because a Panel is a container, it can hold items just like the main Application component can (which is also a container). So, drop the Label in this Panel, and place it near the top of the Panel.

4. Give the Label the text `My name is:`, and make the text bold. You can apply bold by selecting the label and clicking the Bold icon in the Flex Properties panel in the Style section.

5. Drop a TextInput control under this Label.

6. Drop a CheckBox control under the TextInput.

7. Give the CheckBox the label `I'm a Flex Expert!`. (You modify its label the same way as most components, by double-clicking it on the stage.)

There you are—you have created the user interface for your first Flex application. Let's run it in a browser by clicking the Run button (remember the green arrow?).

Flex Speaks Your Language

So, I mentioned you should say "hi" in any way you like, and I meant it. If "hello" to you is Olá, 你好, or こんにちは, you're in luck. Because Flex supports UTF-8, you can insert characters from most languages without hassle. You can do this in both Source and Design mode, so you can make a Flex application in any language. If you don't expect everyone to have the proper fonts available on their machine, you can always embed fonts into a Flex application (see Chapter 14 for how to embed fonts and other assets). While this will increase file size, it will ensure that characters display just as you envisioned them.

Save and Launch

When you attempt to run a project but haven't yet saved changes, you'll be greeted with a dialog box asking whether you want to save your work (see Figure 3-12). You'll see a nice option at the bottom of the dialog box allowing you to "Always save resources before launching." This is convenient, because you can then click Run after modifying your project, and your work will be saved, built, and then run. I usually leave this check box turned on, because it saves time and effort.

Figure 3-12. Save and Launch dialog box

You should see your application in a browser window (see Figure 3-13). Feel free to type your name in the text input and turn on the check box that says "I'm a Flex Expert!" It will give you a feel for how these components work and, anyway, you deserve it!

Figure 3-13. Your first application

Summary

Now you're comfortable with Design mode, and you're able to create an application by using the standard Flex components. You still have a few skills to learn to make your applications interactive and fun, but you're well on your way to mastering Flex. In the next chapter, you'll look at the code that was generated from Design mode and start to write your own.

CHAPTER 4

USING SOURCE MODE

In this chapter, you'll go right into the heart of Adobe Flex 3, MXML. Using the code that was generated automatically in the previous chapter, you'll get a feel for what makes MXML tick. Once you're comfortable with the basics, you can start to write your own code using the built-in editor.

What Design Mode Does

What Design mode does is create MXML code for you. When you drag a component onto the stage, Design mode writes a corresponding tag in the main application's *.mxml* file. If you modify the MXML code in Source mode, Design mode updates and shows those changes.

Open the application you started in the previous chapter, then switch to Source mode to look at the code that Design mode created for you.

Typing Stereotypes

The great thing about Flex Builder's Design mode is that you might never "grow out" of it. I've been developing in Flex for years, and while I know MXML by heart and can get most tasks done very quickly, I still find myself using Design mode on occasion. As good as MXML is, it's still so much more intuitive to design an application visually, and besides, a ton of features in Design mode make it worthwhile. So, don't listen if someone says you're not a real developer if you don't do everything in a text editor. The goal of any developer is to use the right tools for the job, and Design mode is often the right tool.

Anatomy of a Flex Application

Looking at the source code for this simple **HelloWorld** example, you'll see something like the following:

```
<?xml version="1.0" encoding="utf-8"?>
<mx:Application xmlns:mx="http://www.adobe.com/2006/mxml"
    layout="absolute">
    <mx:Panel x="10" y="10" layout="absolute" title="Howdy Ya'll">
        <mx:Label text="My name is:" fontWeight="bold" x="10" y="14"/>
        <mx:TextInput x="5" y="41"/>
        <mx:CheckBox label="I'm a Flex Expert!" x="10" y="71"/>
    </mx:Panel>
</mx:Application>
```

Now I'll break this code down for you. The first line contains an XML declaration, which is just some optional XML-specific stuff. It's the next line with the **Application** tag where the "Flex" begins.

Every Flex application will begin with a root tag. For Flex applications that are deployed to the web, that root tag is called **Application**. For AIR applications, the root tag is called **WindowedApplication** and is pretty much the same, with just a few desktop-specific features. For your application, which is going to be viewed in a browser, you'll see **<mx:Application>** displayed at the root. Notice the attribute **layout="absolute"** in this tag. That's one of those defaults that Flex throws in, and it means "make everything placed here need *x*,*y* coordinates." Because an Application is a container, it has the ability to either require *x*,*y* coordinates or lay components out in a horizontal or vertical stack (more on this topic in the box "X and Why?: A Note about Coordinates").

The **Panel** tag within the **Application** tag is also a container, and it has its default layout set to **absolute** as well. Notice the attributes **x="10"** and **y="10"**, which tell Flex to place the panel 10 pixels from the left corner of the Application. The **Label**, **TextInput**, and **CheckBox** tags also have their coordinates set, but these coordinates are relative to the panel container in which they appear.

Of course, these tags have other attributes as well. Take a look at the Panel, which has its title set via the **title** attribute. In addition, the Label uses the **text** property to set its text and has a style property called **fontWeight** to make it bold. Finally, the CheckBox uses a property called **label** to set its label.

Try editing the code and changing some of the properties. You could, for instance, change the label on the CheckBox to read "I'm a Flex Genius!" When you're done, switch to Design mode to see the changes.

Components Added in Source Mode

Now try modifying the UI by typing the MXML to add a component. Right below the CheckBox but still within the **Panel** tag, add a button component by typing `<mx:Button label="Click me"/>`.

Switching back to Design mode, you might notice that the button is placed on top of everything else and probably not where you envisioned it (below the CheckBox). That's because you haven't set the *x,y* coordinates for the button yet, and Flex defaults to **x="0"** and **y="0"**. Now, you have the choice of guessing the coordinates and typing them in Source mode or moving the button in Design mode. Actually, you have another option. If you want a vertical layout for the items in your panel instead of having to set every item's *x,y* coordinates, you could change one property of the panel. You guessed it: **layout**. Change the panel's **layout** property to **vertical** either by typing in Source mode or by changing it in the Properties panel.

Now the items are stacked on top of each other vertically, and that's great. But they're stuck to the left edge of the panel in a not-so-attractive way. That's where the property **paddingLeft** comes into play. If you set the **paddingLeft** property of the panel to 5, you will create a pleasing amount of space between the left edge of the panel and its contents.

Titles, Labels, and Text

You might have noticed that the Panel, TextInput, and CheckBox controls each have a different property for what essentially sets their label. Why not just have a property called **label**? Well, actually the panel does have that property, but it's not used to display in the title bar. It uses the label to identify itself when used in navigation controls, which I'll discuss in Chapter 11. The panel also has a property called **status** that displays some text in the upper-right corner. I suppose for the Label, giving it a property called **label** didn't make sense aesthetically, but the main reason is that it shares the **text** property with other text display controls like Text, TextArea, and RichTextEditor. This concept might seem confusing at first, but you'll soon get the hang of which properties are used for what.

X and Why?: A Note about Coordinates

If you've ever studied geometry, you're familiar with *x,y* coordinates. You might remember that *x* means placement along a horizontal axis, and *y* refers to placement along a vertical axis. And you might have noticed something different about how *x,y* coordinates work in Flash. A Cartesian coordinate system, shown in Figure 4-1, will have an origin point at 0,0 and *x* and *y* values that increase as you go toward the top or toward the right. So, a point at **x="3"** and **y="5"** will be placed up and to the right of the origin.

In Flash, the origin is at the top left of the stage, and the *x* and *y* values increase as you go toward the ***bottom of the screen*** or toward the right. So, in essence, the *y* values are backward in Flash. That's why giving a button a *y* value of 20 will place it 20 pixels from the top, and a *y* value of -20 will move it nearly out of view—right off the top of the stage.

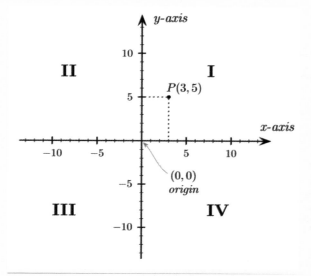

Figure 4-1. A Cartesian coordinate system

Code Completion

You've no doubt seen that Flex Builder pops up a list of autocomplete entries when you start to type something in the editor in Source mode. This auto-completion is one of its most useful and powerful features. Typos and misspellings can wreck your project, and accepting a little help can go a long way toward preventing errors and frustration.

When you begin to type an attribute, Flex Builder pops up suggestions, and the most likely one (the one at the top of the list) is already selected (see Figure 4-2), so pressing Enter inserts the complete text for you. This auto-completion is useful not only for attributes but also for tags. If you're about to insert a button, you don't even have to begin writing the mx: part—simply typing the left bracket and the first few letters gets you started. And if you ever want the autocompletion to pop up faster, or to pop up again after it is closed, just press Ctrl+spacebar, and it comes to save the day.

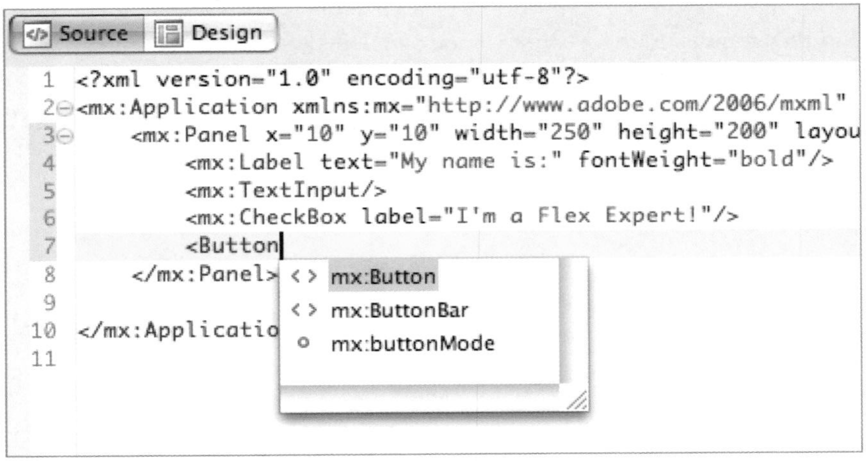

Figure 4-2. Autocompletion menu

MXML in Depth

MXML is the heart of your source code. It's relatively easy to read and write, and understanding just a few rules will take you a long way in getting the job done. Because MXML is a type of XML, it's worth going over some of the basics of XML.

The *XML* in MXML

One of the first books I read that had anything to do with programming was a book about XML. I wasn't studying computer science at the time, though I'd always had a keen interest in programming and web design. I just remember wondering what this fancy language was that I kept hearing about. Much to my surprise, I discovered I had been using it all along with HTML (specifically XHTML).

It's all about structure

I learned that XML was just structured text, *any* text, that uses angle brackets (< and >). That was the way it represented data, just by structuring via tags created with angle brackets. There wasn't much of a vocabulary to it, because the author of XML decided his or her own vocabulary. XML was purely syntax and structure.

You're reading a book right now, so you certainly know that a book contains different parts such as chapters and sections. If you wanted to represent a book in XML, you could create your own tags like **<book>**, **<chapter>**, and **<section>** and then add information to a document using those tags.

```
<book>
    <chapter>
        <section/>
    </chapter>
</book>
```

XML stands for Extensible Markup Language, and the *extensible* part is in creating your own tags. The *markup* part means it can include text as well as extra information about that text, via tags. In the case of HTML, you can use tags to provide text as well as information such as formatting for that text. As an example, early text-only word processors required writers to use tags equivalent to **<i>** and **<b>** to add italic and bold formatting (respectively) to a document. These tags would be converted to the proper format when printing, and this same type of markup is used in HTML today.

More importantly for a Flex application, XML shows hierarchy and structure. MXML is, if you will, a vocabulary of XML, created to provide a way to easily write the structure of a Flex application. So, lucky for us Flex developers, we can describe an application by simply writing it.

A few ground rules

If you follow these few simple rules, you'll have worry-free development:

All that is opened must be closed: An important fact to remember about XML is that each tag must be complete. That is to say, if a tag is opened, it has to be closed at some point. Computers are awfully logical, and they get upset when rules aren't followed. A tag definition, as you've seen, is created with a left bracket (<), some text that is the tag's name, followed by a right bracket (>), for example, the tag **<book>**. This is considered an open tag. To show that a tag is completely finished and won't have anything else inside it, it must be closed by using a forward slash (/).

You can ensure all tags are closed in a couple ways. The first is by creating an end tag for each beginning tag. So if you create the tag **<book>**, you must eventually close it with the end tag **</book>**. Another, shorthand way to close a tag—if it doesn't have any nested tags—is by adding a forward slash immediately before the right angle bracket of the same tag, like this: **<book/>**. So **<book></book>** is equivalent to **<book/>**.

Case matters: XML is case-sensitive. That is to say, uppercase letters and lowercase letters aren't considered the same. So, **<book>** and **<Book>** aren't the same in XML. And that means **<mx:Text>** and **<mx:text>** are different as well.

Declarations are optional, but polite: The first line of an XML document may (optionally) contain a line declaring that it's XML and what encoding it uses. The declaration looks like this:

```
<?xml version="1.0" encoding="utf-8"?>
```

All MXML files created through Flex Builder automatically contain this declaration, so you don't need to worry about it.

Because MXML is a version of XML, MXML inherits all of these rules.

The Anatomy of a Tag

A tag can contain information in two ways, either by *content* or by *attributes*. Content is simply the text that exists between two tags, and attributes are text inside the opening tag only, with their information enclosed in quotes. Check out the following XML:

```
<book title="Learning Flex" author="Alaric Cole">
    <chapter title="Getting Up to Speed"/>
    <chapter title="Setting Up Your Environment"/>
</book>
```

In this example, **<book>** is the root tag, and the title and author of that tag are placed as attributes of that book. The code also has two child tags representing two chapters. Compare the previous code to the following, which contains the same information but arranged in a different way:

```
<book>
    <title>Learning Flex</title>
    <author>Alaric Cole</author>
    <chapter>
        <title>Getting Up to Speed</title>
    </chapter>
    <chapter>
        <title>Setting Up your Environment</title>
    </chapter>

</book>
```

This code is essentially the same as the first, but you'll notice the second one is a bit more verbose. The first uses attributes, and the second uses nested tags. So, attributes can be useful as a more compact way to represent the same information as nested tags—and more compact means more readable. Compare this code to the same example in MXML.

You're probably used to seeing something like this:

```
<mx:Label text="Learning Flex"/>
```

But did you know you could do the following?

```
<mx:Label>
    <mx:text>Learning Flex</mx:text>
</mx:Label>
```

Those two code examples are essentially the same, one using an attribute to add the **text** property and the other using a nested tag. You'll usually want to use attributes in MXML for the reasons I stated earlier: compactness and readability.

However, occasionally you'll need to use nested tags for properties, instead of using attributes. Because nested tags allow more complex content instead of simply a single-line piece of text or numbers, they're useful for plugging in data that can't be represented in an attribute. Consider the case of the **text** property. If the text were a whole paragraph, it would look strange to place it inline as an attribute. Even more important is when a component expects structured data. You might need to set the data provider of a list control, which would be an array of items, not just a single line of text. The same is true for other properties that accept an array of items, such as the **columns** property of a DataGrid. The **columns** property lets you set properties on individual columns, and you can see an example of this by dragging a DataGrid control to your application in Design mode. You'll probably see code like this generated:

```
<mx:DataGrid>
    <mx:columns>
        <mx:DataGridColumn headerText="Column 1" dataField="col1"/>
        <mx:DataGridColumn headerText="Column 2" dataField="col2"/>
        <mx:DataGridColumn headerText="Column 3" dataField="col3"/>
    </mx:columns>
</mx:DataGrid>
```

The **columns** property of the DataGrid can't really be written as an attribute because it expects a list of **DataGridColumn** tags, which in turn have their own properties to set.

The *MX* in MXML: Namespaces Explained

You'll notice that each tag in the MXML example contains by default the designation **mx** followed by a colon. This is an XML *namespace*, stating that the **Button** and **Panel** tags belong to the **mx** namespace. What's a namespace? Take a look at the word itself: *name + space*. A namespace is a designation of what a name for something is in regard to its placement in some type of structure. Say, for the sake of this example, that your name is John Smith. Of course, lots of other John Smiths exist, so how can you distinguish yourself? Well, you could use your location, like your home address, because it's highly unlikely that several John Smiths live at that address (unless you've named your son John Smith, but that's a different story. Anyway, he'd at least have a "Jr." or

Namespaces in Nested Properties

Notice that you must use the namespace (usually **mx:**) within a nested property of an MXML tag. So while attempting to make a property into a nested tag instead of an attribute, you might be tempted to write the following (incorrect) code for assigning text to a Label:

```
<mx:Label>
   <text>Some Text</text>
</mx:Label>
```

However, because the **text** property is its own tag, it must use the namespace **mx:** as well, to match it with its parent tag:

```
<mx:Label>
   <mx:text>Some Text</mx:text>
</mx:Label>
```

If you're using Flex Builder to write your application, autocompletion will usually insert this namespace for you, so you don't have to think about it.

Roman numeral attached to his name to differentiate himself). So, in terms of XML namespaces, you could refer to yourself as *123.PineStreet:JohnSmith*; that's a name you're unlikely to witness anywhere else!

So, namespaces help distinguish different components (which may have the same name) by their location. In terms of MXML and ActionScript, the namespaces refer to the package structure of your components (what folders they're organized in), but I'll explain the details of packages later. For now just accept that the Flex components are in the **mx** namespace because the source for these components is located in a special grouping of folders. If you were to create your own button-like component and wanted to name it Button, you could do so, because you'd be placing the source for your special button code in a different location than the Flex button component. You might then refer to your button in MXML as something like **<special:Button/>** to differentiate it from **<mx:Button/>**.

What if you aren't planning to use your own components? Why not just make **mx** the default namespace and omit all the extra **mx:** designations? That is, why can't you just see the tags **<Button/>** and **<Panel/>** instead of **<mx:Button/>** and **<mx:Panel/>**? Well, the truth is you can if you'd like. Looking at the beginning of a typical MXML file, you'll see the following:

```
<mx:Application xmlns:mx="http://www.adobe.com/2006/mxml">
```

Note the part that says **xmlns:mx="http://www.adobe.com/2006/mxml"**. Translated to English, that means "Create an XML namespace called 'mx' and point it to the location 'http://www.adobe.com/2006/mxml'."

Where Does This Namespace Point?

If you try to point your browser to *http://www.adobe.com/2006/mxml*, you probably won't see anything interesting. Although it looks like a web address, it's really just an identifier. Using the web address paradigm assures that you won't have any conflicts in naming. This way, if you eventually create your own identifier, you have the option of using your web address, which makes it unlikely another person will have the same identifier.

By default, the namespace for Flex components is set up to be **mx**, but you can change it. For instance, instead of mx, you could use the name **flex** by doing the following:

```
<flex:Application xmlns:flex="http://www.adobe.com/2006/mxml">
```

This line of code lets you use **<flex:Button/>** instead of **<mx:Button/>** in your MXML file. Now, if you want to be able to use simply **<Button/>**, change the namespace to an empty name:

```
<Application xmlns="http://www.adobe.com/2006/mxml">
```

NOTE

*Notice how the **Application** tag, which declares this namespace, is also affected by it.*

Using this code, the default namespace will be empty, so when you type `<Button/>`, you're referring to the Flex button. If you had created your own, you'd still need to use your namespace to distinguish your components from the Flex defaults.

When you start using third-party components or begin creating your own, you're more likely to see a package name used as a namespace identifier. Instead of something that looks like a web address, you'll see something like `xmlns:components="best.flex.components.*"`. I'll go over packages more in depth in later chapters, but for brevity, just accept that a namespace in MXML lets you distinguish between different sets of components by the folder in which they're located.

I Do Declare

The beauty of using markup languages for laying out an application is that they're *declarative*. Declarative means you're stating something. (Remember all those grammar exercises in school? Wait, that was an interrogative sentence. Oh, but that one was declarative. Find me an imperative sentence. There it was!) In essence, you can just say, "I think a button should go here," and Flex will listen. (Well, you do have to type it, unless you have a really good speech-to-text program.) So instead of building your UI in scripts and dealing with procedures, you just place a `Button` tag where you want a button to exist, and Flex takes care of implementing it.

By comparison, ActionScript, the scripting language for Flex, is *imperative*. That means you create commands that you want the computer to follow.

I'll show a couple of examples to demonstrate this idea. Here's how create a panel with a button inside it in ActionScript:

```
import mx.containers.Panel;
import mx.controls.Button;

var panel:Panel = new Panel();
var button:Button = new Button();

addChild(panel);
panel.addChild(button);
```

This code instantiates a panel and a button and places the button within the panel. (`addChild()` is the method for adding components to the display list, which is the container that holds visual objects in your application.) Notice how you're issuing commands. ("Computer, import! Computer, add child! Am I talking to myself?")

Compare this script with the same thing in MXML:

```
<mx:Panel>
    <mx:Button/>
</mx:Panel>
```

What Does MX Mean?

MX is an undisclosed acronym that is also used for the name MXML and for previous versions of Macromedia products (Flash MX, Dreamweaver MX). Some think it stands for "Maximum eXperience," but you can make it whatever you like.

That's much less verbose, isn't it? And it's not necessary to really read the code and follow its flow to understand what's happening; you can quickly scan the MXML and visualize the structure.

Not only that, but now the code is super easy to modify. Say you decided that the button should be outside the panel instead of inside it. You'd simply move the **Button** tag outside the **Panel** tag, and it would work fine. For the ActionScript version, you'd have to follow the logic of the script and know that you needed to change the method **panel.addChild(button)** to just **addChild(button)**, because you want to add the child to the main stage and not the panel.

Summary

Now you've learned enough to really get moving with Flex and Flex Builder. You know how to work with Design mode as well as with Source mode and got your feet wet writing simple code. You've learned the basics of XML and how it relates to MXML. Now you're ready to get moving. Next up on the agenda: making your applications interactive. For that you'll need to learn a little more about ActionScript.

CHAPTER 5

LEARNING THE BASICS OF SCRIPTING

ActionScript is the glue that holds your application together. While you'll use MXML for the layout and structure of your application, you'll generally need (at least a little) ActionScript to make things happen. How much you'll need depends on the application, but then, as they say, a little goes a long way.

Knowing where to optimally place scripts, how to create reusable code, and other basics of ActionScript programming will help you to build more powerful Flex applications. Also, recognizing how ActionScript and MXML work together is key to understanding the Flex framework. In this chapter, you'll gain the knowledge you need to get going with this powerful—and surprisingly simple—programming language.

Getting Ready

In this chapter, you'll learn to make your HelloWorld application from Chapter 3 "do something." So go ahead and open that project again; we'll be using some of it to do some hands-on learning.

Often, buttons are the main point of contact for making something happen, so that's where you'll start. The button in your HelloWorld application says "Click me," so it makes sense to start with it.

As an example, I'll show you how to autofill the TextInput with your name when you click this button. That means you'll be referring to this TextInput in ActionScript to access the text properties. To do that, the TextInput will need a name. That's where the **id** attribute comes into play. Using the Flex Properties panel in Flex Builder's Design mode or using Source mode, add an **id** attribute to the TextInput, calling it `fullNameTextInput`.

> ## Naming Conventions
>
> One popular naming convention, and the one I use for components, is appending the type of component to the **id**. For example, the TextInput in the HelloWorld application is used for inputting your name. So, you could call it **fullName**. (You can't call it **full name** because spaces aren't allowed in **id** attributes.)
>
> However, you might later create a Label that also displays your name, so you wouldn't want to call them both **fullName**, you'll want to differentiate the two. It's an easy trick to call one **fullNameTextInput** and another **fullNameLabel**, which is just adding the component's type to its **id**. If this technique results in too many letters for you, you can instead append the initials of the component type, calling it **fullNameTI**.

Inline ActionScript

Inline ActionScript is script placed in an MXML tag. Typically in an application, the program responds to certain events that occur, such as clicking or dragging the mouse, or typing with the keyboard (more on this topic later). You can respond to these events by telling a component to wait for a specific event and then do something in response. A typical scenario is a person clicking a button and that button changing the property of another component. For that, you can use inline ActionScript:

```
<mx:Button id="myButton" click="someComponent.someProperty =
    'something'" />
```

All you had to do was add a **click** attribute to the Button and within that attribute place ActionScript. Here's a real example for the application:

```
<mx:Button label="Click me" click="fullNameTextInput.text =
    'John Smith'"/>
```

This code says, when the button is clicked, make **fullNameTextInput**'s **text** property equal to "John Smith." The **fullNameTextInput.text = 'John Smith'** part is ActionScript, placed inline. That's scripting at its easiest, placed right in an MXML tag.

Dot Notation

Previously, you added attributes to a tag to change the properties of a component. For instance, adding a **label** attribute to an **<mx:Button/>** tag changed the Button's **label** property. This same behavior is available in ActionScript as well, through the use of *dot notation*. Having created a TextInput called **fullNameTextInput** in MXML, you can easily modify its **text** property via the **text** attribute:

```
<mx:TextInput id="fullNameTextInput" text="John Smith"/>
```

But, you can also change this **text** property in ActionScript. You do this by typing the **id** of the component, **fullNameTextInput**, followed by a period and then immediately followed by the name of the property you want to modify:

```
fullNameTextInput.text
```

The period, or *dot*, is a way to say you want to access something that belongs to this specific TextInput. The same would work for a Button called **myButton**. To access its **label** property, you'd type the following:

```
myButton.label
```

Assignment

To change the value of such a property, you use something called *assignment*. You want to assign the value of a property to another value, which you can do with the equal sign (=) followed by the value. So, to change the **text** of a TextInput control, you could use the following ActionScript:

```
fullNameTextInput.text = "John Smith";
```

What's the difference between setting the **text** property this way and setting it in MXML through attributes? Technically, there is no difference. However, in an MXML attribute, you're setting the property on the component as it's created. In ActionScript, you can set a property any time you wish, or delay an assignment until an event occurs, such as when someone clicks a button.

You might have noticed the use of single (') quotes instead of double (") quotes inside the **click** attribute. The single quotes appear simply because double quotes would confuse the compiler as to when the **click** attribute was finished. The funny thing is, you can actually switch the single and double quotes, just as long as whatever begins the quote also ends it:

```
<mx:Button label="Click me" click='fullNameTextInput.text =
    "John Smith"'/>
```

Now what if you wanted to do two or more things at once, all when someone clicks a button? It's just as easy, because you can add multiple statements within the **click** attribute. Say you want to automatically select a CheckBox when someone clicks the Button. All that takes is a little more code. Be sure to first give the CheckBox an **id** of **expertCheckBox** and then modify your code to include a little more in the **click** attribute:

```
<mx:Button label="Click me" click=" fullNameTextInput.text='John Smith';
    expertCheckBox.selected=true "/>
```

In this case, you're setting the **selected** property of the CheckBox to **true**, which means it's selected and displays a check mark. This is also a property assignment and is done the same way, using the equal sign. Notice that a semicolon (;) separates the two assignments. The semicolon tells the compiler you have two different statements occurring on the same line.

As you can see, however, the code is starting to get a little messier. If you had three or four assignments, the **click** attribute would get fairly long. Luckily, functions let you place the code in a more convenient place, and you'll get a few benefits besides.

Functions

A *function* is a piece of code that you create for reusability. You place some ActionScript code within a function, give the function a name, and when you want to run that code, you reference that function. In the following section, you'll put your previous code, which sets the text of the TextInput and the selection of the CheckBox, inside a function. To do so, you need to move your code from inside the tag to another location.

Where to Place a Function

To place code elsewhere in the MXML file, you use a tag called **<mx:Script/>**. The **<mx:Script/>** tag is a special tag that you can add only in Source mode, because it's not a visual component—but you're not going to be writing code in Design mode, so that's fine. Here's what the tag looks like:

```
<mx:Script>

    <![CDATA[

        //Your code goes here

    ]]>

</mx:Script>
```

You might be curious as to what that cryptic **CDATA** tag is all about. **CDATA** is a special XML entity that tells the compiler not to look at the contents of this tag as XML. Because you'll be writing ActionScript here, which may have characters such as quotes and angle brackets (**<** and **>**) that can confuse the XML parser, you wrap it in a **CDATA** block. It's all cryptic-looking, so you're unlikely to type such a thing by accident! Don't worry if it looks too complicated to remember, because using code completion with an **<mx:Script/>** tag inserts all this code for you. Just place the insertion point after your **<mx:Application/>** tag, begin typing **<mx:Script**, and then press Enter. Flex Builder inserts all the necessary mumbo jumbo automatically. You can also add a CDATA block by selecting Source→Add CDATA Block in Flex Builder.

NOTE

In the following examples that show ActionScript, all the code would be placed inside an **<mx:Script/>** *tag.*

How to Create a Function

To create your function, use the keyword **function** followed by the name you want to give it, followed by a couple of parentheses:

```
function setForm()
```

Following this function statement, place a couple of curly braces ({ and }). These braces act as containers for the function—everything in them is considered part of the function. So, add the braces, and place the code that you had in the **click** attribute inside them:

```
function setForm()
{
    fullNameTextInput.text = 'John Smith';
    expertCheckBox.selected = true;
}
```

Now you have your code, which does two things, placed nicely in a function. All you have to do is *call* that function (tell it to run), and this code will execute. How do you do that? You call the function by using its name followed by the parentheses:

```
<mx:Button label="Click me" click="setForm()"/>
```

Now when the button is clicked, both the TextInput and CheckBox selection will be set.

Function Access

You'll typically see access modifiers such as **public** or **private**, placed before function definitions. These set the *access* of the function, or the ability for the function to be seen and used. By default, the access is set to **internal**, which means the function can be used by the current application as well as any components within its package. (In Chapter 12, I'll discuss packages in detail.) Often, you'll see functions set as **public**, meaning they can be accessed from anywhere, and this is what I'll typically use in my examples. The keyword **private** would make the function accessible only in that Application.

If you're not sure which to use, just set access to **public**. This makes the function available for use anywhere in your code, so you won't run into any confusion. Later on, you can always change the access to something else, if you want to be more restrictive.

Why would you ever want to restrict access? You might have functions in your code that apply only to the current application—or component, if you start creating your own. For instance, you may have a helper function that is only useful where it is created, and don't want other components to have access to it, because such access is unnecessary.

> **NOTE**
>
> *Actually, access applies not only to functions, but to any variable declaration. I'll explain variables a little later on in this chapter.*

Function Parameters

What about those parentheses? You put them there because they help designate something as a function. When you see them in your code, you'll instantly know something is a function. But the parentheses are more than just aesthetics—you can use them to pass information, called *parameters*, into the function. This, in essence, gives the function dynamic information at the time of its call. Say you wanted to tell the function which text to set on the TextInput like you did in the inline MXML. You can do that by using a parameter for the function:

```
public function setForm(txt)
{
    fullNameTextInput.text = txt;
    expertCheckBox.selected = true;
}
```

This code creates a variable called **txt** of type String that's available just to the function. You give **txt** a value when you call the function by passing a value in the parentheses:

```
<mx:Button label="Click me" click="setForm('John Smith')"/>
```

Now the text for the input isn't set in stone; it can change on the fly via this function.

You can also pass multiple parameters to a function:

```
public function setForm(txt, sel)
{
    fullNameTextInput.text = txt;
    expertCheckBox.selected = sel;
}
```

Now you can call the function like this:

```
<mx:Button label="Click me" click="setForm('John Smith', true)"/>
```

A useful feature is setting defaults for the parameters, which lets you decide whether to pass in values when you call the function. If you don't pass a value, the parameter will use the default value. You set defaults by setting the parameter to a value when it's declared:

```
public function setForm(txt = "John Smith", sel = true)
{
    fullNameTextInput.text = txt;
    expertCheckBox.selected = sel;
}
```

Now you call the function with zero, one, or two parameters. Here's none:

```
<mx:Button label="Click me" click="setForm()"/>
```

Here's one:

```
<mx:Button label="Click me" click="setForm('John Smith')"/>
```

And here's two:

```
<mx:Button label="Click me" click="setForm('John Smith', true)"/>
```

Methods

Now that you've learned about functions, it's time you learned about methods. This topic is going to be an easy one, because basically functions are methods. When talking about a method, I really mean a function that is part of a class. You created a function called **setForm()** in your code. What happens is that the **setForm()** function becomes a method of your main application. Most classes have methods as well as properties, and the most common controls and other classes you'll be using may have some useful methods as well.

One method you've already learned about is **addEventListener()**, which registers event listeners. Another is **addChild()**, which places instances of components on the display list. Another fun one is **setFocus()**, which is available on all controls and makes that control the active control. For a TextInput, it places the cursor so that you can begin typing, very useful for forms so that you don't have to use the mouse to be able to start typing in a field.

Now you'll use this function to make your little application more usable. You'll want to call **setFocus()** on the **fullNameTextInput** control once the application is ready. (Calling **setFocus()** too soon may not work as you'd like.) So, you'll register an event listener with the **applicationComplete** event. Add the following attribute to your **Application** tag:

```
applicationComplete="fullNameTextInput.setFocus()"
```

NOTE

Now when your application loads, the TextInput control is ready to accept keyboard input. Note that there may be issues with the focus of Flash Player, meaning you may have to click somewhere within the application to actually set the focus to Flash Player and not the browser.

Variables

A variable is a way to store information that you can use in your applications. For example, you may have an application that stores the name of a user, and you can store this name in a variable. You create a variable in ActionScript by using the **var** statement followed by the name of the variable.

```
var userName;
```

You can then assign a value to the variable:

```
username = "Tom";
```

Actually, when you create a variable, you can set its value in the declaration:

```
var username = "Tom";
```

Also, just like with functions, you can set the access of a variable:

```
public var username = "Tom";
```

You've already been using variables quite a bit, because the properties of components you've used are actually variables. For instance, the **text** property of a TextInput was declared as a variable within the source code of the TextInput component.

Data Types

Typing can mean more than just pressing keys on the keyboard. In programming, *typing* refers to a way to designate the kind of values a variable can have. The intent is to force the developer to think about what kind of information is needed. It also helps the program know the type of information, which results in much better performance.

Another great reason for typing is that each data type has certain properties and methods available to help you. (You'll use a few basic or fundamental data types regularly, as described in Table 5-1. After reading this table, you'll be a pro at typing.) You'll certainly want to do different things with text than you would with numbers, so if you do a little planning, you'll make life easier in the long run.

Table 5-1. Fundamental data types

Name	Description	Example	Default Value
String	Text, plain and simple. Can be one character or many. String is short for "string of characters."	`var hi:String = "Hello!"`	`null`
Number	A numeric value that can be a fraction (decimal value).	`var pi:Number = 3.14`	NaN ("Not A Number")
uint	An "unsigned" integer—a whole number that can't be negative. Can be in the range from **0** to **4,294,967,295**.	`var ultimate:uint = 42`	`0`
int	Any integer (a whole number, no fractions or decimals). Can be in the range from **-2,147,483,648** to **2,147,483,647**.	`var neg:int -12`	`0`
Boolean	A true/false value, like a switch. Valid values are **true** and **false**.	`var isHappy:Boolean = true`	`false`

void	A special value for functions, meaning the function returns nothing. The only value it can have is **undefined**.	`function doNothing():void`
		`{`
		`}`
			`undefined`

Say your application has a form that asks for user information, such as name and age. Obviously, name information is what's called a String, and the age would be a numeric value. But which numeric value? Well, it would be a positive whole number, so looking at Table 5-1, you can see that the type uint would be a good choice, but Number would work as well.

When declaring a variable or function, you can set its type pretty easily. You use a colon (:), placed directly after the variable's name (or after the parentheses in the case of a function). So to type a variable called **userName** to a String, you'd do the following:

```
var userName:String = "Hello";
```

All you did here was insert a colon followed by the data type String. The same applies to a number. The following code creates a variable called **pi** and types it as a Number:

```
var pi:Number = 3.14;
```

For functions, it's similar. Functions have the ability to return values, and the value they return can be typed. Just place a colon and the return type after the parentheses, and return a value using the **return** keyword. This next function returns the sum of 2 and 2:

```
public function doSomeMath():Number
{
    return 2 + 2;
}
```

To access this value in code, you can assign the returned value of a function to a variable:

```
var myMath:Number = doSomeMath();
//the value of myMath would then be 4
```

So, knowing all this fancy stuff, you can fix your **setForm()** function you made earlier to include typing. Because you declared variables as parameters, you can type them, and you can type the function as well:

```
public function setForm(txt:String = "John Smith", sel:Boolean =
    true):void
{
    fullNameTextInput.text = txt;
    expertCheckBox.selected = sel;
}
```

You know the **txt** parameter will be a String of text, and you know the **sel** parameter will be a Boolean, because a CheckBox has only two options (either selected or not selected). But the function doesn't return anything, does it? In that case, you use a special data type, which really isn't a data type at all. It's called **void**, and it's just a way of saying "This function isn't going to return anything, so don't expect it." It's good practice to include this.

NOTE

You can determine the type of a property by hovering over the property with the mouse. After a moment, a tooltip will display with more information about that property, including the data type.

Objects

Everything is an object. That's right, in an object-oriented programming language such as ActionScript, everything you deal with is an object of some kind; that's why you'll notice the word object mentioned throughout this text. "But that still doesn't tell me what an object is!" you say? Okay. Here goes.

An *object* is, in a way, a container for anything else. It can hold a piece of text or some numbers, it can have logic that manipulates pieces of data, and it can even hold other objects. It can be thought of as something that has both state and behavior, meaning it can have variables (state) and methods that work with those variables (behavior). It's the basic building block of any Flex application, because, again, everything is an object. Your application is an object. The Button inside your application is also an object, and any variables you create are objects, such as the properties of a Button. And so on.

As an example, I'll show you how to create your own object. Say you want to create a new object called **car** and give it some properties that you expect a car to have, such as the car's type and color. You'd do that in ActionScript with the following code, first creating an instance of an **Object** and then giving it properties:

```
var car:Object = new Object();
car.type = "sports car";
car.color = "red";
car.topSpeed = 170;
car.isInsured = false;
car.driver = undefined;
```

Now you have a fast sports car with no insurance. You're living dangerously. Now you'll create a driver for this car by creating another object:

```
var person:Object = new Object();
person.name = "Steve";
person.age = 19;
```

Now, because you have a perfect match for your car (an object), you can modify the **driver** property (also an object) of the car to include this person (an object as well):

```
car.driver = person;
```

Now what if you expected the program to have lots of cars and drivers and you wanted to make sure they all had a defined set of properties? Classes are a better way to deal with such things.

Classes

If everything is an object, then what is a class? A *class* is like a blueprint for the kinds of information and properties an object will have, and an object is an *instance* of a class.

When you created a **car** object, you gave it a few properties such as **color** and **type**. If you wanted to create another car, you'd do the same thing, giving it properties as you saw fit. But if you wanted to get organized, you could create a **Car** class, setting it up with all the properties you expected to use. That way, when you created a new **car** instance, you'd already have a blueprint of what properties were available. This would give you a few benefits, such as not having to worry about typos or forgetfulness ("Was the property called **hasInsurance**, **isInsured** or was it something else?"). It also would give you code completion in Flex Builder.

The **car** class would look like this in ActionScript (don't worry about trying to compile this code; just consider it an example):

```
public class Car
{
    var type:String;
    var color:uint;
    var topSpeed:int;
    var isInsured:Boolean;
    var driver:Person;
}
```

Notice that the **driver** property of the **Car** class is typed as **Person**. This means a **Person** class exists, such as this:

```
public class Person
{
    var name:String;
    var age:int;
}
```

Notice all the properties of these classes are *strongly typed*, meaning you can expect the **age** of a **Person** to be an integer and the **isInsured** property of a **Car** to be a Boolean. You even know now that the **driver** property is a **Person**. Now when you create new instances of cars or people, you know what properties to expect and what type they should be. Create a **Car** and a **Person** again, taking advantage of the new classes:

```
var car:Car = new Car();
car.type = "sports car";
car.color = 0xFF0000;
car.topSpeed = 170;
car.isInsured = false;
car.driver = undefined;

var person:Person = new Person();
person.name = "Steve";
person.age = 19;

car.driver = person;
```

While this might seem like overkill this early on, you've actually benefited from classes already, because the controls that you use in Flex are all made from classes. For instance, the Button is actually from a **Button** class, and when you use it in ActionScript or MXML, you know its properties are always going to be the same. And while you may never need to create your own classes in ActionScript, it helps to be familiar with the concept, because it will come up frequently as you program with Flex.

MXML and ActionScript Work Together

MXML doesn't completely replace ActionScript. Rather, ActionScript and MXML complement each other. As you'll soon discover, scripting is still very useful and usually necessary for interactivity. In fact, MXML isn't necessary at all, because you can build a full application in pure ActionScript. However, I'm sure you'll find that MXML is the best tool for the job of building your application's structure, because it's easier to read and write.

ActionScript's Relationship with MXML

Flex is composed of two languages, MXML and ActionScript. MXML is great for laying out structure, and ActionScript is built for interactivity. What is the difference between the two? In many ways they're the same thing.

MXML = ActionScript

MXML markup is actually turned into ActionScript by the Flex compiler. You can think of it like this: ActionScript is the core language of Flash Player, and everything in Flex can be distilled into ActionScript. In this regard, you could create a Flex application using an ActionScript project, and use only ActionScript. However, because of the benefits of using a markup language, MXML can be a more intuitive way to create applications.

Tags Are Classes

A tag placed declaratively in a Flex application is turned into the appropriate code in ActionScript when it is compiled. For example, to create a Button in MXML, you'd write the following code:

```
<mx:Button id="myButton" />
```

This could get compiled into the equivalent ActionScript code:

```
import mx.controls.Button;

var myButton:Button = new Button();

addChild(myButton);
```

Knowing this, you can use such ActionScript to create components dynamically, not having to rely on MXML. The choice is yours, depending on the needs of your application.

Attributes Are Properties

When you add attributes to a tag, you're essentially changing the properties of an instance of that component. For example, to change a Button's **label** property, you do the following in MXML:

```
<mx:Button id="myButton" label="Click Me"/>
```

which has the equivalent ActionScript:

```
import mx.controls.Button;

var myButton:Button = new Button();
myButton.label = "Click Me";

addChild(myButton);
```

NOTE

To compile means to convert, or translate, source code into another language. So a compiler is something that compiles source code. To build means to assemble all the necessary pieces of a Flex project and compile them.

Looking at this ActionScript in more depth, you'll see the first line contains an **import** statement, importing **mx.controls.Button**. This is the way to tell the compiler you want to ready a certain component or group of components for use.

The second line declares a Button called **myButton**. This is equivalent to using the **id** attribute in MXML. This way, you can reference this particular Button later in your code.

Notice that a bit more is going on in the second line. For instance, the colon followed by the word **Button** is a typing declaration, saying that this **myButton** variable should be a Button. Because a variable can be anything, this is the way to tell ActionScript you want a Button here, not a Panel or a piece of text or something else.

This same line contains an equal sign and the statement **new Button();** at the end of the line. Entering **new** followed by a class's *constructor* is how you create things in ActionScript. The constructor is really a method of the same name as the class, and it's used to create new instances of classes. Just stating a variable and giving it a type doesn't usually make it into anything until you use the equal sign and assign the variable to some value. For fundamental data types, you can assign a variable directly and do not need to use a keyword, such as a String (**var name:String = "hello"**) or Number (**var num:Number = 23**). But you can use this syntax if you like:

```
var name:String = new String("hello");
```

Attributes Are Styles

A component can have many types of properties, as you saw in Chapter 3 when I discussed the Flex Properties panel. You may have noticed that, under the Category view of this panel, there is a section called Styles. Styles are special properties of Flex components that are used to control the look and feel of the component. While they can be considered properties, they are not directly accessible in ActionScript using dot notation. In MXML, you can easily set styles using attributes. However, because of the way that styles are implemented in Flex, there is a different syntax for accessing style properties in ActionScript, using the methods **getStyle()** and **setStyle()**.

For example, the **cornerRadius** style property sets the roundness of a Button control, and you could set this style with the following MXML:

```
<mx:Button id="myButton" cornerRadius="14" />
```

Being a style property, you cannot access it directly. Therefore, the following code is incorrect:

```
myButton.cornerRadius = 14;
```

NOTE

These concepts may seem daunting at first, and you might worry that you'll never remember what you need to import, but Flex Builder is here to help. If you use code completion when typing **Button**, *or any other class, Flex will import it for you by writing the necessary import statement.*

Instead, you must use the **setStyle()** method. This method takes two parameters. The first is the name of the style property, and the second is the value you want to assign it to.

```
myButton.setStyle("cornerRadius", 14);
```

NOTE

I'll explain styles in depth in Chapter 14. For more details on how to learn all the properties, style properties, and available events for a particular component, see the sidebar "Reading Flex Documentation" in the next chapter.

The method **getStyle()** allows you to get the value of a style property. It takes a single parameter, which is the name of the style you'd like to access, and returns a value representing the style. To get the **cornerRadius** of **myButton**, for example, you could use the following ActionScript, which stores the value in a variable called **roundness**:

```
var roundness:Number = myButton.getStyle("cornerRadius");
```

Attributes Are Event Listeners, Too

Event listeners are the way to tell a component to respond to an event, such as a mouse click. You've already used them by setting up a **click** attribute for a Button. However, while these listeners are set via an attribute in MXML, they are not actually properties of the component. Instead, they are set via a special method.

So, while to add a **click** listener to a Button in MXML, you'd do this:

```
<mx:Button id="myButton" click="doSomething()" />
```

the following would be done in ActionScript:

```
import mx.controls.Button;

var myButton:Button = new Button();
myButton.addEventListener("click", doSomething);

addChild(myButton);
```

Behind the Scenes

Want to see all the ActionScript code Flex generates from MXML? Within your project's properties dialog (Project→Properties), go into the compiler options by choosing Flex Compiler from the list at the left. Here you'll see a field called Additional compiler options. Within this field, add the compiler argument **–keep**, separating it from any other compiler arguments with a space.

This will save the ActionScript code the compiler creates from MXML, and place it in a folder called **generated** that you can look through. It's nice to see all the work Flex does for you. (Note that the **generated** folder this creates will be overwritten each time you compile, so modifying it won't do you any good.)

Notice that the ActionScript way to register events uses the **addEventListener()** method. This method takes two parameters: the name of the event (**click** in this case) and the name of a function to call when that event occurs (**doSomething**). Unlike inline ActionScript placed within a tag, this **addEventListener()** method doesn't allow you to make assignments such as **fullNameTextInput.text = txt**. You're allowed to place such assignments only within a function and register that function. So, now you have yet another reason to be familiar with functions.

When using the **addEventListener()** method, you place only the name of the function you'd like to call in the second parameter. Don't include parentheses following the function name. For example this code is incorrect:

```
myButton.addEventListener("click", doSomething() );
```

Comments?

You'll often find you need to comment your code, either to make a note for yourself or others or to temporarily remove a piece of code or an application. Commenting syntax is different between MXML and ActionScript.

In ActionScript, you can comment either one line or a block of code. To comment out a single line, use the double forward slash syntax:

```
//This code won't be run
//public var foo:String = "No Comment";
```

For multiple lines, it's more convenient to use the slash-asterisk syntax:

```
/*
    public var foo:String = "No Comment";
    public var bar:String = "Don't want to see it";
*/
```

Because MXML is XML, the way it's commented is entirely different from ActionScript. It uses special tag syntax to create a comment, namely, the characters **<!--** and **-->**. You may have seen this in HTML as well.

```
<!-- This is a comment in MXML -->
<mx:Button label="Button to Keep"/>
<!-- <mx:Button label="Button to Remove"/> -->
```

The ability to use comments is yet another benefit of using a markup language to create applications. Using comments, you can remove an entire piece of an application but keep the source code available to add at another time. For example, your application might have a preferences panel for customizations, but you might have been pressed for time and couldn't finish the panel. Simply commenting the Panel allows you to keep your code for later use but doesn't compile it into the final application.

NOTE

It's easy to add a comment in Flex Builder without knowing the proper syntax. You just select the text or code that you want to comment, and select Source→Add Block Comment. Whether you're editing ActionScript or MXML, the proper comment syntax will be inserted. When commenting, be sure you've selected whole tags or blocks of code, or you'll get a compile-time error.

Summary

It's not the goal of this book to make you an expert in ActionScript but instead to give you an overview. I've given you enough information that you can create simple interactivity; however, being a pro in ActionScript will take further study. I recommend the Learning Series book *Learning ActionScript 3.0: A Beginner's Guide* (O'Reilly) for an easy-to-understand introduction to this powerful language.

CHAPTER 6

ADDING INTERACTIVITY WITH ACTIONSCRIPT

Handling user input is what makes an application tick. Dealing with mouse clicks, dragging, typing on the keyboard, and such is where the fun is. Otherwise, you wouldn't have an application; you'd have just an animation or a static image, and that's, well, comparatively boring.

However, understanding what someone using your application does and responding to that action takes some planning and work. You have to account for every interaction that you think is important. Basically, you're thinking about what a user might want to do and preparing for that. Of course, this can be a challenge, but it can be really rewarding as well.

Understanding Events

A Flex application responds to user input by something called an *event*. An event is something that happened, either by user interaction, or by other things happening such as a photo appearing or data returning from a server. (Getting data from a server is covered briefly in Chapter 10.) When a user clicks a button, for instance, an event occurs. (The event for clicking something is called—you guessed it—**click**.) And when a button is created, an event also occurs. (This event is called **creationComplete**.) When the event happens, you say the event *fired* or was *dispatched*. To respond to such an event, you set up something called an event *handler* or *listener*.

Handling Events Inline

MXML makes listening for events very simple. All you have to do is add the proper event attribute to a tag and tell it what to do. This could mean calling a function or just modifying a property. The following code example shows a Button (**myButton**) that changes the text of a Label (**myLabel**), as shown in Figure 6-1, by modifying the Label's **text** property. You do this simply by adding the attribute **click** to the Button:

```
<mx:Label id="myLabel" text="The Button will change my text" />
<mx:Button id="myButton" label="Change it!" click="myLabel.text = 'Some
    new text'"/>
```

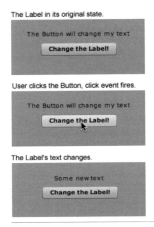

Figure 6-1. The click event play-by-play

The same goes for other events, such as when a TextInput's **text** changes by a user typing into the component. That's a *change* event, so the following code would cause a TextInput to modify the Label:

```
<mx:Label id="myLabel" text="The TextInput will change my text" />
<mx:TextInput id="myTextInput" change="myLabel.text =
    myTextInput.text"/>
```

This code modifies the Label's **text** to match the TextInput's **text** any time the TextInput's **text** changes. There's actually a better way to make a property update itself automatically when another property changes, and that's called *data binding*. I'll go into more detail on that in Chapter 7.

While there's no limit to the number and names of events that a component can use, you will see a few old standards. Table 6-1 lists the most common types of events.

Table 6-1. The most common events

Event Name	Constant	Description
change	`Event.CHANGE`	Fired when a selection changes in a list or navigation component such as a TabBar, or when a text component's **text** is changed.
click	`MouseEvent.CLICK`	Fired when a user clicks an element. This means someone pressed the mouse button down and released it on the same component.
creationComplete	`FlexEvent.CREATION_COMPLETE`	Fired when a Flex component is created.
mouseDown	`MouseEvent.MOUSE_DOWN`	Fired when someone presses the mouse button down on a component.
mouseUp	`MouseEvent.MOUSE_UP`	Fired when someone releases the mouse button on a component.
resize	`Event.RESIZE`	Fired when the application is resized because of the browser or window being resized.
rollOut	`MouseEvent.ROLL_OUT`	Fired when the mouse pointer moves out of the component area.
rollOver	`MouseEvent.ROLL_OVER`	Fired when the mouse pointer moves into the component area.

Of course, tons more events exist, and many are specific to certain controls, but knowing the events in Table 6-1 will get you pretty far. You can see what kinds of events a specific control offers in a few other ways:

- In Design mode, click a control that's been added to the stage, and look at the Flex Properties panel's Category view. Check out the Events section in that list, and you'll see every event available for that component.

- In Source mode, when using code completion on a component, all of its properties will pop up. The events will be listed with a little lightning bolt icon next to them.

- Check out the documentation for a component by selecting Help→ Help Contents and searching for a component or by selecting a component in Source mode and then selecting Help→Find in Language Reference. At the top of every component's documentation page are links to its properties, methods, and events. Check out its list of events for details. (See the sidebar "Reading Flex Documentation" for more information.)

Reading Flex Documentation

Flex comes with some of the best documentation of any programming language. You can access this documentation by going to Help→Help Contents when in Flex Builder, or you can access it online at http://livedocs.adobe.com/flex/3/.

The Flex documentation contains a number of articles on using every aspect of Flex, so once you're keen on using the documentation, you can find pretty much everything you need to build your skills, including lots of example code. Often, you'll find exactly what you're looking for by using the search functionality in the documentation.

One of the most useful parts of the documentation is the Flex 3 Language Reference, which contains all the information you need to use Flex components. It might seem daunting at first, but once you get the hang of it, you'll find yourself visiting it quite a bit.

There are a few ways to get to the Language Reference. One is to search for a component by name, such as Button. Another is when you're using Flex Builder in Source mode—from there you can get the details for a specific component by selecting the component and going to Help→Find in Language Reference. Otherwise, you can browse for the Language Reference by using the table of contents, where you'll choose Adobe Flex 3 Help, then Adobe Flex 3 Language Reference. Typically, you'll access the reference when you're looking for the specifics of a component, so I recommend either searching for the component or using the Find in Language Reference feature of Flex Builder.

Once you look at the reference for a particular component, you'll see something similar to Figure 6-2. At the top of every component's reference is a list of its available properties, methods, events, styles, and so on—even a link to examples is included.

To see the available events for a component, you could click the Events link at the top, or scroll your browser to the Events heading. There you'd see the list of events as pictured in Figure 6-3. However, like other properties of a component, there may be a large list of inherited events which you can see by clicking "Show Inherited Events." Components typically inherit functionality from a higher-level class, so to view the properties of the base classes, you can choose to view the inherited events. You'll find it valuable, because many of the properties you'll want to access may be inherited from a higher class. In the case of Button, it inherits its **click** event from the class UIComponent (which is actually the base class for all visual Flex components).

Figure 6-3. The Flex Language Reference for Button - Events

The Flex 3 Language Reference is your one-stop shop for everything you need to use components in ActionScript and MXML, and you'll find it an indispensable resource when you start developing in Flex.

Figure 6-2. The Flex Language Reference for Button

Using Event Constants

A *constant* is a fixed value in Flex, which means it's a way to store a value that you don't expect will change, to make it easier to remember. Constants are usually used to give a name to some numeric value, because, let's face it, words are easier to remember than numbers. Can you remember π (pi) to the fifteenth decimal place? I didn't think so. What about the ASCII value for the Caps Lock key? That's why some smart person invented constants. Get a piece of the pi by using the constant `Math.PI`, or get the keyboard code for the Caps Lock key with `Keyboard.CAPS_LOCK`.

But numeric values aren't all constants are good for. Flex often uses constants for strings as well, and the most common place you'll see them is in event types. For instance, the event for when the user's mouse goes out of the Flex application's bounds is called `mouseLeave`. Because the string "mouse leave" or "mouse-leave" isn't sufficient, Flex has a constant set up so you don't have to remember the specifics: `Event.MOUSE_LEAVE`.

You might be thinking to yourself, "That's not any easier to remember!" True, but if it makes you feel any better, because these constants are properties of a class (`MOUSE_LEAVE` is a property of the `Event` class, `PI` is a property of the Math class, and so on.), they're available using code completion. That means you don't have to worry about typos. Type the first few letters, and Flex Builder will fill in the rest for you.

You've probably noticed by now that constants are all in uppercase—that's to distinguish them as constants. Though this capitalization is not necessary, it's considered a best practice. And because it's difficult to distinguish separate words in all-uppercase text, the standard is to place an underscore (_) between the words.

Making Things Happen

Returning to the HelloWorld application, you'll now make some things happen.

First, you'll add a few more sources of user input. You have a name field already, so now you'll add an age field. Place another Label with the text "My age is:" below the name text input, place a NumericStepper control below that, and give them the **id** attributes `ageLabel` and `ageNS`. The NumericStepper control is like a TextInput control that accepts only numbers and has special keyboard and mouse interactions to make increasing or decreasing the numbers easy. You'll want to set a couple of properties on the NumericStepper to customize it. The property `maximum` will set the top value allowed, and the `minimum` property will set the minimum. Set these to a maximum of 120 and a minimum of 18. This additional code should look like the following:

```
<mx:Label id="ageLabel" text="My age is:"/>
<mx:NumericStepper id="ageNS" maximum="120" minimum="18" />
```

Using Pop-up Alerts to Display Information

Now that you have a basic form, you'll display the data in a pop-up. To do that, you'll create a function that uses the class called Alert, which is used to display pop-up alerts:

```
import mx.controls.Alert;

public function showInfo():void
{
    Alert.show("Your name is " + fullNameTextInput.text +
        " and your age is " + ageNS.value);
}
```

Notice the **import** statement that imports the Alert class necessary for this function. Remember that when you use code completion, most imports will be written for you automatically.

This function has a few features you haven't learned about yet. One is the **show()** method on the Alert class. This is a *static method*, one that exists on the Alert class itself, that displays a window centered above everything else.

Static Properties and Methods

Take a look at the code for displaying an alert, and notice the **show()** method. This has a different syntax than you may be accustomed to using, because it exists on the Alert class instead of an instance of that class. That is to say, you're using the class name (Alert), and calling the method using dot notation on the Alert class.

Just like constants, which are properties that are attached to a class, static methods are attached to a class. Instead of creating a variable of Alert type, (such a calling **new Alert()**), and then calling the **show()** method on that instance, you call the method on the Alert itself.

Constants are generally static properties of a class, meaning they are variables attached to the class itself, and that is why you use a similar syntax for constants and static methods. (These are actually created using the **static** access modifier when creating such methods or variables in ActionScript.)

Also note the **value** property of the NumericStepper control. Because the **value** property behaves similarly to a TextInput control, you might expect the property you're looking for is **text**. However, the NumericStepper actually holds numeric data, so its property is called **value** instead. Because it is a Number, you can do math calculations with its **value** property, like **ageNS.value + 10** to add 10 years to your age. (On second thought, maybe taking away 10 years from the age would be better.)

This addition calculation brings up another point. Plus signs (**+**) are used in ActionScript to both add numbers and piece together text. The use of the plus signs in the case of adding years to your age would be addition, but in the case of the **" and your age is " + ageNS.value**, the plus sign is used for *concatenation*, or the linking together of data. What you're doing in your application is creating a phrase that has dynamic information gathered from your form fields. Although the **value** property, as you just learned, is numeric, Flex is smart enough to realize that it can't add a number to a string of text such as **" and your age is "** so it changes the numeric value into a text value for you. This might not even be something you would've noticed, but it's good to recognize, because this functionality may not work as expected in all situations. See the box "Conversion, Coercion, and Casting" for more information.

Conversion, Coercion, and Casting

So, now you understand the idea of typing your variables. You've thought it out and decided what types your variables should be, you've typed everything nicely, and you feel confident that your code is clean and optimized. Then you wake up one morning and realize you need to change one data type into another. What to do?

A few methods of conversion are available to you, the Flex and ActionScript guru that you are. One is *coercion*, or implicit conversion. This happens when you have a variable of a numeric type but you imply in your code that this number should be displayed as a string. Such is the case when setting a TextInput's **text** property to a number. In some cases, this will be fixed for you automatically, but sometimes the compiler will complain. Then you need to do an explicit conversion, also known as *casting* or *typecasting*. This kind of casting means you want to tell the compiler to convert, at least temporarily, the type of a value to another type. In the case of using a number in the text property, you want to change a numeric value to a text value.

You have lots of ways to accomplish an implicit conversion at your disposal. One way is to use the constructor of the desired type to convert the value. The constructor is the special method used to create a new instance of a class, such as **new String()**. It's the method of the same name as the class. Using the constructor and passing in a value will convert the value. For instance, you could use the code **fullNameTextInput.text = String(ageNS.value)**. An additional means of casting is using the keyword **as**. This tells the compiler to think of a value in another way. Use the code **fullNameTextInput.text = ageNS.value as String** to do that. A final means of conversion is to use the **toString()** method, which most classes in Flex have implemented. The **toString()** method returns a string representation and is a useful method to know. In that case, you could use the code **fullNameTextInput.text = ageNS.value.toString()**.

One last thing to notice in the example is the way the code breaks across two lines, even though it's considered one entity. Usually you'll need to put everything that is a complete statement on one line, such as passing a long parameter into the **show()** method. But, when you have plus signs or commas, you're allowed to bend the rules and break the line. For readability, you place an indentation in front of the following line to show that it is a continuation of the previous line. Of course, you could still place all this code on one line, but that may make it difficult to read for some users with smaller screens, causing them to have to scroll horizontally to read all the code.

The next step is to remove the previous **setForm()** function you created and to register the button's **click** event with your new **showInfo()** function so that when a user clicks the button, a pop-up alert displays. Do that, and then go

NOTE

A good rule of thumb is to set a maximum line length of 80 characters of text in your source code. That way it will be readable to most people.

ahead and run it to see your work. You should see an alert similar to the one in Figure 6-4. The full code for your application so far may look like this:

```xml
<?xml version="1.0" encoding="utf-8"?>
<mx:Application xmlns:mx="http://www.adobe.com/2006/mxml"
    layout="absolute"
    applicationComplete="fullNameTextInput.setFocus()">

    <mx:Script>
        <![CDATA[
            import mx.controls.Alert;

            public function showInfo():void
            {
                Alert.show("Your name is " + fullNameTextInput.text +
                    " and your age is " + ageNS.value);
            }
        ]]>
    </mx:Script>

    <mx:Panel  id="panel" x="10" y="10" width="250" height="200"
        layout="vertical" title="Howdy Ya'll" paddingLeft="5">
        <mx:Label text="My name is:" fontWeight="bold"/>
        <mx:TextInput id="fullNameTextInput"/>
        <mx:Label id="ageLabel" text="My age is:" fontWeight="bold"/>
        <mx:NumericStepper id="ageNS" maximum="120" minimum="18" />
        <mx:CheckBox id="expertCheckBox" label="I'm a Flex Expert!"/>
        <mx:Button label="Click me" click="showInfo()"/>
    </mx:Panel>

</mx:Application>
```

Figure 6-4. An Alert displaying some information

Using Change Events

So far you've worked only with **click** events, which occur when a Button or other control is clicked. Now you'll learn how to deal with another type of event, a **change** event. These often occur when a selection changes or a text or value changes on a control. When a NumericStepper or TextInput changes, the controls fire **change** events. So, add a listener for the **change** event on your NumericStepper control that runs the **showInfo()** function:

```
<mx:NumericStepper id="ageNS" maximum="120" minimum="18"
    change="showInfo()" />
```

Now, when the value of the NumericStepper changes, this event fires, and you'll see the pop-up alert. The change will occur when either using the mouse to change the value via the arrow buttons, using up and down arrows on the keyboard, or typing in the NumericStepper and then confirming the change (by pressing the Tab key or using the mouse to select another component). Notice that both a Button's **click** event and this NumericStepper's **change** event are registered with the same **showInfo()** function. It's totally fine to do that. Registering multiple functions to listen to one event is part of the power of programming.

What Flex Does When You're Not Looking

You might be wondering at this point how Flex does what it does. You write some MXML or create your masterpiece in Design mode, but what happens when you push that little green button?

Flex is, in one respect, a compiler for MXML and ActionScript. When using Flex Builder to compile your application, a script runs in the background that does the following:

1. Converts all MXML into ActionScript
2. Converts all metadata into compiler arguments
3. Compiles the generated ActionScript into bytecode (**.swf** file)

ActionScript is still the main language for Flash applications. MXML is great for easily creating applications and has great options like styling and creating services and effects. But the Flex compiler converts your MXML into a web of ActionScript classes, essentially taking your high-level code and creating lots of lower-level code. All this code gets recompiled into SWF bytecode, which is a set of instructions for Flash Player. It also looks at special metadata (the stuff in square brackets) and injects that into the SWF as well; things like embedded assets, settings for frame rates, and so on.

Debugging for Kicks

While showing how to display an alert helps in learning how events can work, displaying such a pop-up alert with every little change can be annoying. Because this isn't really a feature you'd want to implement in your application, but more of a way for you to learn from and test your application, there's a better way to display information in regard to an event. It's called *debugging*. While the name implies that there's a *bug*, or glitch, in your software that you're trying to locate, you'll see there's really more to debugging than that. Debugging in Flex is a great way to show the innards of your application or to display information while you're developing.

Outputting Information to the Console

To debug your application, you'll use a method called **trace()** that will display some text in the Console panel. Simply replace the **Alert.show** method with **trace**, as in the following:

```
public function showInfo():void
{
    trace("Your name is " + fullNameTextInput.text +
        " and your age is " + ageNS.value);
}
```

Now, just running the application won't actually display this information. To use **trace**, you'll have to be debugging your application. How do you do that? Pretty easily—I'm glad you asked. Instead of running the application by using the green arrow button, you'll click the green bug icon to its right. Clicking this icon launches the application in debug mode. In most cases, it will look the same to you, but now when you change the NumericStepper, the string of text will be output to the Console panel.

NOTE

The Console panel is, by default, located at the bottom of your Flex Builder window, next to the Problems panel. If your Console panel isn't visible, make it visible by selecting Window→Console.

Debug your application, click the NumericStepper a few times, and then switch back to Flex Builder to see the information in the Console panel. The same information that was previously in a pop-up alert is now output to a new line of text in the Console panel, as shown in Figure 6-5.

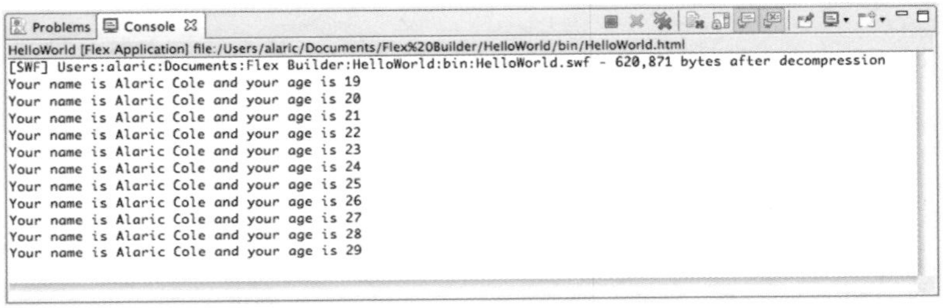

Figure 6-5. The output of a **trace** *in the Console panel*

The **trace** statement is deceptively simple. However, coupled with debug mode, it will be one of your most powerful tools as you grow as a developer. Next you'll learn how to use debugging to find out more information about an event.

Using Event Parameters in Debugging

Remember those parameters you learned about that you could pass to a function? You'll now add a parameter to your **showInfo()** function called **event** and make it of type Event. (You could call it whatever you like, but I usually just call it *event* in lowercase.) Now in the **trace** statement, you'll be able to get some details about the event, namely, two properties called **type** and **currentTarget**. Your function should look like this:

```
public function showInfo(event:Event):void
{
    trace("The type is " + event.type +
        " and the current target is " + event.currentTarget);
}
```

What's going to happen is an event object will be passed to this function. It is of type Event, which is a general type that has properties attached to it which are helpful in learning about the event. The **type** property contains the name of the event type, which in this case is a **change** event ("change"). The **currentTarget** property contains a reference to the object that passed the event, which is whatever called the function.

You might have realized that making this work requires one more step: you have to actually pass the parameter to the function when you call it. There's a special parameter in Flex called **event** that is used to pass event objects to functions, and you're going to use it. It's built in. You haven't created any variable called **event**, but Flex will create one at compile time. Think of it as a feature. Pass in the event by using the following code for your **change** event on the NumericStepper:

```
change="showInfo(event)"
```

And pass in the event for the button by using this for your **click** event on the button:

```
click="showInfo(event)"
```

Because the function expects an **event** parameter to be passed in, failing to pass it when calling the function results in a compile-time error.

Now when you debug the application and change the NumericStepper, you'll get a message in the Console panel like "The type is change, and the current target is HelloWorld0.panel.ageNS." Make sense? You knew the type of the event would be **change**, but that current target value is a little cryptic. Notice the *ageNS*, which is the **id** of the NumericStepper. But what's the *HelloWorld0.panel* part? Well, when Flex creates your application, it actually creates a class based on the name of the application. In this case, Flex added zero to the end of the name. As for the *.panel* part, that's the **id** of the panel in which the NumericStepper is located. So, in terms of a hierarchy, **ageNS** is considered part of panel, which is in turn part of the HelloWorld application.

When clicking the button, the **trace** statement will display slightly different information. Because the event registered on the button is a **click** event, the trace will display the event type as "click." Also, you'll see that the **currentTarget** is the button. (If you haven't given the button an **id**, the Flex compiler creates one for you, and it may be displayed here as "Button0" or "Button23" or something like that.)

This event information is handy when creating functions, because you can make the functions highly reusable. You could create one function that changes what it does based on who called it (the **currentTarget**) or what type of event occurred (the Event type).

Using Breakpoints

Next you'll learn a pretty advanced technique, but it's one I find so essential that it merits explaining. I'm talking about using breakpoints in your code to really see what's happening.

A *breakpoint* is a place in the logic of your code at which you'd like to stop everything. Because some programming constructs can get complicated, it's really useful to be able to say, "Hold up a minute!" and check how things are going. A breakpoint allows you to do that, letting you pause the application and view its current status before continuing.

To use a breakpoint, double-click in the *gutter*, the area where the line numbers appear to the left of your code. Do this next to the line of code in which you want to create a breakpoint. In this case, you'll want to create a breakpoint in the only place it makes sense, the only place you really have application logic, within your one and only function. So, place a breakpoint to the left of your **trace** statement, as shown in Figure 6-6.

```
 8
 9            public function showInfo(event:Event):void
10            {
11                trace("The type is " + event.type +
12                    " and the current target is " + event.currentTarget);
13            }
```

Figure 6-6. A breakpoint placed on line 11

Now when you debug the application, whenever the NumericStepper is changed or the button is clicked, the function will be called and the breakpoint will be set. You'll probably be prompted the first time with a dialog box from Flex Builder similar to Figure 6-7, which asks you whether you'd like to switch to the Flex Debugging perspective. I recommend turning on the checkbox that says "Remember my decision" because this will launch the right perspective when breakpoints are set. Click the Yes button, and you'll have a whole new perspective.

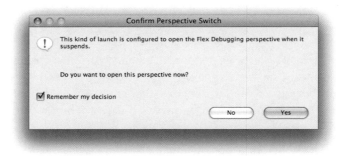

Figure 6-7. Confirm Perspective Switch dialog box

Seeing a New Perspective

Perspectives in Flex Builder are just a way of specifying and remembering a panel layout. When you're developing in Flex Builder for the first time, you're using the Flex Development perspective, which contains panels like Flex Properties and Flex Navigator. When debugging, you'll be using a few new panels specific to that task, and they're contained in the Flex Debugging perspective.

One of these new panels you'll see, now that you're in the Debugging perspective, is the Variables panel. By default it's located in the top right of Flex Builder. Flex Builder also allows you to move and resize panels easily just by clicking and dragging the title bar of the individual panel. Because this panel is a tree list that needs a lot of vertical space, I really recommend moving it so that it takes up the whole right side of Flex Builder. Just click and drag the panel, moving your mouse to the far right side of the Flex Builder window. You'll see a thin black outline, which is your feedback as to where the panel will be placed. You can also drag the panel outside the Flex Builder window, and it will be placed in its own pop-up window.

Whether you clicked the button or changed the NumericStepper, the Variables panel will display information about your application in its current state, at the breakpoint you set. You should see two items in a tree list, one called **this** and another called **event**. The item **this** refers to the application as a whole, and the item **event** refers to the **event** parameter that you passed to the function.

Click the arrow to the left of the **event** item to display the child nodes. You'll focus on the items in the **[inherited]** node, so click the arrow to display them. You'll see all the properties of this **event** object, including the beloved **type** and **currentTarget** properties, displayed with their current values, as shown in Figure 6-8.

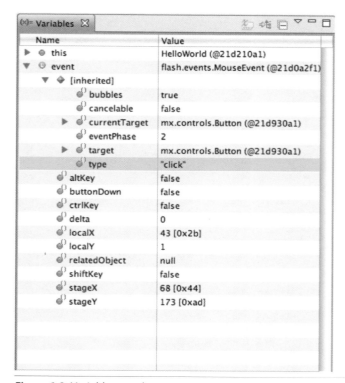

Figure 6-8. Variables panel

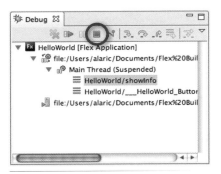

Figure 6-9. Debug panel

Ending Your Debug Session

Feel free to poke around here as you wish. You might want to return to this later, because it will tell you a lot about how Flex works, so keep it in mind. For now, close this perspective, and end your debug session. Note that debugging may lock up your browser, because it pauses Flash Player. So, the way to end the session is by clicking the red, square button located both in the Console panel and in the Debug panel, as shown in Figure 6-9. You can also access this command by selecting Run→Terminate. That will terminate the debugging session. When you're done, you'll also want to return to the Flex Development perspective by using the toggle button bar at the top right of Flex Builder or by selecting Window→Perspective→Flex Development.

Summary

Now you've learned a bit more about what events are and how to use them in your application. Don't worry if some of this is overwhelming; interactivity can be a very challenging part of development. If you need to return to this chapter later for a refresher, feel free. While your application may not be looking that different yet, you've learned some very important concepts in creating interactivity that you'll be able to use very soon.

In the next chapter, you'll get into some of the powerful features of Flex. Then you'll really start to make your application into something useful.

CHAPTER 7

USING DATA BINDING

Say your application knows someone's display name (Jed90210) and you'd like to show that name in various places: on a button to sign out, on the person's profile page, and on the welcome screen to say "hello." You could just store a variable with the display name and reference that variable throughout the application. But what if that person decides to change their display name to Jed75961? In such a case, you'd need to write code to listen for changes to the display name, updating all references to it explicitly. If you've referenced the name in quite a few places, that would be a lot of code.

With Flex, you have another option. You can store the display name in one place and reference it all you want. If the display name were updated, all references to it would change automatically, without any need to write tedious code to listen for changes. You can accomplish all this through the magic of *data binding*.

What Is Data Binding?

Data binding is one of those features that makes Flex so great: it gives you the ability to easily pass information around. It is simply a way to reference a piece of data and watch for changes to that data in an intuitive way. This data can be anything from a piece of text, such as a display name, to a structured list of information, such as a bunch of stock quotes, and anything in-between—data is simply information, in any form. Essentially, data binding makes it natural for developers to share information across their applications. You can use data binding: between one component's properties and another, between a component's properties and a data model, and between different data models.

How to Use It

Data binding is surprisingly easy to use, considering how powerful it can be. You can take advantage of it in a number of ways. Depending on your situation and coding style, you can choose the best way to implement it in your application.

Basic Usage

The most basic example is binding a property of one control to a property of another. Consider the following Label control's text that is bound to a TextInput control's text:

```
<mx:TextInput id="helloTextInput" text="Hello, World"/>
<mx:Label text="{ helloTextInput.text }"/>
```

In this example, the phrase "Hello, World" will appear in both the TextInput and Label controls. This is because the **text** property of the Label control is bound to the **text** property of the TextInput control. You specify this by using curly braces (**{** and **}**) to surround the name of the property being bound to. The curly braces are used to distinguish bindable information from regular text in your MXML—without them the Label's **text** property would be set to the text "helloTextInput.text". This is the simplest and most common usage of data binding in Flex.

Not only will the text be the same when the application runs, but changes in the TextInput will be reflected in the Label. That means the text typed into the TextInput will display in the Label, automatically and immediately.

Multiple Applications in a Project

If you want to play around with some of the example code here or write your own to get a feel for these concepts, please do so. If you're afraid to mess with the main project that you've been working with, you can easily create a new project using the skills you learned in Chapter 2.

Alternatively, you can create a new application within your main project. Yes, Flex projects can have multiple applications within them. To create an application within a project, select the project in the Flex Navigator, and select File→New→MXML Application. Complete the dialog box to create a new application, and you're good to go.

Note that while a Flex project can have multiple application files, one application always is considered the default application. What *default application* means is, "What application does the green Run button launch when no application is selected?" If a project has more than one application, the Run button has a few rules it goes over before deciding which application to launch when clicked:

- If an application is being edited in Design or Source mode, clicking the Run button runs that one.
- If nothing is being edited, clicking the Run button launches the application that is selected in the Flex Navigator.
- If nothing is selected in the Flex Navigator, clicking the Run button launches the main application.

Also worth noticing is that the Run button has a drop-down list next to it. This list is populated by the applications contained in the project currently selected in the Flex Navigator. You can use this drop-down list to select which application you want to run.

Note that you don't want to bind the Label control to the TextInput control itself but to the TextInput control's **text** property. Thus, the following is incorrect:

```
<mx:TextInput id="helloTextInput" text="Hello, World"/>
<mx:Label text="{ helloTextInput }"/>
```

This code would not cause an error, but the result would be less than spectacular. What would happen is that Flex would assume you wanted the fully qualified **id** of **helloTextInput**, and your label would read something like "ApplicationName0. helloTextInput."

As another example, you'll see how to create two variables for a first name and a last name, using the **String** tag. The **String** tag creates a String variable that is set up for binding. You'll then bind the first name to the text of a **label**.

```
<mx:String id="firstName">Alaric</mx:String>
<mx:String id="lastName">Cole</mx:String>

<mx:Label id="nameLabel" text="{firstName}"/>
```

Notice the curly braces surrounding the variable name **firstName** in the **text** attribute. The curly braces tell the Flex compiler to place the value of **firstName** as a string of text into the Label control's **text** attribute. Without curly braces, Flex would place the literal string "firstName" as the text of the Label control. Curly brace syntax also tells Flex to listen for changes to the variable. If "Alaric" were changed to another name, the Label control would update itself accordingly. Curly braces signal to Flex that something is a binding.

NOTE

*Using data binding is one of those situations where giving your components an **id** is essential. You must give an **id** to the component that is the source of a data binding expression so that you can reference it.*

The variable **firstName** is the *source* of the data binding expression. The text of the Label control is the *destination*.

Multiple Destinations

I mentioned binding a display name across multiple parts of an application earlier. Data binding isn't limited to one source and one destination, though; it can have the same source data bound to multiple destinations. Consider the following code, which binds a display name to the text of a Label control *and* the label of a Button control:

```
<mx:String id="displayName">Jed90210</mx:String>

<mx:Label id="nameLabel" text="{displayName}"/>
<mx:Button id="nameButton" label="{displayName}"/>
```

Concatenation

You're not limited to just a variable name or a property in binding expressions. You can also *concatenate* (piece together) and otherwise manipulate the information inside the curly braces. If you want a label to greet the person, you can do that easily:

```
<mx:String id="displayName">Jed90210</mx:String>

<mx:Label text="{'Hello, ' + displayName}"/>
```

This code combines the string "Hello, " with the display name "Jed0210," because it uses the plus sign (+) to put together two strings.

More complex combinations can also occur where you might combine the first and last names and add a greeting. It's important to point out that when either the first or last name changes, the label's text will update:

```
<mx:String id="firstName">Alaric</mx:String>
<mx:String id="lastName">Cole</mx:String>

<mx:Label text="{'Hello, ' + firstName + ' ' + lastName}"/>
```

Another way to concatenate a string is by using multiple sets of curly braces. Instead of concatenating strings via quotes and plus signs, you can simply place more than one binding expression within an attribute. Thus, the following is equivalent to the previous example:

```
<mx:Label text="Hello, {firstName} {lastName}"/>
```

In this code, regular text is being mixed with a binding expression. The Label control contains the text "Hello, " followed by a binding expression, then another space, and then another binding expression. Of course, when the application runs, the Label control displays the text "Hello, Alaric Cole" in my case.

You can put white space between the curly braces and the property you want to bind, because it will not affect the actual values. While white space will be part of the actual created value if it's outside the braces and this can be used to help form strings for display, white space within the braces doesn't matter.

In fact, a lot of Flex developers like to place a bit of space between the interior of the curly braces and the variable reference to aid in readability, such as the following:

```
<mx:Label text="Hello, { firstName } { lastName }"/>
```

See Figure 7-1 for details.

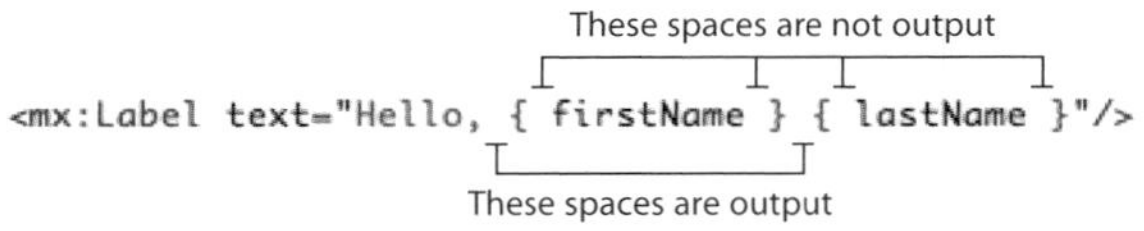

Figure 7-1. How white space is seen in a binding expression

More Uses for Curly Braces

You've used curly brace syntax to modify or piece together strings for data binding and to cause fields to update automatically. So, what the braces are actually doing is twofold: declaring bindable properties and distinguishing regular text from dynamic text. You can actually use the curly braces just for dynamic text without any bindings. The following example shows a simple math operation placed inline, mixing regular text with dynamic text:

```
<mx:Label text="Eleven times forty-two equals {11 * 42}"/>
```

Here's an example using more than one set of curly braces:

```
<mx:Label text="Hey {firstName}, eleven times forty-two equals
    {11 * 42}"/>
```

The <mx:Binding/> Tag

In larger applications, you may find it useful to separate your binding declarations. In previous examples, a Label tag, through the use of the curly braces in its text attribute, told Flex it wanted to be bound to a specific variable, like a first name. This is fine and is the typical way to set up bindings. However, because of your coding style or the way in which your project in structured, you may find that this makes the Label control "know" too much about what it's bound to. That's because, in the case of binding to someone's first name, the Label tag would refer to that firstName variable explicitly.

Basic usage

If you prefer to keep things separated and declare bindings outside of component tags, you can set up bindings in MXML in another way. Specifically, you can use the <mx:Binding/> tag to declare what's bound to what:

```
<mx:String id="firstName">Alaric</mx:String>

<mx:Label id="nameLabel"/>

<mx:Binding source="firstName" destination="nameLabel.text"/>
```

The <mx:Binding/> tag just says you want to bind the firstName variable to the text property of the Label control called nameLabel. This is where it's useful to think of the source and destination of your binding, because the <mx:Binding/> tag has a source property and a destination property that you need to set up. Because the <mx:Binding/> tag must refer to both the firstName variable as well as the Label control, the Label control needs to have an id.

Multiple sources

I've talked about binding a source to multiple destinations and showed earlier that someone's display name could populate both a Label and a Button. One of the benefits of using the <mx:Binding/> tag is that you can specify

NOTE

You don't use curly braces within the **source** *and* **destination** *properties of the* **<mx:Binding/>** *tag. So,* **<mx:Binding source="{firstName}" destination= "{nameLabel.text}"/>** *is incorrect.*

multiple sources for one *destination*. For example, it is possible in Flex to bind a Label control's text to two or more sources. You can't accomplish this by writing multiple destination attributes for a `<mx:Binding/>` tag, but you can by using multiple `<mx:Binding/>` tags:

```
<mx:Binding source="oneTextInput.text" destination=
    "confusedLabel.text"/>
<mx:Binding source="anotherTextInput.text" destination=
    "confusedLabel.text"/>

<mx:TextInput id="oneTextInput"/>
<mx:TextInput id="anotherTextInput"/>

<mx:Label id="confusedLabel"/>
```

In this code, one Label's **text** property is bound to two different TextInputs. Whenever **oneTextInput** changes its value, that value is copied into the Label. If **anotherTextInput** changes value, that value then becomes the Label's text.

It isn't necessary to use `<mx:Binding/>` tags for both binding declarations in this example. While curly braces alone can't designate multiple sources, curly braces can be used in conjunction with an `<mx:Binding/>` tag. However, using curly braces with an `<mx:Binding/>` tag can get confusing. Consider the following code, which has identical functionality to the previous example but uses one `<mx:Binding/>` tag along with curly brace syntax to bind the Label control's text to two different TextInput controls:

```
<mx:Binding source="oneTextInput.text" destination="confusedLabel.
    text"/>

<mx:TextInput id="oneTextInput"/>
<mx:TextInput id="anotherTextInput"/>

<mx:Label id="confusedLabel" text="{anotherTextInput.text}"/>
```

Binding Tags vs. Curly Brace Syntax

The `<mx:Binding/>` tag offers essentially the same functionality as curly braces, just a different way to get to it. Using the `<mx:Binding/>` tag, you can put all your binding declarations in one place. One benefit of this is that you can easily modify the bindings placed in a central location. However, one of the drawbacks is the loss of the ability to easily create complex bindings. Because you're limited to one source and one destination, you can't create more intricate bindings like you can with multiple sets of curly braces. However, you can do this by separating your data into a separate location, explained shortly in the section "Storing Complex Data."

NOTE

You can place `<mx:Binding/>` tags anywhere within the top level of your application, meaning you can place them between the opening and closing **Application** *tags but not within containers. A good practice is to place them all in one location, preferably near the top of the application code. If you try to place an `<mx:Binding/>` tag within a container or another place it shouldn't be, Flex will issue the warning "<mx:Binding> is not allowed here." That's straightforward enough, right?*

Implementing Two-Way Bindings

By nature, a binding is a one-way road. You specify a source and a destination, and the binding copies the information from the source into the destination. You're not limited to one-way bindings, however. If you want a binding to go both ways, you can simply set up two bindings that copy from each other:

```
<mx:TextInput id="oneTextInput" text="{anotherTextInput.text}"/>
<mx:TextInput id="anotherTextInput" text="{oneTextInput.text}"/>
```

In this case, two TextInputs are bound to each other. When one changes its text, the other matches. You can accomplish this same thing in an `<mx:Binding/>` tag with the following code:

```
<mx:Binding source="oneTextInput.text" destination=
    "anotherTextInput.text"/>
<mx:Binding source="anotherTextInput.text" destination=
    "oneTextInput.text"/>

<mx:TextInput id="oneTextInput"/>
<mx:TextInput id="anotherTextInput"/>
```

Storing Complex Data

Flex makes it easy to store structured information in a data model. A *data model* is a single object with multiple properties that you can declare, so that you can store lots of information in one place. For example, instead of holding a first name and a last name in separate variables, wouldn't it be nice to hold them in one variable called **name**, which has properties like **first**, **middle**, **last**, and even **title**, **suffix**, and so on? This would be a data model. You could go even one step further and make a data model with information like address, phone number, email, and even this **name** object itself, creating a data model to store user information.

Basic Usage

Data models are a great way to organize your code and are very practical as well. If you'll eventually be accessing data from a server (which I'll discuss in Chapter 9), it's good practice to grab lumps of similar data all at once. Instead of making separate calls to get someone's name, email, and address, you'd make just one call and store the result in a model for later use. You can store data models by using `<mx:Model/>`. Here's an example that creates a data model called **model** that uses the `<mx:Model/>` tag:

```
<mx:Model id="model">
    <info>
        <name>
            <firstName>Tim</firstName>
            <lastName>O'Reilly</lastName>
        </name>
```

Yet Another Way to Bind

You can set up bindings in Flex in one more way. Because it's not used so frequently and is a fairly advanced topic, it's outside the scope of this book to go into it in detail, but it's good to know it's there. Using a class called **BindingUtils**, you can create bindings in ActionScript. Why would you want to do this? Well, if you need fine-grained control of when bindings fire or need to turn bindings off and on at will, scripting is the way to go. If you find that the `<mx:Binding/>` tag or curly brace syntax isn't going to cut it, check out the Adobe Flex 3 Language Reference for the **mx.binding.utils.BindingUtils** class, available by going to Help→Help Contents.

```
            <email>tim@oreilly.com</email>

            <phone>(707)827-7000</phone>

        </info>
    </mx:Model>

    <mx:Binding source="areaCode.phone" destination="nameLabel.text"/>

    <mx:Label id="nameLabel"/>
```

The <mx:Model/> tag is an MXML-only tag that lets you enter structured data in XML format. In this case, you're using it to store user information in one central location that's easy to read and understand. There is information about a user's name, email, and phone number, which are created using XML tags. Notice that the root node of this is a tag called <info/>. A root tag must be there to make this valid XML, but you can call it anything you like—the word "info" isn't necessary.

To access this information in a binding expression, you refer to the data model's **id** followed by a dot and the property you want to access. For instance, to get the phone number, you'd use the expression model.phone.

Multilevel Bindings

Now here's the interesting part: you can use binding expressions *within* a model! The following code creates a string variable called **areaCode** that contains the text "707". By using a curly brace binding expression within an <mx:Model/> tag, the area code is added it to the beginning of the phone number that exists inside the data model.

```
    <mx:String id="areaCode">707</mx:String>

    <mx:Model id="model">
        <info>
            <name>
                <firstName>Tim</firstName>
                <lastName>O'Reilly</lastName>
            </name>

            <email>tim@oreilly.com</email>

            <phone>{areaCode}827-7000</phone>

        </info>
    </mx:Model>

    <mx:Binding source="model.phone" destination="nameLabel.text"/>

    <mx:Label id="nameLabel"/>
```

As before, the Label control's **text** is bound to the phone number in this data model. If you were to run this, you'd see the text "707827-7000" displayed in the Label control.

In other words, a multilevel binding has occurred. First, the phone number is constructed using a binding to the country code. Then, the Label control is bound to the phone number. If the country code changes, the phone number will change as well, triggering the binding in the Label control. That's very powerful stuff.

You can use all the features of curly brace data binding in data models, making data coercion very easy. That means you can concatenate strings and use multiple sets of curly braces inside a model. This is sometimes called *data massaging*, meaning piecing together, running calculations on, and possibly formatting data for display (which I'll discuss in Chapter 9). You've seen a simple example of this, when you put together an area code and a phone number to get a full phone number. You could take it a step further and really expand on this data model:

```
<mx:Model id="model">
    <info>

        <name>
            <title>Mr.</title>
            <firstName>Tim</firstName>
            <lastName>O'Reilly</lastName>
            <displayName>{model.name.title} {model.name.lastName}
                </displayName>
        </name>

        <greeting>Hello, {model.name.displayName}</greeting>

        <email>tim@oreilly.com</email>

        <areaCode>707</areaCode>

        <phone>{model.areaCode}827-7000</phone>

    </info>
</mx:Model>

<mx:Binding source="model.greeting" destination="nameLabel.text"/>
```

This code is a bit complex, but it shows just how deep you can go with multilevel bindings. In this case, you've created a **displayName** property that is bound to the title and last name of a user. This, in turn, is being used by a **greeting** property, which is then bound to a Label control. Whew!

Creating Bindable Variables in ActionScript

So far you've used **<mx:String/>** tags, **<mx:Model/>** tags, and properties of controls to create bindings, and everything has worked fine. However, when creating your own variables in ActionScript, you need to explicitly declare them as bindable. If you don't, bindings will work when your application starts up, but changes to the variables won't be reflected. That is to say, the

NOTE

For more complex massaging of data, you may find a class-based model more efficient. Refer to the Flex documentation about class-based models for more information on this advanced topic.

variable's initial value would be copied, but if the variable changed, anything bound to it wouldn't be updated.

`<mx:String/>` tags, `<mx:Model/>` tags, and most properties of Flex components work automatically with data binding. But when creating bindable variables in ActionScript code, you have to do a little extra work. To specify that you want an ActionScript variable to be bindable, you use a *metadata* declaration, which is a special instruction to the Flex compiler that uses square brackets ([and]). The metadata tag you will use is **[Bindable]**, placed before the variable declaration:

```
<mx:Script>
    <![CDATA[
        [Bindable]
        public var firstName:String = "Alaric";

        [Bindable]
        public var lastName:String = "Cole";
    ]]>
</mx:Script>
```

This code is equivalent to the `<mx:String/>` tags used earlier, but it's written in ActionScript instead of MXML.

Why bindable metadata? When you create bindable variables, either through a tag or via script, Flex actually writes a ton of ActionScript for you behind the scenes, setting up listeners for changes to the variables. Without your ability to declare what is bindable and what isn't, Flex would have to create a bunch of useless code for variables that you may not want to be bindable. This useless code might make your application larger and slower than it could be.

Determining When Data Binding Isn't Appropriate

As you've seen, data binding is a great way to move data around in your application. As great as it is, why would you want to use anything else? Well, the truth is, data binding isn't the solution to everything. Sometimes it isn't the best tool for the job. If your application relies on some sort of timing mechanism to display its data, data binding may not be the right choice, because you don't have much control over when a binding is triggered. (This limitation can be overcome by setting up bindings in ActionScript, as discussed in the box "Yet Another Way to Bind.")

A binding is fired whenever the source value changes, and if you have a number of properties that rely on a source that is very large and frequently updated, the bindings may fire more frequently than you'd like. This may cause performance issues because of too much going on at once. In such cases, it may be better to manually set values for variables by scripting. However, in most cases you'll probably find data binding indispensable.

Putting Data Binding to Work for You

Now that you know so much about data binding, you can put it to the test. Start a new Flex project called **ContactManager**, and place the following code in the main application file. Save the file as *ContactManager.mxml*.

```
<?xml version="1.0" encoding="utf-8"?>
<mx:Application
    xmlns:mx="http://www.adobe.com/2006/mxml"
    layout="absolute">

    <mx:Panel
        x="10"
        y="10"
        layout="vertical"
        title="Contact Editor"
        paddingLeft="5"
        width="200"
        height="300">

        <mx:Label
            text="First Name"
            fontWeight="bold"/>
        <mx:TextInput id="firstNameTextInput"/>
        <mx:Label
            text="Last Name"
            fontWeight="bold"/>
        <mx:TextInput id="lastNameTextInput"/>
        <mx:Label id="ageLabel"
            text="Age"
            fontWeight="bold"/>
        <mx:NumericStepper id="ageNS"
            maximum="120"
            minimum="18"/>
        <mx:CheckBox id="dogsCheckBox"
            label="Likes Dogs"/>
        <mx:Label
            text="Favorite Color"
            fontWeight="bold"/>
        <mx:ColorPicker id="favoriteColorPicker"
            selectedColor="#FFFFFF"/>

    </mx:Panel>

</mx:Application>
```

This code creates a Panel control called "Contact Editor" that contains a few different controls. A new one that you haven't seen before is the ColorPicker, which works like a color picker in design applications such as Adobe Photoshop or like the color picker in Flex Builder's Design mode in the Flex Properties panel. It simply lets you select a color via a drop-down list of swatches. In this case, you've set the **selectedColor** property to a hexadecimal value, which is a compact way to designate a numerical value. (See the box "Roses are FF0000, Violets are 0000FF" for more information.) Thus, the color is represented by a numerical value, and this value, just like text, is bindable. (You'll see that in a moment.)

NOTE

*Formatting the MXML isn't necessary. But for the sake of readability, you can format the MXML such that the **id** attribute is placed on the same line as the tag and all other attributes are on their own line.*

Roses are FF0000, Violets are 0000FF

Hexadecimal, or *hex* for short, is one way of representing 24-bit color in a compact way. Hexadecimal is really just a means of concisely representing large numbers, but for these purposes, I'll refer to its use in colors. Colors in Flex are displayed in what are called *hex triplets*, the format being RRGGBB, where RR specifies the amount of red, GG stands for the amount of green, and BB represents the amount of blue. It's beyond the scope of this book to really explain hexadecimal, but suffice it to say that hexadecimal is a way of representing base-16 numbers, that is, a numerical system that is based on 16 (as opposed to the numbering system we're all used to that's based on 10). Thus, 16 values are available: 0–9 and A–F, which represent 10 through 15. So, the 16 possible values are 0, 1, 2, 3, 4, 5, 6, 7, 8, 9, A, B, C, D, E, and F. For example, black is 000000, meaning no red, green, or blue. Pure red is FF0000, because it's the full value for the red element and zero for the blue and green values. 00FF00 is full green, and 0000FF is complete blue. Mix and match as you like to get other colors. If you remember anything from art class, red and blue mixed together make purple. So, it would make sense that pure red (FF0000) mixed with pure blue (0000FF) would make a purple shade (FF00FF). If you remember that white is actually a mix of all colors, you could've guessed that white can be represented as FFFFFF.

It's of course not necessary to write this stuff yourself, but it does help make your code less mysterious. It's worth noting that you can represent hexadecimal values in Flex in a couple of ways. One is via a hash character (**#**) followed by the value. That is to say, to show red, you'd place a hash before the value, like so: #FF0000. This is the way it is done in CSS, and MXML works with this just fine. Another way to show that a value is hexadecimal is by starting it with 0x. This would display red as 0xFF0000. This is the way it's used in ActionScript, so if you're working with colors or hexadecimal values in ActionScript, that's the way you'd need to represent it. For the beginner, if you need a hexadecimal value for a color, you can simply use Design mode in Flex Builder. The Flex Properties panel contains a few color pickers that allow you to visually select a color.

If all this talk about base-16 has tickled your fancy, you may be interested in the history of the word *hexadecimal*. *Hexa* comes from the Greek ἕξ (hex) meaning "six," while *decimal* is derived from the Latin for "tenth." If this all seems like Greek to you, well, it's worth noting that some people think the word should be *sexadecimal*, that being a purely Latin form.

Next, create another panel called "Contact Details" to which you'll add a few Label controls that are bound to the input controls in the Contact Editor panel. Place the following code under the first Panel control (but before the closing **Application** tag, of course):

```
<mx:Panel
    layout="vertical"
    x="227"
    y="10"
    width="200"
    height="300"
    paddingLeft="5"
    title="Contact Details">
    <mx:Label
        text="Full Name:"
        fontWeight="bold"/>
    <mx:Label
        text="{firstNameTextInput.text} {lastNameTextInput.text}"/>
    <mx:Label
        text="Age:"
        fontWeight="bold"/>
    <mx:Label
        text="{ageNS.value} years old"/>
    <mx:Label
        text="Likes Dogs:"
        fontWeight="bold"/>
    <mx:Label
        text="{dogsCheckBox.selected}"/>
```

```
<mx:Label
    text="Favorite Color:"
    fontWeight="bold"/>
<mx:Canvas
    width="60"
    height="60"
    backgroundColor="{favoriteColorPicker.selectedColor}"/>

</mx:Panel>
```

This is a simple example of data binding using input controls in one Panel control and displaying controls in the other. In Contact Editor, you'll see some TextInputs, a NumericStepper, a CheckBox, and a ColorPicker. The values of these controls are updated on the fly in the Contact Details Panel. Running this application, you should see something similar to Figure 7-2.

Figure 7-2. A simple application showcasing data binding

Worth noting is the use of a Canvas container to show your favorite color. It has a **backgroundColor** style property, which is bound to the selected color of the ColorPicker. The **backgroundColor** property expects a numerical value, which is given by the ColorPicker. So now when the ColorPicker's selection changes, the Canvas will draw its background with that color. As you'll learn more about in Chapter 10, a Canvas is a layout container that lets components be placed via *x*,*y* coordinates. But it also works in a pinch as a simple graphical component used to display, in this case, a square of color.

You may be tempted to set the background color of your main application using a binding similar to what you've built with a ColorPicker and a Canvas. The application shares the style property **backgroundColor** with Canvas and other containers, so this makes sense. However, binding isn't supported for properties of the **<mx:Application/>** tag.

To set the background color of the application based on a ColorPicker, you would need to do so in script. The easiest way would be to listen for changes to the ColorPicker and set the background color of the application explicitly. You do so through a method of the **<mx:Application/>** tag called **setStyle()**.

NOTE

The **<mx:Binding/>** *tag wouldn't work when trying to bind* **backgroundColor**. *This is because* **backgroundColor** *is a style property and is handled differently from other properties. While it works through curly brace syntax because the Flex compiler will detect style properties versus other properties, the* **<mx:Binding/>** *tag only takes properties.*

Actually, this method is shared among all Flex components, so it's good to get familiar with it. This method takes two parameters, a String that's the name of the style property you want to modify and the value to which you want to change the style. In the case of background color, the style property is the String **backgroundColor**, and the value you'd want to set it to is the selected color of the ColorPicker instance. Thus, the full method call would be **setStyle('backgroundColor', favoriteColorPicker.selectedColor)**. You'd want to call this method when the ColorPicker changes its value. A **change** event is fired when this happens, so you'd want to set up a listener for the **change** event by doing the following:

```
<mx:ColorPicker id="favoriteColorPicker"
    change="setStyle('backgroundColor',
        favoriteColorPicker.selectedColor)"/>
```

Now, when the ColorPicker changes, it calls this method, which changes the background color of the application.

However, this event isn't fired when the application starts up, so you might end up with an initial background color that doesn't match the current selection of the ColorPicker. To resolve this, you'll need to call this method again on a special event of the **<mx:Application/>** tag called **applicationComplete**. This event is fired when the application loads and all of its top-level components have been created. This simply means, when this event fires, you can be sure that **favoriteColorPicker** has been created and you can access its properties. Other events such as **initialize** occur during startup, but **applicationComplete** is the one you want because it's the last one that's fired and therefore the safest bet.

It is good coding practice, and useful for you besides, if you create a function that calls the **setStyle()** method and in turn calls this function in both the **applicationComplete** event and the **change** event, like in the following code:

```
<mx:Application
    xmlns:mx="http://www.adobe.com/2006/mxml"
    layout="absolute"
    applicationComplete="modifyBackgroundColor()">

<mx:Script>
<![CDATA[
    public function modifyBackgroundColor():void
    {
        setStyle('backgroundColor', favoriteColorPicker.selectedColor);
    }
]]>
</mx:Script>

<!-- More code would go here -->

<mx:ColorPicker id="favoriteColorPicker"
    selectedColor="0xFFFFFF"
    change="modifyBackgroundColor()"/>

<!-- More code would go here -->
```

Binding and Coercion

The way in which different types of values change as a result of data binding merits an explanation. Notice the CheckBox in the example. It has a value of **true** (when selected) or **false** (when it's not selected). This is a Boolean value. However, when you bind that value to the text of a Label control, something happens that you might not have noticed. The Label's **text** property expects a String value, meaning it expects text, not a Boolean value. So, data binding is actually converting a Boolean value to text. In this case, **true** is converted to the string "true," while **false** is converted to the string "false."

This conversion is also occurring in the binding to the NumericStepper's **value** property. The **value** property is a Number, which again is converted to a String. If you're interested in the details, I'll explain what Flex is actually doing. Every object in ActionScript has a **toString()** method, which returns a String value. In the case of a Number, the **toString()** method returns a textual representation of the Number. What Flex does is call that method on a binding when necessary. Without that, you would get runtime errors complaining that a Number isn't a String and can't be converted to one. Luckily, Flex will convert the string for you.

However, this only works for string assignments. For instance, if you try to bind that same NumericStepper's **value** property to the **text** of a Label—that is, try to reverse the binding—you'll get an error. Flex will complain "Implicit coercion of a value of type String to an unrelated type Number," which means it can't convert text to a numeric value.

To get around this, you can convert text to a numeric value by casting. For instance, you could coerce the String value into a Number like this:
`<mx:NumericStepper value="{Number('33')}"/>`.

Summary

Now you understand what those curly braces are all about. You've seen that data binding is an invaluable tool for moving information around in your application, and you know more than one way to go about it. You've even built a simple example that shows that even colors are bindable in Flex.

You will continue to use and expand on this important concept throughout the book, since data binding is used so frequently in Flex applications. Knowing these basic concepts will take you far. With all this knowledge, you can move on to the next set of skills. Next up, I'll explain how to lay out your applications.

LAYING OUT YOUR APPLICATIONS

Having a mechanism for layout is yet another one of the great features of Flex. If you've ever developed applications using the Flash integrated development environment (IDE), you know that layout can be one of the greatest challenges. Sometimes you will be developing something that works fine with a static size. In that case, it's okay if all of its components are set to one location and one size, never needing to resize or reposition themselves. For this, the Flash IDE has worked great. More often than not, however, you'll want more flexibility in your layout, and Flex provides this.

With today's multitude of screen resolutions, having a layout that can expand is often essential. If someone is viewing your application in a browser, they can resize their browser. If your application is deployed to the desktop with AIR, you'll probably want the ability to resize that window as well. You may even want to be able to move components around based on the size of the application.

The Flex layout system is built using the web paradigm of layers and constraints, so having a background in web design or development doesn't hurt. However, Flex Builder's Design mode will help you build a beautiful layout, even if you've never heard of Cascading Style Sheets (CSS).

Types of Layouts

You can lay out components in your application in many ways. You can use coordinates, layout containers, constraints, or a mixture of all three to find the perfect layout.

Absolute Positioning

When creating a new Flex application in Flex Builder, the `Application` tag is given the attribute `layout="absolute"`. This makes the application have an *absolute* layout, meaning components are positioned by an *x,y* coordinate.

This lets you stipulate where you want items to be placed within their parent container, by specifying *x* and *y* coordinates on each of them. It's called *absolute*, in contrast to *relative* positioning, because absolute positioning doesn't take into account other components in the same container. That is, each component within a container has its placement without regard to others. Absolute positioning gives you complete control over where components appear and can even allow the overlap of components.

For a quick-and-dirty approach to laying out your application, absolute positioning is great. In Design mode, you can simply place components where you like, and their *x,y* will be written for you automatically. However, for most interfaces, you need more control over positioning and may even need to adjust the sizes of your components in addition to where they're placed. You can accomplish all this by using constraints or relative positioning using specific layout containers.

The Canvas container, while being a layout container, lets you use an absolute layout. However, most other containers have a predefined system for relative layout.

Relative Positioning

Relative positioning is laying out the parts of your application by their relationship to one another. You typically do this by using layout containers.

I went over layout containers briefly in Chapter 3, but they merit a deeper explanation here. *Containers* are special components that can have layout controls (and even other containers) placed within them. You do this in MXML by creating a container tag, such as **<mx:Panel/>**, and placing components inside that tag. Thus, you could create a Panel container with a single TextInput control inside it using the following MXML code:

```
<mx:Panel>
    <mx:TextInput/>
</mx:Panel>
```

Simple enough, right? Because the **<mx:TextInput/>** tag is inside the two **<mx:Panel>** **</mx:Panel>** tags, it makes sense that the TextInput would be drawn inside the Panel. In Flash terminology, the TextInput is considered a *child* of the Panel. Conversely, the Panel is called the TextInput's *parent*.

Two major types of relative layout exist:

Vertical

> This lays children out in a vertical stack. The attribute **layout="vertical"** accomplishes this.

Horizontal

> This lays out children in a horizontal stack. The attribute you use is **layout="horizontal"**.

Some containers, such as HBox and VBox, accomplish a specific type of layout (horizontal for HBox and vertical for VBox). This is fairly straightforward.

An HBox or VBox can take any number of components, lining them up one by one.

Other containers such as Panel and Application have three options for the type of layout they will create. These may be known as *hybrid* containers, because they may act like other containers, depending on the properties set. They are useful because you can use one container, changing its layout just by switching the `layout` property to one of `vertical`, `horizontal`, or `absolute`.

To really understand the usefulness of layout containers, it's important to first understand the concept of the display list in Flex. Once you grasp that, you'll make better decisions with your layout.

The Display List

The *display list* in Flex, and in all Flash-based content, is the name for the list of all graphical elements in a particular application. For a Flex application, you can think of it as a hierarchy of components, from the Application root to a Panel within it to a Button that resides in that Panel. It's actually much more than this. For instance, a Button contains multiple graphical elements itself such as its label and the graphics that make it look like a button. But for beginning Flex developers, it's convenient to think of it in terms of components and containers.

How It Works

If you're used to design programs, you might be familiar with the concept of *layers*. This concept is similar to a display list in that the layers are a list of elements, with more recent layers overlapping older ones.

What happens when you add items to a Panel in MXML is that each item is added to the Panel's display list in order of its location in the MXML. If you're familiar with layers, you can imagine the newest element overlapping the previous. In programming, you would refer to the new items as having a higher *index*. The first component added to a container has the lowest index, and that index increases on each addition. Check out the following MXML, which adds three Canvas containers to a Panel container, each Canvas having a different color:

```
<mx:Panel id="colorsPanel"
    width="250"
    height="250"
    layout="absolute">

    <mx:Canvas id="redBox"
        x="70"
        y="70"
        width="50"
        height="50"
        backgroundColor="#FF0000" />
```

> ## There're Defaults, and Then There're Defaults
>
> By default, a new Flex application created in Flex Builder will begin with absolute positioning. In other words, Flex Builder will automatically add the attribute `layout="absolute"`. This is the same for the Panel container, if you're using Design mode to drag and drop a Panel onto the stage. However, it's worth noting that the default layout for both Application and Panel is actually vertical. That is, if you create an Application or Panel control without specifying a layout attribute, the layout will be vertical. Flex Builder overrides this setting by placing the attribute `layout="absolute"`.

```
                              <mx:Canvas id="greenBox"
                                  x="90"
                                  y="90"
                                  width="50"
                                  height="50"
                                  backgroundColor="#00FF00" />
                              <mx:Canvas id="blueBox"
                                  x="100"
                                  y="60"
                                  width="50"
                                  height="50"
                                  backgroundColor="#0000FF" />

                          </mx:Panel>
```

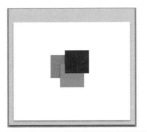

Figure 8-1. Three colored boxes overlapping in an absolute layout

This code adds **greenBox** to the Panel's display list after **redBox**, because **greenBox** is after **redBox** in the MXML. Similarly, **blueBox** has the highest index because it was added last. You can see how this works by looking at the output of this code in Figure 8-1.

Accessing Children

The display list, being a list, means you can access each child of a container by its index. You just use a method in ActionScript called **getChildAt()**. This method takes one parameter, an integer corresponding to the index of the child you want. It's zero-based, meaning that 0 is considered the first, 1 the second, 2 the third, and so on. In the case of the previous code, calling **getChildAt(0)** returns **redBox**, while calling **getChildAt(2)** returns **blueBox**.

Adding and Removing Children

In Chapter 4, I briefly mentioned the method **addChild()**. This is the ActionScript way of *adding* children to containers and the display list. Creating a component in ActionScript doesn't actually add it to the display list, so you must specifically add it using this method. The ActionScript equivalent of the previous MXML would be the following function:

```
//import the required classes
import mx.containers.Panel;
import mx.containers.Canvas;

public function createBoxes():void
{
    //create a Panel
    var colorsPanel:Panel = new Panel();
    colorsPanel.layout = "absolute";
    colorsPanel.width = 250;
    colorsPanel.height = 250;

    //add the Panel to the Application
    addChild(colorsPanel);

    //create a red box
    var redBox:Canvas = new Canvas();
```

```
redBox.x = 70;
redBox.y = 70;
redBox.width = 50;
redBox.height = 50;
redBox.setStyle("backgroundColor", 0xFF0000);

//create a green box
var g:Canvas = new Canvas();
greenBox.x = 90;
greenBox.y = 90;
greenBox.width = 50;
greenBox.height = 50;
greenBox.setStyle("backgroundColor", 0x00FF00);

//create a blue box
var blueBox:Canvas = new Canvas();
blueBox.x = 100;
blueBox.y = 60;
blueBox.width = 50;
blueBox.height = 50;
blueBox.setStyle("backgroundColor", 0x0000FF);

//add the boxes to the Panel
colorsPanel.addChild(redBox);
colorsPanel.addChild(greenBox);
colorsPanel.addChild(blueBox);
}
```

Just like the equivalent MXML example, the Canvas **greenBox** is added to the Panel container after **redBox**, because the method **panel.addChild(greenBox)** was called after **panel.addChild(redBox)**. Therefore, **greenBox** has the index of 1, while **redBox** has the index of 0, just like before. Again, this means **greenBox** is higher on the display list than **redBox**, and **blueBox** is the highest overall.

If you were to switch the layout of the Panel to vertical, the boxes would line up in a vertical stack. Their order would be the same as their order in the MXML, as shown in Figure 8-2.

NOTE

Simply placing the **createBoxes()** *function in an* **<mx:Script/>** *tag in an MXML file won't actually run the function. You'll have to call the function by setting up an event listener somewhere.*

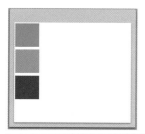

Figure 8-2. Three colored boxes lined up, one below the other in a vertical layout

Just as you can add items to a display list, you can remove them; you merely use the method called **removeChild()**. If you decided you didn't want a blue box anymore, you could remove it by calling **colorsPanel.removeChild(blueBox)**.

NOTE

Just as creating an item in ActionScript doesn't add it to the display list, removing an item from the display list doesn't mean the item doesn't exist anymore. It simply removes it from view. You can always add it back later.

***Figure 8-3.** The green box placed higher in the display list*

***Figure 8-4.** A vertical layout showing the green box highest in the display list*

NOTE

You can use the `swapChildren()` *method to switch the location of two items on the display list. For example, to swap the location of the red and green boxes, you could use* `colorsPanel.swapChildren(redBox, greenBox)`.

Rearranging Children

What's great about a display list is that it lets you rearrange items as you want. For instance, if you later wanted **greenBox** to be on top, you could use ActionScript to make that happen. First you would use the method `colorsPanel.removeChild(greenBox)`, which would remove **greenBox** from the Panel's display list. Then you would call `colorsPanel.addChild(greenBox)`, which would add **greenBox** to the display list. Because it was added last, **greenBox** would be at a higher index than both **redBox** and **blueBox**, as shown in Figure 8-3. Again, if you were to switch the Panel to a vertical layout, **greenBox** would be at the bottom of the Panel, just like in Figure 8-4.

For a better understanding of the display list, try the following code, which adds a click event listener to each of the colored boxes. When you click a box, that box is placed higher on the display list.

```
<mx:Script>
    <![CDATA[
    public function moveUp(event:Event):void
    {
        //we expect the "current target" of this event to be a Canvas
        var box:Canvas = event.currentTarget as Canvas;

        //remove the box that was clicked
        colorsPanel.removeChild(box);

        //place it back at a higher point
        colorsPanel.addChild(box);
    }

    ]]>
</mx:Script>

<mx:Panel id="colorsPanel"
    width="250"
    height="250"
    layout="absolute">

    <mx:Canvas id="redBox"
        x="70"
        y="70"
        width="50"
        height="50"
        backgroundColor="#FF0000"
        click="moveUp(event)" />
    <mx:Canvas id="greenBox"
        x="90"
        y="90"
        width="50"
        height="50"
        backgroundColor="#00FF00"
        click="moveUp(event)" />
```

```
<mx:Canvas id="blueBox"
    x="100"
    y="60"
    width="50"
    height="50"
    backgroundColor="#0000FF"
    click="moveUp(event)" />

</mx:Panel>
```

Try this code with different layout attributes on the Panel, and see how moving items around on the display list affects the way they are shown.

Note that the Panel, in turn, is part of the Application container's display list. Just as you can move elements around in a particular display list, you can also move them in and out of others. This means the colored boxes aren't even limited to the Panel but can be moved around anywhere, such as another container or the Application itself.

If you have two Panels, one called `panel1` and the other `panel2`, you can move children from one to the other. If `panel1` has a child with an ID of `someChild`, you can move it by first calling `panel1.removeChild(someChild)` and then calling `panel2.addChild(someChild)`.

Sizing

You can control the size of components by specifying a height and width. This is typically done by specifying the number of *pixels*. Pixels are a measurement of size corresponding to the smallest discrete area of illumination on a computer's screen. If you were to enlarge part of your computer screen, you would see lots of little squares. Each of those squares is a pixel.

However, there's more to controlling component size than simply specifying a width or height in pixels. Containers not only help with providing arrangement, but they also have the ability to allow a two-way effect of either resizing themselves to fit their children or resizing their children to fit them.

Explicit Sizing

You can set an explicit size on a component via its `width` or `height` property, or a component can have a default size. If a container such as a VBox, HBox, or Panel doesn't have a size set on itself, it will resize to fit the components within it.

If the container does have a size set or if it runs out of available space, it may *clip* its content. This means, because it's not able to display its contents completely, it will cut off the rest from view. In the case of many containers, a scroll bar will appear, allowing the unseen content to be viewed by scrolling.

Figure 8-5. Percentage-based width

NOTE

While in MXML, you can set a width or height of either a numerical value or a percentage value; the width and height properties in ActionScript expect only a numerical value. To set percentage widths in ActionScript, use the properties percentWidth *and* percentHeight, *which will accept a numerical value in the range 0–100, corresponding to a percentage amount.*

NOTE

When using relative, or percentage-based, sizing on container children, it's best to set a width on the parent container. Otherwise, both sizes will revert to the default size of the child.

Relative or Percentage-Based Sizing

You can also size components within a container using relative sizing. This means using percentages instead of pixels. While a Button, for instance, can have a width of 22, meaning 22 pixels, it can alternatively have a width of, say 50 percent, which means it should resize itself to take up 50 percent of its parent's width.

Consider the following code, which creates an HBox that is 400 pixels wide, with a Button inside set to a width of 50 percent:

```
<mx:HBox width="400">
    <mx:Button label="Button" width="50%"/>
</mx:HBox>
```

Figure 8-5 shows the result, where the Button takes up half the available space of its container, the HBox.

Because its container is 400 pixels wide, the button will size itself to half of that, or 200 pixels. You could also set the HBox to a relative size, say 100 percent. This would allow the HBox to resize to fit all the available space of its container (the Application itself), and then the button would take up half of *that*. If the application were resized, the widths of the HBox, and therefore the button, would also change.

What would happen if you then removed the `width` property from the HBox? The button's width is expecting to be 100 percent of its parent's width, but no width would be set on its parent. So, the button would want a width of 100 percent, but 100 percent of what? In this case, the button would simply revert to its default size (which is based on the size of its label).

Remember that containers have the ability to resize to fit their contents. If using explicit or default widths on container children, it helps to know that you have these choices for the container:

- *Do* set a size on the container. Content will be clipped if the sum of the children's sizes are larger than the container's size.

- Do *not* set a size on the container. The container will resize as needed to contain its children. If the container runs out of available space, content will be clipped.

Minimum and Maximum Sizes

You also have control over the minimum and maximum widths or heights that you want a component to have. This is especially useful when using percentage-based sizes. Say, for example, that you have a button's `height` set to 100 percent, but you don't want it to actually grow more than 300 pixels high. You could accomplish this by adding the property `maxHeight`:

```
<mx:Button height="100%" maxHeight="300" />
```

The same goes for width, using the `maxWidth` property.

If you want to ensure that a component never goes below a certain size, you can use the properties `minWidth` and `minHeight` to control minimum allowable width and height, respectively.

Layout Container Options

When using a layout container such as an HBox or Panel, you have a few options to help you get the look you want.

Padding Layout

If you've used much CSS, you're probably familiar with the concept of *padding*, which lets you specify the number of pixels of space with which you want to pad a container. This allows some visual separation from the container and its children. In Flex, you use the properties `paddingLeft`, `paddingRight`, `paddingTop`, and `paddingBottom`.

For example, placing a few Buttons within a Panel with a vertical layout will have the Buttons placed at the top and left of the Panel in a vertical stack. They will be hugging the edges of the Panel. If you want more space between the edges, you can change this using the different padding properties, showcased in Figure 8-6.

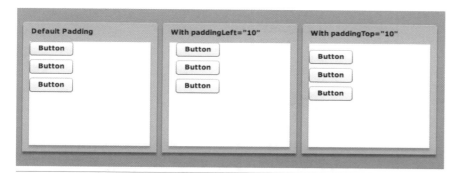

Figure 8-6. Panels with different padding applied

It's important to note that padding properties are not used just on containers; they are also used in some controls, such as List. In this case, the properties designate the amount of padding between the border of the control and its content.

Gaps

Gaps are distances between child components when using many layout containers. You have both `horizontalGap` and `verticalGap`, which you can set independently to control how much space you want between components. You can easily understand this by looking at Figure 8-7.

NOTE

Components will compete for available space when using percentage-based sizes. For instance, if two Buttons are placed within a HBox that has a width of 300 pixels and each Button is given a width of 100 percent, their actual widths will be half the available space, or 150 pixels. If three Buttons were placed within this container, each with a width of 100 percent, their actual width would be divided into thirds (33 percent, or 100 pixels each). For a couple of Buttons, the first with a width of 100 percent and the second with a width of 70 percent, the result would be around half the requested space—the first about 60 percent, the second around 40 percent.

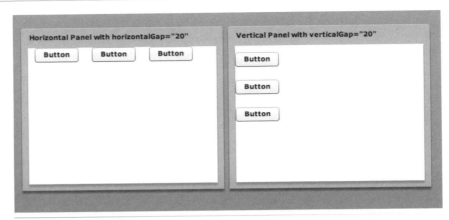

Figure 8-7. Panels with different layouts and gap styles

NOTE

While these properties are easy to set and modify in MXML, it's important to note that they are style properties. As such, you cannot access them in ActionScript through dot notation. That is, the script `panel1.paddingLeft = 10` *isn't valid. You must access such style properties using the* `setStyle()` *method.*

The Flex Layout Process

The layout mechanisms in Flex are quite advanced, and they take into account a huge number of variables. This usually works seamlessly for the developer, allowing you to spend less time worrying about your layout. If you're interested in how this works, Figure 8-8 gives a quick overview. Essentially, calculating layout involves three steps. First, components like Buttons and CheckBoxes that can resize themselves to fit their labels are given the chance to do so if they don't have an explicit size already. Then, component sizes are gathered. This measurement begins at the components that are deepest in the tree of the application. For example, for the following code, the Button is the most deeply nested component, followed in turn by the Panel, then the Canvas, and finally the HBox:

```
<mx:HBox>
    <mx:Canvas width="300">
        <mx:Panel width="100%">
            <mx:Button width="50%"/>
        </mx:Panel>
    </mx:Canvas>
</mx:HBox>
```

Only pixel-based sizes are gathered, because percentage-based sizes can be determined only in the next step. The final stage of the layout process applies size and placement, in the reverse order from the previous step. For the previous code, the HBox would first have its size changed to allow it to fit the Canvas that is 300 pixels wide. After this would come the Canvas. Because the Canvas already has an explicit width, no changes would occur, and it would remain at this width. The layout mechanism would then move onto the Panel. Because the Panel has a width of 100 percent, it would be sized so that its width fills the parent

Canvas. Finally, the Button would have its width applied, being sized so that it fills half its parent Panel.

This process begins again if any components are added, removed, or resized (whether through code or by someone resizing the application window).

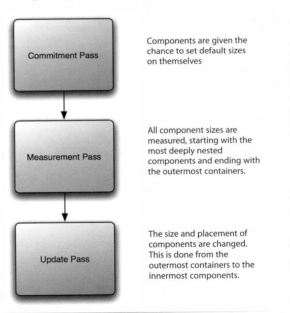

Components are given the chance to set default sizes on themselves

All component sizes are measured, starting with the most deeply nested components and ending with the outermost containers.

The size and placement of components are changed. This is done from the outermost containers to the innermost components.

Figure 8-8. The three steps in the Flex layout process

Advanced Containers

Going further than simple vertical or horizontal layout, a few containers provide advanced functionality. Figure 8-9 shows a mixture of advanced containers.

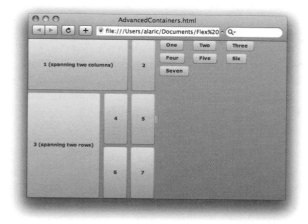

Figure 8-9. A mix of advanced containers: a Grid on the left, a Tile on the right, and the overall layout provided by an HDividedBox

Divided Boxes

While HBoxes and VBoxes can line children up in a horizontal or vertical fashion, a couple of containers add a little more functionality. HDividedBox and VDividedBox are just like their equivalent HBox and VBox, but they allow resizing.

Between each child of a divided box, the Divided box draws a draggable section divider. Moving the divider resizes that section. Divided boxes are especially useful when using relative sizing.

Tiles

If you want a layout that can really roll with the punches, Tile is a great choice. The Tile container arranges children like tiles, lining them up horizontally until the available space is used up, and then it starts a new row. While laying out in horizontal rows is the default behavior, Tile has a **direction** property that you can set to vertical, and it will arrange by columns instead of by rows.

All these tiles will have the same size and will be arranged in a perfect grid. The largest child will set the size for all other tiles, unless you explicitly set a `tileWidth` or `tileHeight` on the Tile container.

For example, consider that in your application you had a list of toolbar items. You placed these items in an HBox at the top of your application to mimic the toolbars in Microsoft Word. However, you realized that there were just too many buttons to fit in the HBox, and the buttons got clipped. This HBox could be replaced with a Tile container, and when space ran out, the buttons would just get placed on a new row.

Grid

If you've ever used a Hypertext Markup Language (HTML) table, you already know what a grid is. If not, suffice it to say that a Grid container can lay out components in a tiled fashion similar to the Tile container. However, a Grid allows the various items to span columns or rows. If you've ever used a spreadsheet, you may have found that one cell in the spreadsheet needed more horizontal space, so you allowed it to span multiple columns, meaning you let one cell stretch to contain the space of the adjacent cell.

NOTE

If all this sounds too complicated, Grid is probably not the container for you. You can accomplish most of what it does by using constraints, explained a little later in this chapter. However, if you've been using HTML tables a great deal, you may find that Grid is a great choice for you.

To accomplish this, the Grid expects its immediate children to be GridRow or GridItem containers (which correspond roughly to `<tr/>` and `<td/>` tags in an HTML table). It works with these containers to accomplish tasks like column and row spanning, using the `colSpan` and `rowSpan` properties.

When using Design mode, dragging a Grid container onto the stage will prompt you with a dialog box asking for the number of rows and columns you want. This is an easy way to create a Grid, because it will then write the code for you, inserting the necessary GridItem and GridRow containers. From there you can simply drag and drop components into the individual GridItem containers. You can put multiple children inside a GridItem container as well, which can provide a lot of flexibility.

Form

The Form container creates a layout for its children in a way that mimics an HTML form. It does this by working with a special container called a FormItem. FormItem containers take an input control and provide it with a label, without the need to use a Label control. An example follows:

```
<mx:Form>

    <mx:FormItem label="A Short Label">
        <mx:TextInput/>
    </mx:FormItem>

    <mx:FormItem label="A Very, Very Long Label">
        <mx:TextInput/>
    </mx:FormItem>

</mx:Form>
```

Figure 8-10. A simple Form layout

NOTE

FormItems have additional functionality that help with form validation. I will discuss this more in depth in Chapter 9.

This creates a layout like Figure 8-10, causing the form fields (the two TextInput controls) to line up vertically, while also lining up their corresponding labels. The labels are matched in width, so that if you have a long label and a short label, the longest label pushes the form fields to the right so that it all fits nicely.

Forms can also take a FormHeading control, which provides a title for the form. The FormHeading also lines up with the form fields automatically.

In Flex Builder's Design mode, forms are easy to create. Just drag a Form container onto the stage. Then when you drag form fields such as TextInputs, NumericSteppers, or DateFields, Flex Builder automatically generates a FormItem, and you can double-click the FormItem to change its label. If you don't want a label at all, it's fine to enter an empty string or go into Source mode and remove the **label** attribute from the FormItem altogether.

To really understand this container, return to the ContactManager project you created in Chapter 7. In this chapter, you'll rework the layout to take advantage of this new container. Either re-create it in Design mode or modify your code to replace the Panel containers with Form and FormItem containers:

WARNING

For Form fields to line up properly, you must enclose them in a FormItem container, so even if you don't want a label displayed, keep the FormItem in place.

```
<mx:Form>
    <mx:FormHeading
        label="Contact Editor"/>
    <mx:FormItem
        label="First Name">
        <mx:TextInput id="firstNameTextInput"/>
    </mx:FormItem>
    <mx:FormItem
        label="Last Name">
        <mx:TextInput id="lastNameTextInput"/>
    </mx:FormItem>
    <mx:FormItem
        label="Age">
        <mx:NumericStepper id="ageNS"
            maximum="120"
            minimum="18" />
    </mx:FormItem>
    <mx:FormItem>
        <mx:CheckBox id="dogsCheckBox"
            label="Likes Dogs" />
    </mx:FormItem>
    <mx:FormItem
        label="Favorite Color">
        <mx:ColorPicker id="favoriteColorPicker"/>
    </mx:FormItem>
</mx:Form>

<mx:Form x="300">
    <mx:FormHeading
        label="Contact Details"/>
    <mx:FormItem
        label="Full Name">
        <mx:Label
            text="{firstNameTextInput.text} {lastNameTextInput.text}"/>
    </mx:FormItem>
    <mx:FormItem
        label="Age">
        <mx:Label
            text="{ageNS.value} years old"/>
    </mx:FormItem>
    <mx:FormItem
        label="Likes Dogs">
        <mx:Label
```

Tabbing Through Fields

People expect to be able to easily navigate through an application with more than the mouse. The most commonly used navigation button is the Tab key. People expect to be able to use this key to move through input fields in an application, and not providing this functionality will be more than frustrating for most people.

Usually, you won't even have to think about this one, because Flex provides a default system of tab navigation. Based upon the proximity of a particular control or form field to the currently selected field, focus will generally move to the expected field when using the Tab key. When using containers such as Form, the tab navigation will move from the current field to the adjacent field in a way that you can predict.

If you find that you need more fine-grained control, components have a property called **tabIndex** that you can modify. This property expects an integer that gives the order in which the particular component should be given focus when tabbing through controls. Note that for this to work properly, you must set the **tabIndex** of every single control. Usually, using containers that lay controls out in the right order is a better way to accomplish this.

```
            text="{dogsCheckBox.selected}"/>
    </mx:FormItem>
    <mx:FormItem
        label="Favorite Color">
        <mx:Canvas
            width="60"
            height="60"
            backgroundColor="{favoriteColorPicker.selectedColor}"/>
    </mx:FormItem>
</mx:Form>
```

Your ContactManager application should now look like Figure 8-11. Keep this for now, because you'll continue building upon this application throughout this book.

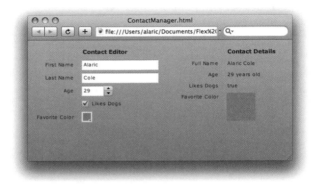

Figure 8-11. ContactManager with a new Form layout

Layout Controls

A few *controls* are useful for layout. These controls help with relative layouts by taking up space in containers.

Spacer

The Spacer is an invisible control that, when used in conjunction within layout containers, will push other children around. Although it's invisible, it can still have a width and height, and it accepts all other sizing options such as percentage-based sizes and minimum and maximum values.

For instance, a Spacer placed inside an HBox can separate the controls to its left and right, pushing them apart. If you gave the Spacer a width of 100 percent, this can provide a layout where two visual controls are pushed to the opposite edges of the HBox, as shown in Figure 8-12:

```
<mx:HBox width="250">
    <mx:Button label="Left"/>
    <mx:Spacer width="100%"/>
    <mx:Button label="Right"/>
</mx:HBox>
```

Figure 8-12. A representation of a Spacer at work in an HBox

Planning Your Layout

Like all aspects of software development, designing a great interface layout can benefit from a bit of planning. I've found that creating a simple diagram of my application really helps, especially if I plan to use a lot of layout containers. This helps me think about how different components relate to one another.

Flex's layout mechanism does a lot of calculations when determining optimal size and placement, so having too many nested containers can cause a performance degrade. That's why it's good to plan for your layout in order to ensure you have only the pieces you need. Remember, for instance, that the **Application** tag is a container itself. Thus, the following code, which attempts to line up two Buttons vertically, isn't optimal:

```
<mx:Application
      xmlns:mx="http://www.adobe.com/2006/mxml"
      layout="absolute">

      <mx:VBox>
            <mx:Button/>
            <mx:Button/>
      </mx:VBox>

</mx:Application>
```

You could easily reduce this code by removing the VBox and replacing the layout by changing the **Application** tag's layout property to vertical:

```
<mx:Application
      xmlns:mx="http://www.adobe.com/2006/mxml"
      layout="vertical">

      <mx:Button/>
      <mx:Button/>

</mx:Application>
```

The trick is to simplify and use only what you need. This not only makes your applications run better, but it makes your code easier to understand, navigate, and maintain.

HRule and VRule

HRule and VRule controls work similarly to Spacer controls, but they have chrome that shows a thin horizontal or vertical line by default. For example, you could use an HRule in a Form container to visually separate different sections. You can see how an HRule looks in Figure 8-13.

NOTE

You can use the Label control like a layout control in some situations. Because setting its width or height to a larger number doesn't affect the actual text size, it can provide an additional means of controlling layout.

Figure 8-13. An HRule helps separate the sections of a Form container

Visualizing the Structure of Your Application

Flex Builder provides a couple of ways to easily understand (and navigate) the hierarchy of your application.

Using the Outline panel shown in Figure 8-14 (accessible by selecting Window→Outline if not visible in your workspace), you can see the structure of your application in a tree list. When you select an item in this list, the selection is matched on the stage, and vice versa.

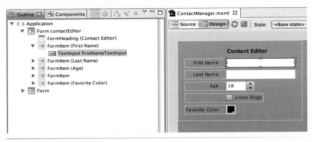

Figure 8-14. *The Outline panel*

Another great option is the Show Surrounding Containers feature. You can toggle this by selecting Design→Show Surrounding Containers. What this does is highlight the containers that enclose the currently selected component, as

shown in Figure 8-15. This helps you visualize the hierarchy of containers, especially those containers that don't have much of a visual representation. It also helps when dragging and dropping components to the stage, because it provides extra padding around the current selection, making it easier to drop components where you want.

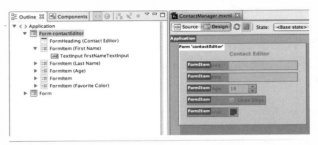

Figure 8-15. *An example of showing the surrounding containers*

You can even use the Outline panel and the Show Surrounding Containers feature together for a very powerful and intuitive way to understand your application. This enables you to view and select containers and controls either in the tree view or directly on the stage.

Alignment

Many Flex containers like HBox and VBox can support both horizontal and vertical alignment. This happens through the **horizontalAlign** and **verticalAlign** properties, which accept values of **left**, **center**, or **right**. Take, for example, a VBox with a width and height of 400 pixels that is lining up three buttons. By default, the VBox's **horizontalAlign** property will be set to **left**, meaning the Buttons will all be aligned to the left edge of the VBox. You can make them centered, however, by changing the property to **center**, as shown in the following code:

```
<mx:VBox
    width="400"
    height="400"
    horizontalAlign="center">

    <mx:Button label="Button"/>
    <mx:Button label="Button"/>
    <mx:Button label="Button"/>

</mx:VBox>
```

An alternative system for layout that lets you both center components and anchor them to the left or right edge is a constraints layout.

WARNING

Alignment won't make any difference if no explicit size has been set on the container. Because a container with no size will simply fit its contents, alignment wouldn't show because there would be no space between the container and its children.

Constraints-Based Layout

You can use another, very powerful way to lay out your application, and it can work in conjunction with layout containers. It's a *constraints-based* layout, and it not only provides a way to position components but works for sizing as well.

Typical Usage

You can think of constraints as extensions to normal absolute positioning, because they are used with the Canvas container or other containers such as Application or Panel that have their layout set to absolute. They provide a way to anchor a component to an edge of its container so that resizing that container causes the component to either move or resize itself to stay anchored to that point.

The best way to understand constraints is to convert an absolutely positioned layout to a constraints-based layout.

Consider the following code, which places a Button in an Application with an absolute layout. In Flex Builder's Design mode, the Button is placed 5 pixels from the bottom and right of the stage, which happens to be an **x** of 600 and a **y** of 400 (see Figure 8-16).

```
<mx:Application
    xmlns:mx="http://www.adobe.com/2006/mxml"
    layout="absolute">

    <mx:Button label="Button" x="600" y="400"/>

</mx:Application>
```

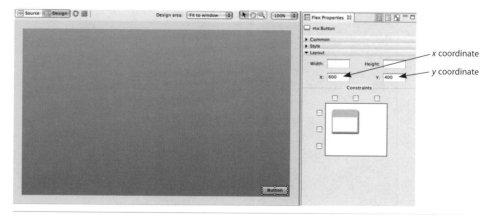

Figure 8-16. The Layout section showing typical x and y coordinates

To convert to a constraints layout, use the Layout section in the Flex Properties panel. You will find not only fields for width and height and *x* and *y*, but you will also see near the bottom a utility for creating constraints. Turning on the top-right and bottom-left checkboxes in this section generates the constraints code for you (see Figure 8-17). This creates constraints for the right edge and the bottom edge, using the properties **right** and **bottom**:

```
<mx:Application
    xmlns:mx="http://www.adobe.com/2006/mxml"
    layout="absolute">

    <mx:Button label="Button" right="5" bottom="5" />

</mx:Application>
```

Notice how the **x** and **y** attributes have been replaced by the constraint attributes **bottom** and **right**.

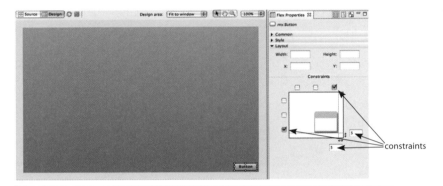

Figure 8-17. The Layout section showing a converted constraints layout

Instead of the Button control being locked into place at an **x** of 600 and a **y** of 400, it's now anchored 5 pixels from the bottom and 5 pixels from the right edge. Figure 8-18 shows how the application looks when resized.

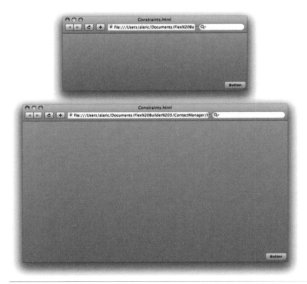

Figure 8-18. The Button is anchored to the bottom-right edge and stays there when the application is resized

You can add multiple constraints, which can even cause the Button to resize. Using this same example, return to Design mode, and resize the Button so that it takes up the entire Application, leaving just a few pixels of space as in Figure 8-19. It may now have a large width and height set.

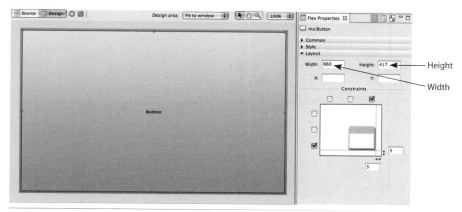

Figure 8-19. The Button with a width and height that match the currently visible Application in Design mode

Next, add **left** and **top** constraints by turning off the two top-left checkboxes in the Layout section. This replaces the Button's width and height (see Figure 8-20). The code created should be something like the following:

```
<mx:Application
    xmlns:mx="http://www.adobe.com/2006/mxml"
    layout="absolute">

    <mx:Button label="Button" right="5" bottom="5" left="5" top="5"/>

</mx:Application>
```

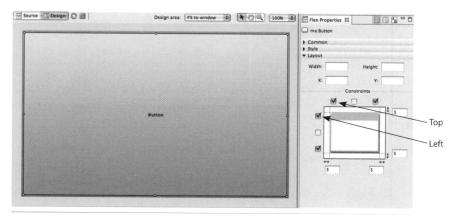

Figure 8-20. The Button, now sized according to constraints all around

Now, the Button resizes to stay anchored to all four corners of the Application tag, as shown in Figure 8-21.

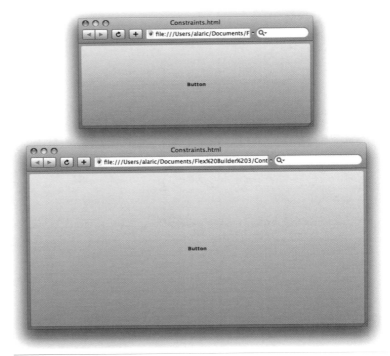

Figure 8-21. The Button is anchored to the four corners of the application and will grow or shrink as needed when the application is resized

You can also use constraints to center components both vertically and horizontally. To understand this, you'll need to create a little example. So, start with a blank application. In Design mode, place a single Panel anywhere on the stage. Returning to the Layout section, this time turn on the top center and left center checkboxes. This converts the current *x,y* coordinates into center constraints called **horizontalCenter** and **verticalCenter**. The number that is showing the input fields next to these checkboxes specifies the number of pixels you want the Panel to be from the horizontal center and vertical center, respectively. To anchor the Panel perfectly in the center, set both fields to 0, as shown in Figure 8-22. This generates the following code:

```
<mx:Application
    xmlns:mx="http://www.adobe.com/2006/mxml"
    layout="absolute">

    <mx:Panel
        width="250"
        height="200"
        layout="absolute"
        horizontalCenter="0"
        verticalCenter="0">
    </mx:Panel>
</mx:Application>
```

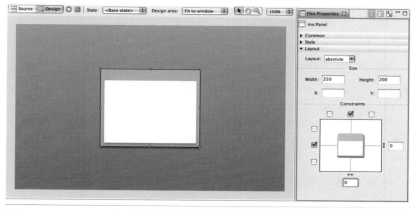

Figure 8-22. A Panel that has been centered via constraints

Now, whether the Panel has its width or height changed or even if the Application is resized, it will stick right in the center.

NOTE

Mixing left *or* right *anchors with* horizontalCenter *anchors can lead to somewhat unpredictable results. Similarly,* top *and* bottom *anchors aren't best mixed with* verticalCenter *anchors. They are not mutually exclusive, but it doesn't necessarily make sense to be anchored, for instance, to the left edge and be centered horizontally. If you specify both a center constraint and an edge constraint in code, the size of the component is calculated from the edge constraints, while its position is determined by the center constraint. In Design mode, Flex Builder keeps you from doing this by removing anchors that aren't compatible.*

Bindings in Layout

You can use bindings in size and layout attributes to create powerful layouts. Just as you can bind two TextInput's **text** properties together, you can also bind two Panel's **width** properties together, ensuring that they always remain the same width as one another.

Similarly, you can bind a Panel's **width** to its **height**, making the Panel stay square. You can bind **x** and **y** attributes and anchors as well. For instance, using an absolute layout, you can bind the **x** of one Panel to the **x** and **width** of another, mimicking a relative layout:

```
<mx:Panel id="onePanel"
    x="{anotherPanel.width + anotherPanel.x + 10}"
    width="{anotherPanel.width}"
    height="{anotherPanel.height}" />

<mx:Panel id="anotherPanel"
    width="250"
    height="200" />
```

You can also use the bindings to create calculations in coordinates or sizes. The options are truly limitless.

One caveat of this approach, however, is that Flex Builder won't be able to show the layout binding in Design mode.

Constraint Rows and Columns

There's actually more to constraints than I've discussed. You can use constraint rows and columns to gain further control over your constraints. These rows and columns are imaginary (invisible) boxes that you can place around your application and then anchor components to them. Instead of simply anchoring a component to the edge of a container, you can now anchor it to any point you want.

When you create a constraint column using the tag **<mx:constraintColumn/>**, Flex places that column at the leftmost edge of the application. You then set the **width** attribute on that column. Flex places the next column you create to the right of the previous column.

Constraint rows, created with the tag **<mx:constraintRow/>**, appear from top to bottom. Creating the first constraint row puts it at the top of the application. You then set its **height** attribute, which determines how far down it extends. The next row created will begin right below the first row, as set by the first row's height.

To anchor components to rows, you use almost the same syntax as with typical anchors. However, to show that you want the component anchored to a specific row or column, you *prepend* that row or column ID to the property. For example, in a typical constraint layout not using rows or columns, you would anchor a Button control 5 pixels from the top of its container by using **<mx:Button top="5"/>**. To instead anchor it 5 pixels from a constraint row called **row2**, you would prepend **row2** to that value, followed by a colon: **<mx:Button top="row2:5"/>** (see Figure 8-23).

Figure 8-23. The syntax for anchoring to constraint rows or columns

You can create multiple rows or columns, attaching components to any one of them. This allows a grid layout, supporting columns and row spans as well.

Try the following code, which maps some HRules and VRules to constraint rows and columns. Because constraint rows and columns are invisible, this lets you see where the constraint rows and columns are located. It then places four Buttons in a grid, anchoring them to the rows and columns, as shown in Figure 8-24.

```
<mx:Application
    xmlns:mx="http://www.adobe.com/2006/mxml"
    layout="absolute ">

    <!--Create two columns, one from the left edge until 200 pixels,
        Another from 200 until the far right edge
    -->
    <mx:constraintColumns>
        <mx:ConstraintColumn id="col1" width="200" />
        <mx:ConstraintColumn id="col2" width="100%" />
    </mx:constraintColumns>

    <!--Create two rows, one from the top edge until 100 pixels,
        Another from 100 until the bottom
    -->
    <mx:constraintRows>
        <mx:ConstraintRow id="row1" height="100"/>
        <mx:ConstraintRow id="row2" height="100%"/>
    </mx:constraintRows>
```

```
<!--Use VRules and HRules to map the locations of the
    constraint rows and columns
-->
<mx:VRule height="100%" left="col1:0" />
<mx:VRule height="100%" left="col2:0" />

<mx:HRule width="100%" top="row1:0" />
<mx:HRule width="100%" top="row2:0" />

<!--Place Buttons in a grid layout -->
<mx:Button
    label="column 1, row 1"
    left="col1:5"
    right="col1:5"
    top="row1:5"
    bottom="row1:5"/>

<mx:Button
    label="column 1, row 2"
    left="col1:5"
    right="col1:5"
    top="row2:5"
    bottom="row2:5"/>

<mx:Button
    label="column 2, row 1"
    left="col2:5"
    right="col2:5"
    top="row1:5"
    bottom="row1:5"/>

<mx:Button
    label="column 2, row 2"
    left="col2:5"
    right="col2:5"
    top="row2:5"
    bottom="row2:5"/>

</mx:Application>
```

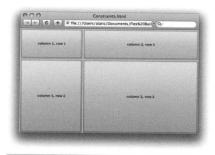

Figure 8-24. Four Buttons placed in a grid layout and anchored to constraint rows and columns

Summary

In this chapter, you learned a great deal about laying out applications in Flex. You discovered some new types of layouts and learned how to use the display list, which allows you to easily move components around, even in and out of other containers. You now know how to size your components with both explicit sizes and percentage-based sizes, which gives you a lot of flexibility in your layouts. You learned about a few new containers as well and made your ContactManager application better looking because of it. You've also learned some very advanced techniques for constructing layouts using constraints. There was plenty to cover in this chapter, but everything you've learned has an immediate use. In the next chapter, you'll learn more about the Form container and how to create rich experiences with Forms and user input.

CREATING RICH FORMS

Have you ever filled out an HTML form on a website, submitted it, and waited for the result—only to find that one of the fields had an error or omission? How easy was it to find your mistake? Was it something silly like not putting parentheses around the area code of a phone number (or putting them in if they weren't needed)? Wouldn't it be nice if that never happened again?

With Flex, the tasks of validating input and formatting the results are second-nature. Built into the most common controls is a great way to give feedback to people using your application if something they've entered isn't correct, and there's also an easy way to format their input. With Flex validators and formatters, you'll be able to give your applications an easy-to-use UI.

Preparing the Application

First, you'll return to the ContactManager application you modified in Chapter 8 to take advantage of the Form container. In this chapter, you'll add a few fields and modify the application so it really looks like an address book. You'll add phone number, email, address, and zip code fields, and you'll replace the current CheckBox with one to designate whether a contact is a company. You'll also get rid of the NumericStepper, because an actual birth date makes more sense to store (you'll learn how to calculate an age later in this chapter). You'll learn a great way of entering dates using the DateField control, which provides a pop-up calendar interface.

To start, make sure the ContactManager application is open, and go ahead and add a DateField to the Contact Editor Form. Once added, set the DateField's **editable** property to **true**. Setting the editable property to **true** lets people type in the DateField, instead of having to use the mouse to navigate to a date.

Next, add a TextInput control for the phone number field. You'll also create a way for someone to select the type of the phone number, be it mobile, home, or some other kind. Because you want to accept one of three values, a CheckBox isn't going to do, because a CheckBox has only two values:

IN THIS CHAPTER

Preparing the Application

Validating Data

Restricting Input

Formatting Data for Display

Summary

NOTE

Remember that you can use Design mode to easily wrap your form fields in FormItem containers. Simply drag the control you want to use into the Form, and Flex Builder will create a FormItem automatically.

Figure 9-1. The Insert Radio Button Group dialog box

on (**true**) or off (**false**). Radio buttons are great for letting someone select one of a few values, so you'll create a set of radio buttons in this chapter.

To do so, go into Flex Builder Design mode, and drag a RadioButtonGroup into the FormItem for the phone number. You'll be prompted with a dialog box similar to Figure 9-1, which lets you configure your group. Give the group a name of **phoneRadioButtonGroup**, and set up three radio buttons corresponding to three types of phone numbers: mobile, home, and other. You can add a new one by clicking the Add button. Once you click OK, Flex Builder generates a **<mx:RadioButtonGroup/>** tag and three **<mx:RadioButton/>** tags like the following, that you can see in Source mode:

```
<mx:RadioButtonGroup id="phoneRadioButtonGroup" />

<mx:RadioButton label="mobile" groupName="phoneRadioButtonGroup"/>
<mx:RadioButton label="home" groupName="phoneRadioButtonGroup"/>
<mx:RadioButton label="other" groupName="phoneRadioButtonGroup"/>
```

The **<mx:RadioButtonGroup/>** tag isn't a container tag for the RadioButtons; it's a nonvisual control that RadioButtons are connected to, and it lets you access their state, such as which one is selected in the group. RadioButtons are connected to this group by pointing their **groupName** property to this group.

Back in Design mode or Source mode, whichever you prefer, set the first RadioButton in the group to selected so mobile is selected automatically. You can do this by setting that RadioButton's **selected** property to **true**.

You'll want to make sure that at least a first name and email address are entered. The first step in doing that is to add a property to the corresponding FormItems called **required**, setting it to **true**. This doesn't actually do anything other than display visual feedback via a red asterisk next to the field. However, you'll learn how to ensure a value is entered very soon by using a validator.

Your code for the Contact Editor Form should look like this:

```
<mx:Form id="contactEditor">
    <mx:FormHeading
        label="Contact Editor"/>
    <mx:FormItem
        label="First Name"
        required="true">
        <mx:TextInput id="firstNameTextInput"/>
    </mx:FormItem>
    <mx:FormItem
        label="Last Name">
        <mx:TextInput id="lastNameTextInput"/>
    </mx:FormItem>
    <mx:HRule
        height="22"
        width="100%"/>
    <mx:FormItem
        label="Email"
        required="true">
        <mx:TextInput id="emailTextInput"/>
    </mx:FormItem>
```

```
<mx:FormItem
    label="Phone">
    <mx:TextInput id="phoneTextInput"/>

    <mx:RadioButtonGroup id="phoneRadioButtonGroup" />

    <mx:RadioButton
        label="mobile"
        groupName="phoneRadioButtonGroup"
        selected="true"/>
    <mx:RadioButton
        label="home"
        groupName="phoneRadioButtonGroup"/>
    <mx:RadioButton
        label="other"
        groupName="phoneRadioButtonGroup"/>
</mx:FormItem>
<mx:FormItem
    label="Address">
    <mx:TextArea id="addressTextArea"/>
</mx:FormItem>
<mx:FormItem label="Zip">
    <mx:TextInput id="zipCodeTextInput"/>
</mx:FormItem>
<mx:HRule
    height="22"
    width="100%"/>
<mx:FormItem
    label="Birthday">
    <mx:DateField id="birthdayDateField"
        editable="true"/>
</mx:FormItem>
<mx:FormItem
    label="Favorite Color">
    <mx:ColorPicker id="favoriteColorPicker"/>
</mx:FormItem>
<mx:FormItem>
    <mx:CheckBox id="companyCheckBox"
        label="Company" />
</mx:FormItem>
</mx:Form>
```

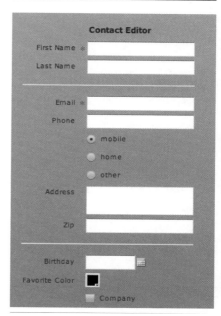

***Figure 9-2.** The new and improved Contact Editor form*

For now, you can just remove the Contact Details section, because it contains references to controls you're no longer using. (You'll build a new and improved version a little later on.) Then run the application so you can see your new work, which should look like Figure 9-2.

Try using the DateField conrol. Not only can you select a date from the pop-up calendar, but you can enter a date as well. The DateField has built-in data validation and parsing, which allows it to accept many different date formats. For example, to enter a birthday of July 20th, 1979, you could enter **7/20/1979**, **7-20-79**, or even **7 20 1979**. How's that for service? As long as you enter the month before the date, it just works. And even that format is configurable. Using the **formatString** property, you can enter a String value to display the date the way you want. For instance, suppose you prefer to see it in a format with the year followed by the month and date. You can simply add **formatString="YYYY-MM-DD"**. Not only will the displayed format of the

NOTE

*Check the Flex Language Reference for the DateField control to see the possible values for the **formatString** property.*

You might have wondered, if there's a DateField control, why aren't there other data-specific controls for information like zip codes and email addresses? There probably are some out in the wild that you can download and use, but you have a pretty solid set of tools right now. You'll make TextInputs work as great input fields for all your data, coupling them with validators. I'll discuss using third-party components in the next chapter.

date change, but setting this property will make the control expect the date to be entered.

While the DateField looks as though it contains simply text, it has a **selectedDate** property that is actually a Date object. Date is a complex data type that is used just for dates and times. It represents a single moment of time, down to the millisecond. When you type in a date that is validated by the DateField control or when you select a date from the pop-up list, its **selectedDate** property is populated with a Date.

The DateField is a great example of letting someone enter data freely, without worrying that they're going to break the form. You'll take some of that with you as you learn about how to implement validation.

Validating Data

Seeing how great the DateField works, it's painful to think of all those forms on the web that don't have such great validation. User-friendly and beautiful forms are natural to Flex; all you need are some basic validation techniques.

Using Validators

To learn validation hands-on, you'll just go down the line, setting up validation for each of the fields in the Contact Editor. You'll start with the first name field, which you've designated as required on its FormItem. However, the FormItem shows it only as required but doesn't actually do any error checking. For that functionality, you'll use a nonvisual component called StringValidator.

StringValidator

*The **source** property of the **StringValidator** tag, and all validators in general, expects a binding, meaning it expects an actual instance of a control. However, it doesn't expect a binding to the property of the control, just the control. Thus, the following code is incorrect:*

```
<mx:StringValidator source=
"{firstNameTextInput.text}" />
```

A StringValidator is a basic validator that can ensure text has been entered. To use it, simply place an **<mx:StringValidator/>** tag at the top of your MXML file, within the **<mx:Application/>** tag. It's not required to place validators at the top, but it's standard practice to put any nonvisual components there to make them easier to find and modify. The **<mx:StringValidator/>** tag has a **source** attribute that points to the control you want it to watch. The **property** attribute tells it which property of this control should be validated. To set up validation for the **firstNameTextInput** field, your tag should look like this:

```
<mx:StringValidator id="firstNameValidator"
    source="{firstNameTextInput}"
    property="text"/>
```

Now run the application and see what validation does. If you change focus from the first name field (by tabbing to the next field or using the mouse to select another field) and haven't entered a value, a red border surrounds the **firstNameTextInput** field, signaling that something is wrong. If your mouse hovers over that field, a nonintrusive message pops up explaining what is wrong. By default it reads "This field is required."

But you can do better than that. Using the validator's `requiredFieldError` property, you can enter your own message. For a more descriptive and slightly rude alternative, you can add the property `requiredFieldError="I'm sure you've got a name.&#13;Why not enter it here?"` If you noticed the `&#13` characters and thought I was swearing, I'm sorry to let you down. `&#13` is a XML *character reference*, which is a way to insert a special character. Using this character reference inserts a line break into the error string, making it more presentable.

Be sure to run the application and try the new validation techniques. Your application will look like Figure 9-3.

NOTE

In ActionScript, you would use the **\n** *escape sequence to create a line break. So, in ActionScript, the code might look like this:*

```
stringValidator.requiredFieldError
    = "I'm sure you've got a name.
    \n Why not enter it here?";
```

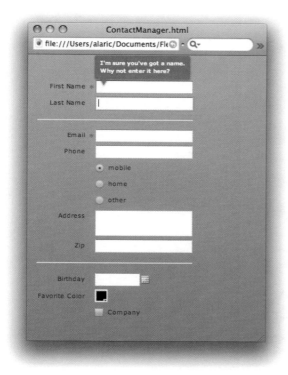

Figure 9-3. The user-friendly form

You'll now continue with the next field you want to validate. For this application, you've specified that a last name isn't required for your form. So, you don't need to validate it, right? Well, that may not be true. A last name isn't required, but if one is entered, you can ensure it's a proper name.

One way to do this is by using another StringValidator, this time setting its `required` property to `false` (which is by default `true`). Because it isn't set as `required`, just pointing this new validator to the last name field won't cause any validation to occur. If you'd like you can use the `minLength` property to enable a very simple check, making sure the name is at least two characters long. This could prevent someone from inputting an initial, when you want a full name.

WARNING

This application showcases validation features. There could be instances where a user's name is actually only one letter long, and such validation could cause irritation. When you're designing validation schemes, always try to think of every possibility you might encounter from your users.

You'll also be able to customize the error message that displays, just like the previous validator. You won't customize it by using a **requiredFieldError**, however, as this error message will display when the text entered is too short. To accomplish this, use the **tooShortError** property:

```
<mx:StringValidator id="lastNameValidator"
    source="{lastNameTextInput}"
    property="text"
    required="false"
    minLength="2"
    tooShortError="What kind of last name is that?"/>
```

Run and test the application, testing the new validation techniques. Your application will look like Figure 9-4.

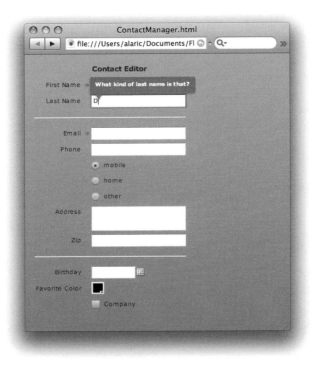

Figure 9-4. The increasingly demanding application

EmailValidator

The next item on the list is the email field. To validate an email address, you use the handy component EmailValidator. It works just like the StringValidator, so add the tag and connect it to the **emailTextInput** control. You can add a custom **requiredFieldError** message as well, just to keep the application cheeky. However, EmailValidator has a ton of other error messages and options for customizing them. It has a **missingAtSignError** message and an **invalidDomainError** and everything in between. You don't need to set a value for all these messages, because the component gives a nice set of defaults. But it's nice to know they're there.

```
<mx:EmailValidator id="emailValidator"
    source="{emailTextInput}"
    property="text"
    requiredFieldError="An at sign (@) is missing in your e-mail
    address."/>
```

Now your application will display a silly warning whenever no email address is entered. Using the standard error messages, it will also display descriptive errors if an invalid email address is entered.

Run and test the application. Your application will look like Figure 9-5.

NOTE

EmailValidator and PhoneValidator do not actually verify that an email address or phone number exists. Like all validators, they are simply ensuring that the information looks like a valid entry. Checking, for instance, whether an email address is actually registered would require a connection to a database or Web service that provides such a service. I'll talk about how to connect to remote data in the next chapter.

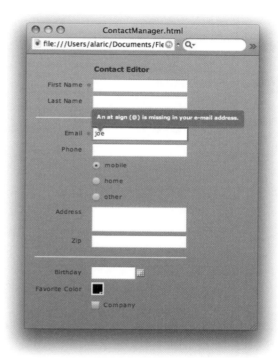

Figure 9-5. The very specific error messages of the EmailValidator

PhoneNumberValidator

Next on the agenda is the phone number. If you haven't already guessed, you're going to use a PhoneNumberValidator to validate this one. This is another case where the field isn't required, but you want to validate any entry that is made.

```
<mx:PhoneNumberValidator id="phoneValidator"
    source="{phoneTextInput}"
    property="text"
    required="false" />
```

What is special about this component is that it will, by default, accept numerous formats for phone numbers without complaint. That means you can enter **(415)555-8273**, **415-5558273**, or even **415 555 8273**, and it will be accepted. However, entering I don't have a phone isn't going to cut it, as shown in Figure 9-6.

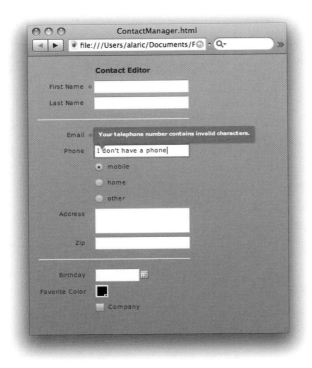

Figure 9-6. No getting past the PhoneValidator

ZipCodeValidator

NOTE

For many client-server applications, validating just on the client side isn't enough. Generally, these applications will have a server-side validation scheme as well, ensuring that no improper information is stored on the server. But that's not your worry at the moment. I'll leave that topic for another book.

You won't need to validate the address field, although you could validate it the same way you did the last name field if you want, ensuring that if a value is entered, it's of the necessary length. So, you'll move on to the zip code. ZipCodeValidator will take care of this one nicely.

The ZipCodeValidator is set up to validate either U.S. zip codes (the default) or both Canadian and U.S. zip codes. You specify this using the **domain** property, which accepts either the string "US Only" or the string "US or Canada." So, you'll allow Canadian zip codes as well.

This is one of those cases where the concept of constants comes into play. You learned about these in Chapter 6. (For a review, see the section titled "Constants" in Chapter 6.) The string "US or Canada" can be easily forgotten or typed in incorrectly, and doing so would cause the ZipCodeValidator to function incorrectly. Instead, you can use a constant value that's available on the `mx.validators.ZipCodeValidatorDomainType` class. Using a binding, you can enter the constant `ZipCodeValidatorDomainType.US_OR_CANADA` for the value of the domain property. This makes it impossible to make a typo, because the compiler will check the value. Using code completion in Flex Builder, the value is very easy to enter.

To make this class available to you, however, you must import it. So, the code you'll need for this validator is in two parts. First you have an **<mx:Script/>** tag that contains an **import** statement:

```
<mx:Script>
    <![CDATA[
        import mx.validators.ZipCodeValidatorDomainType;
    ]]>
</mx:Script>
```

And then you have the validator itself:

```
<mx:ZipCodeValidator id="zipCodeValidator"
    source="{zipCodeTextInput}"
    property="text"
    domain="{ZipCodeValidatorDomainType.US_OR_CANADA}"
    required="false"/>
```

Now your form can validate both U.S. and Canadian zip codes, as shown in Figure 9-7.

NOTE

When using code completion in Flex Builder to enter this constant value, the class will be imported for you automatically.

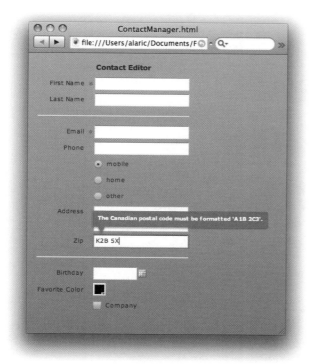

Figure 9-7. The ZipCodeValidator even speaks Canadian

Other available validators

You don't necessarily need to validate the DateField, because the control takes care of it on its own. However, you can use the **DateValidator** class if you'd

There is even a RegExpValidator that you can use to build very powerful validation using regular expressions, which let you find patterns in text. You could even create an advanced validator for the address field by using the RegExpValidator, because you could make sure that an address pattern was entered—such as a city name, followed by a comma, followed by state name or abbreviation.

like, which makes it easy to validate dates. A number of other validators exist as well, such as CreditCardValidator, CurrencyValidator, NumberValidator, and SocialSecurityValidator. Now that you know how to use many of the most common validators, taking on any of these will be easy for you.

Creating That Error Look, Without Error

You've discovered how to use validators to display an error message in a control, and that gives great feedback to the person using your application. But did you know you have another way to display an error message on a control without a validator? Using the property **errorString**, you can cause a red border and pop-up message to display.

For example, you could give the ColorPicker an error message, such as the one in Figure 9-8, using the following code:

```
<mx:ColorPicker id="favoriteColorPicker"
  errorString="Hmm. Not quite the color I was expecting…"/>
```

This property can be very helpful if used in a script so that the error message displays based upon certain events or criteria. To remove the error message, just set the **errorString** back to an empty string, like in the following ActionScript:

```
favoriteColorPicker.errorString = "";
```

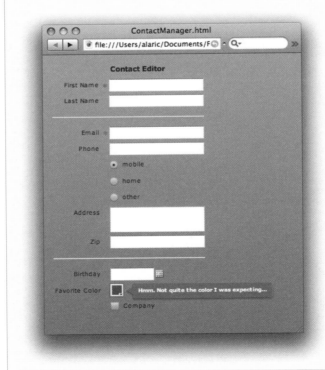

Figure 9-8. Using an error string

Custom Validation Techniques

You might have noticed that these validation components display an error message only once a value is entered (or not entered) and then focus is moved to another field. This is because they work by certain *triggers*, or events that cause the validation to start.

Each validation component has a property called **trigger** that can be set to a component instance. This property defaults to the component that is the validator's **source**. You can also set the **triggerEvent**, which takes the name of the event that causes validation to occur. This defaults to an event called **valueCommit**, which is fired on many input controls when they are sure an entry is finalized; this typically occurs when the focus changes to another control, but it can also happen if the value of a control is changed in script.

For example, to cause validation to fire on the email address field (**emailTextInput**) while someone types in the field, you add the **triggerEvent** with a value of **change**, which is the event that occurs when changes are made on a TextInput. (The **trigger** of the validator is still the **emailTextInput**, as this is the default based upon the validator's **source** property.)

```
<mx:EmailValidator id="emailValidator"
    source="{emailTextInput}"
    property="text"
    requiredFieldError="Please enter your email.&#13;I promise not to
    send spam."
    triggerEvent="change"  />
```

This is a nice concept to help understand triggers, but this code wouldn't be very helpful to those using your application. They would see an error message as they were typing, They may be on their way to entering a valid email address, but the error would complain that the entry was incorrect until they were finished entering it. So, you can make this trigger work for you in another way. You'll add a Button control to your form, which will act as a submit button. (Although you're not actually submitting any data, you're just learning how to build a UI to do so.)

Adding a Button to the form in Design mode will again wrap the Button in a FormItem container, which is used for field labels and proper alignment of fields in Form containers. While the FormItem helps align the Button, it doesn't make much sense to have a label for the FormItem, because the Button has a perfectly good one all its own. So, you can simply enter an empty string for the FormItem's **label**. While you're at it, give the Button an **id** of **submitButton**.

Now you'll change the **trigger** of the EmailValidator to point this button. Because you want the validation to fire when the Button is clicked, you set **triggerEvent** to **click**:

```
<mx:EmailValidator id="emailValidator"
    source="{emailTextInput}"
    property="text"
    requiredFieldError="Please enter your email.&#13;I promise not to
    send spam."
    trigger="{submitButton}"
    triggerEvent="click"  />
```

What will now happen is when someone clicks the **submitButton**, validation will trigger on the email address field. Validation will no longer happen when focusing out of the field; it happens only when the **submitButton** is clicked, because you have overridden the default behavior of this validator.

If you want even more control over what happens in validation, you can use the method **validate()** on a validator's instance to trigger the validation yourself at any time. To try this, first remove any changes you've made to the **trigger** and **triggerEvent** properties in your code. Then you'll create a function that calls the **validate()** method for the EmailValidator:

```
private function validateAndSubmit():void
{
    emailValidator.validate();
}
```

NOTE

Remember to place your ActionScript code in an **<mx:Script/>** *tag.*

Once you set the click event listener on the **submitButton** to point to this function, clicking the button will trigger validation on the email address field. By applying this technique, validation will occur when someone is filling out the form, after values are committed. But by adding this functionality, you're able to double-check once you attempt to submit any data.

To apply this technique for all validators, you don't have to call **validate()** on each one individually. A helper function called **validateAll()** is part of the **mx.validators.Validator** class (the base class for all validators) and is a static method, which means the method is attached to the class itself. Instead of creating an instance of a Validator component and calling the method from that instance, the method is actually called from the **Validator** class. **validateAll()** takes an array of validators as its only parameter. So, make sure to import the **mx.validators.Validator** class, and change your function to the following:

```
private function validateAndSubmit():void
{
    var validators:Array = [firstNameValidator, lastNameValidator,
    emailValidator, phoneValidator, zipCodeValidator];

    Validator.validateAll(validators);
}
```

Now validation will trigger for all these validators at once when the **submitButton** is clicked.

You can do even more to make this user-friendly. When someone clicks a Button, they are probably expecting everything is fine with their form. If it's not, the red borders around the incorrect form fields may not be as noticeable as you'd like. You can use an Alert component that will pop up a message window to help grab the user's attention.

To show an Alert, you simply call the static **show()** method on the **Alert** class, which I mentioned in Chapter 6. This method takes two parameters, the first being the body of the Alert and the second being the text that is shown in the title of the Alert window. So after importing **mx.controls.Alert**, you can pop up an Alert by calling something like **Alert.show("Please fix that stuff.", "There were problems with your form.")**.

To find out whether you actually have errors, the **Validator.validateAll()** method returns an array. Because arrays have a **length** property that tells how many items are in them, checking for a **length** that is greater than zero is the way to know whether you've had any errors. You do this by using a *conditional* statement, which checks whether something is true. The **if** statement is what you want to use. This statement will run certain chunks of code depending on whether a value passed to it is true. It will run the code encased in curly braces if the value is true, and it will skip that code if it's false. So, to make this code work, you take the array that is returned from the **Validator.validateAll()** method and then see whether its **length** is greater than 1. If so, you pop up an Alert.

```
private function validateAndSubmit():void
{
    var validators:Array = [firstNameValidator, lastNameValidator,
            emailValidator, phoneValidator, zipCodeValidator];

    var errors:Array = Validator.validateAll(validators);

    if(errors.length > 0)
    {
        Alert.show("Please fix that stuff.",
                "There were problems with your form.");
    }

}
```

If you're grasping this all right, you can add one more level of complexity to your function. Instead of simply displaying an Alert that says something is wrong, you'll display details about the error in the form submission.

To accomplish this, you'll need to learn one more ActionScript technique, *loops*. Looping lets you run a piece of code repeatedly until certain conditions are met. One of the basic statements for looping is the **for each...in** statement. This calls a chunk of code once for each item in an array (or other object), and it passes that item to the block of code. You can loop through the **errors** array, which is an array of ValidationResultEvents, using the following code:

```
for each (var error:ValidationResultEvent in errors)
{
    Alert.show(error.message, "There were problems with your form.");
}
```

> **NOTE**
>
> *You're diving into some real scripting, so if it doesn't all make sense to you now, you can always return to it later. You've already learned a great deal about validation, and simply using MXML validation tags can get you pretty far.*

This would display an Alert for each error. Note that the **message** property of the ValidationResultEvent is a string of text that corresponds to the error message of the field. The problem with this approach is that too many Alerts will pop up if multiple errors occur. So, you'll finish your validation scheme by storing all the error messages first and then displaying them all at once in a single Alert. You can do so by creating an Array called **errorMessages** and then adding error messages to the Array. You can add items to an Array using the Array's **push()** method. Then, outside the **for each...in** loop, you pop up the Alert. The final function should look like the following:

```
<mx:Script>
    <![CDATA[
        import mx.validators.Validator;
        import mx.validators.ZipCodeValidatorDomainType;
        import mx.events.ValidationResultEvent;
        import mx.controls.Alert;

        private function validateAndSubmit():void
        {
            var validators:Array = [firstNameValidator,
                    lastNameValidator, emailValidator,
                    phoneValidator, zipCodeValidator];
            var errors:Array = Validator.validateAll(validators);
            var errorMessages:Array = [];

            if(errors.length > 0)
            {

                for each (var error:ValidationResultEvent in errors)
                {
                    var errorField:String = FormItem(
                        error.currentTarget.source.parent).label;
                        errorMessages.push(errorField + ": " +
                        error.message);
                }

                Alert.show(errorMessages.join("\n\n"),
                        "There were problems with your form.");
            }

            //Here we could invoke other validators, or submit to
            //a server

        }

    ]]>
</mx:Script>
```

Now the form is looking pretty solid, as shown in Figure 9-9. The next task you can accomplish is limiting what kinds of values can be entered in the TextInputs.

Figure 9-9. An advanced validation scheme

Restricting Input

I don't happen to know anyone with a name like 7*%32$, so why allow some-one to enter such characters? Well, you can actually restrict the allowable characters in a TextInput, preventing people from entering certain numbers or symbols in a field. You can do this, surprisingly enough, by using the **restrict** property. Changing your **firstNameTextInput** to the following tag, you allow only lowercase and uppercase letters to be entered, from *A* to *Z*.

```
<mx:TextInput id="firstNameTextInput"
    restrict="a-z - A-Z"/>
```

However, you've missed one thing. What if someone has a hyphenated first or last name, such as Day-Lewis, or a name that includes an apostrophe, such as O'Reilly? You'll need to add a few more characters to the **restrict** property. The problem is, the hyphen is a special character used by the property to show a range, so how do you let Flex Builder know that you actually want a hyphen? You can use a backslash (\) in front of a hyphen to show that you want the hyphen literally:

```
<mx:TextInput id="firstNameTextInput"
    restrict="a-z A-Z ' \-"/>
```

While you're at it, you can apply this new **restrict** property to the first and last name fields. Now the fields prevent people from typing unwanted characters.

You can use this same idea for the phone number field if you want, restrict-ing it to just numbers, parentheses, hyphens, and so on. You might want to

NOTE

*Restricting allowable characters in a TextInput also prevents special characters from being used, such as those in non-English languages. To get around this, you can use functionality of the **restrict** property, which lets you specify which characters you* don't *want to be entered, instead of specifying what characters you will allow. You do this by prepending the sequence with a caret (^). For example, to exclude only numbers from your TextInput, you could change the property to **restrict="^0-9"**, allowing anything to be entered except 0–9. This is actually regular expression syntax, which you can learn more about by searching this topic in the Flex documentation.*

restrict input on the zip code field as well, limiting input to only digits and hyphens. However, Canadian zip codes use letters as well as numbers, so you'll want to keep things flexible.

Formatting Data for Display

Flex comes with built-in formatters for the most common types of data. Using formatters, you can keep your data in a raw form and modify it as necessary. Say you have some prices of products stored away in a database or an XML file. It's nice to be able to keep them stored as numbers so you can manipulate them (adding discounts, changing currencies, and so on). But you also want to show the prices as dollars for people using your application—complete with a dollar sign, comma separators for the thousands place, and rounded to two decimal points. This is way most people expect to see a price in U.S. dollars.

Formatters can take care of all this. Formatters exist for the most common types of data, such as currencies, dates, numbers, phone numbers, and zip codes. Like validators, these are nonvisual components. To use them, you create a tag for the formatter you want. You don't point the formatter itself to a piece of data but instead use its **format()** function, which returns a string of text. For example, you could declare a **CurrencyFormatter** tag:

```
<mx:CurrencyFormatter id="priceFormatter"/>
```

You later would call its format function, passing in a number: **priceFormatter. format(10243)**. This would return the string "$10,243." Notice that there's even a comma added. This comma separator is a default of the CurrencyFormatter, which you can change with the property **useThousandsSeparator**; just set it to **false** if you don't want it displayed. Particularly useful for formatters are bindings. In Flex you can also bind to the return value of a function, so the following code would place that same string as a TextInput's text:

```
<mx:CurrencyFormatter id="priceFormatter"/>
<mx:TextInput text="{priceFormatter.format(10243)}"/>
```

Of course, you can change many other options for a CurrencyFormatter; one of them is whether to round up or down (**rounding**), and another is how many decimal places to display (**precision**). Say your price is in another currency such as euros, and you wanted to round cents up to the nearest whole number. It's easy if you know which options to modify. In this case, you'd just want to change **currencySymbol** from its default (**$**) to euros (**€**). You could also tell it to round up to the nearest whole number and display two decimal places:

```
<mx:CurrencyFormatter id="priceFormatter"
        currencySymbol="€"
        rounding="up"
        precision="2"/>
```

This would output "€10,243.00."

Of course, other formatters exist for dates, phone numbers, zip codes, and other typical form information. Like in the previous example, you could use a **PhoneFormatter** tag to format a value into a phone number in the (###) ###-#### format:

```
<mx:PhoneFormatter id="phoneFormatter"/>
<mx:TextInput text="{phoneFormatter.format('4795558273')}"/>
```

This would output "(479) 555-8273."

You'll now continue with the ContactManager application by reconstituting the Contact Details panel and adding some formatters. Add a couple right now, PhoneFormatter and DateFormatter. Place them right below your set of validators in the *ContactManager.mxml* file. Again, you don't *have* to place them here, but it's convenient to do so.

```
<mx:PhoneFormatter id="phoneFormatter"/>

<mx:DateFormatter id="dateFormatter"/>
```

Then you'll take advantage of them by adding a Panel with a number of Label controls, bound to the formatters:

```
<mx:Panel id="contactDetails"
    x="346"
    y="10"
    paddingLeft="5"
    paddingRight="5"
    paddingTop="5"
    paddingBottom="5"
    title="Contact Details">
    <mx:Label
        text="Name:"
        fontWeight="bold"/>
    <mx:Label
        text="{firstNameTextInput.text} {lastNameTextInput.text}"/>
    <mx:Label
        text="Phone Number ( {phoneRadioButtonGroup.selectedValue} )"
        fontWeight="bold"/>
    <mx:Label
        text="{phoneFormatter.format(phoneTextInput.text)}"/>
    <mx:Label
        text="Birthday:"
        fontWeight="bold"/>
    <mx:Label
        text="{dateFormatter.format(birthdayDateField.selectedDate)}"/>
    <mx:Label
        text="Company:"
        fontWeight="bold"/>
    <mx:Label
        text="{companyCheckBox.selected}"/>
    <mx:Label
        text="Favorite Color:"
        fontWeight="bold"/>
    <mx:Canvas
        width="60"
        height="60"
        backgroundColor="{favoriteColorPicker.selectedColor}"/>

</mx:Panel>
```

A couple of things are worth noticing in this code. One is the use of the **selectedValue** property on the RadioButtonGroup **phoneRadioButtonGroup**. This gives you the value of the selected RadioButton (either mobile, home, or other). Also worth noting is the binding to the DateField's **selectedDate** property. The DateFormatter is passed this value in its **format** function, and it returns a String that has a nicely formatted date. Without this, the default presentation of the **selectedDate** would be a fairly cryptic-looking string, complete with time values as well. You're not concerned with the actual time of someone's birth, so it's good to use the formatter.

You could go further than simply showing the birthday, however. You could actually calculate a person's age. You can do so using some of the methods of the **Date** class and a little elbow grease. Take a look at the following function, which takes a Date object as a parameter and returns an age:

```
private function calculateAge(birthDate:Date):Number
{
    var today:Date = new Date();
    var ageDate:Date = new Date(today.time - birthDate.time);
    var age:Number = ageDate.fullYear - 1970;

    return age;
}
```

This function creates a new Date, which defaults to the current date and time. To get the person's age, the difference between the date of their birth and the current date is calculated. Note that you can't subtract one Date from another. However, the Date does provide a **time** property, which is a numerical representation of a date on which you can perform calculations. So, in order to calculate the difference between today and the birth date, you take the **time** value of the birth date and subtract it from **time** value of today's date. That value is then converted into the number of years since birth by using the **fullYear** property. (Because a Date object's standard point of reference is 1970, 1970 must be subtracted to get the final age.)

NOTE

*A Date object's **time** property is actually the number of milliseconds since midnight on January 1st, 1970. This is how Date objects store their value internally.*

You can then bind this function's return value to a Label's **text**. You do this by passing in the DateField's **selectedDate** to the **calculateAge()** function and tacking on the string "years old". When the DateField changes value, the Label will be updated with the calculated age. Important to note here is that the initial value of this Label's **text** will be an empty string. It will not display anything when the application first runs, not until a value has been selected in the DateField. Flex realizes that no date is selected on the DateField, so it doesn't run the binding. This is great because the Label won't display the odd text " years old" but will wait until the DateField has a value. Any time the DateField changes, the function will be called, and the binding will update.

```
<mx:Label
    text="{calculateAge(birthdayDateField.selectedDate)} years old"/>
```

If you've added this code to your application and you run it, you may notice something strange. Because the age that you calculated may be a fractional number (with decimal places), a long age value may display, such as "28.662405 years old." That's hardly what you want. Again, formatters come to the rescue.

The final addition to the application for this chapter is to add a NumberFormatter that formats the age. Using the NumberFormatter's **rounding** property, you can make it round numbers down to the nearest whole number, as shown in the following tag:

```
<mx:NumberFormatter id="numberFormatter"
    rounding="down"/>
```

Then you can just pass the **calculateAge()** function's return value to the **format()** function of this NumberFormatter, as shown in the following code:

```
<mx:Label
    text="{numberFormatter.format(calculateAge(birthdayDateField.
    selectedDate))} years old"/>
```

Now, the age displays perfectly. Figure 9-10 shows an example of how your application will look.

NOTE

The Math class has a number of methods for performing calculations and rounding. The method **Math.floor()** *can accomplish the same effect as rounding down. For example, instead of using a NumberFormatter, the* **calculateAge()** *function could perform the rounding. For the last line of the* **calculateAge()** *function, you would simply change* **return age;** *to* **return Math.floor(age);**.

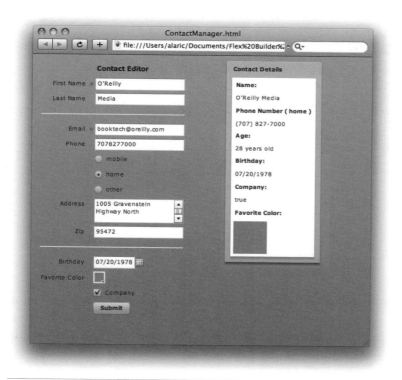

Figure 9-10. Formatters at work in the Contact Details panel

The final code for the Contact Details panel follows:

```
<mx:Panel id="contactDetails"
    layout="vertical"
    x="346"
    y="10"
    paddingLeft="5"
    paddingRight="5"
```

```
                              paddingTop="5"
                              paddingBottom="5"
                              title="Contact Details">
                              <mx:Label
                                   text="Name:"
                                   fontWeight="bold"/>
                              <mx:Label
                                   text="{firstNameTextInput.text} {lastNameTextInput.text}"/>
                              <mx:Label
                                   text="Phone Number ( {phoneRadioButtonGroup.selectedValue} ):"
                                   fontWeight="bold"/>
                              <mx:Label
                                   text="{phoneFormatter.format(phoneTextInput.text)}"/>
                              <mx:Label
                                   text="Birthday:"
                                   fontWeight="bold"/>
                              <mx:Label
                                   text="{dateFormatter.format(birthdayDateField.selectedDate)}"/>
                              <mx:Label
                                   text="Age:"
                                   fontWeight="bold"/>
                              <mx:Label
                                   text="{numberFormatter.format(calculateAge(birthdayDateField.
                              selectedDate))} years old"/>
                              <mx:Label
                                   text="Company:"
                                   fontWeight="bold"/>
                              <mx:Label
                                   text="{companyCheckBox.selected}"/>
                              <mx:Label
                                   text="Favorite Color:"
                                   fontWeight="bold"/>
                              <mx:Canvas
                                   width="60"
                                   height="60"
                                   backgroundColor="{favoriteColorPicker.selectedColor}"/>

                         </mx:Panel>
```

Summary

In this chapter, you learned how to use validation techniques from the very simple to the fairly advanced. You learned to use a variety of validators and even created a robust validation scheme in ActionScript. You also saw how to restrict input fields, limiting the type of characters that are allowed, and learned to use a few new controls such as RadioButtons and DateFields.

This chapter also introduced some basic programming techniques, such as conditionals and loops. You learned how to format your data in detail, even creating a real application that uses the various formatter classes. You also learned to perform calculations on dates and times. All of this, used in conjunction with your new form layout, gives you a way to provide very rich forms in your applications.

CHAPTER 10

GATHERING AND DISPLAYING DATA

Few applications are complete without using some form of data. That is especially true with the advent of web applications. Just think of the web applications you may be using frequently. How many of them would serve you any purpose if they did not access some form of data? It is the ability to seamlessly connect to information that has really made the web what it is today.

Whether the information you send and receive is stored in an XML file, stored in a database, or gathered from one of the many Web services available, you can be sure that, with Flex, connecting to and displaying data is straightforward and simple.

Using List Controls

Flex offers a number of controls known as *list* controls, which make displaying a list of items very easy. All list controls have the ability to accept either a simple list of data or complex, structured data, and they have a number of features that help keep them customizable and reusable. Each list control provides scroll bars if the items cannot be viewed all at once at their current size. A few frequently used controls fall into the list category:

List

This is the backbone of all list controls. It orders its items in a vertical layout.

HorizontalList

This is a list control that arranges its items horizontally.

TileList

This list arranges its items in a tiled pattern.

ComboBox

This is similar to a TextInput, but it provides a drop-down list of possible values for filling the input field. This is similar to the HTML `<select/>` tag.

DataGrid

> This is an advanced list control that can show multiple sets of data arranged in a table. Rows can be sorted, and columns can be resized and even rearranged by dragging and dropping.

Lists of Simple Data

The first piece of data you'll use in this chapter is a simple list of color names. You'll use an *Array* to store this, which is the standard way to store a list of information.

In MXML, you can create an Array using the **<mx:Array/>** tag and fill it with values using a list of tags, such as an **<mx:String/>** tag. For a list of colors, you could use an **<mx:String/>** tag pair, containing a color name:

```
<mx:Array>
    <mx:String>red</mx:String>
    <mx:String>green</mx:String>
    <mx:String>blue</mx:String>
</mx:Array>
```

In ActionScript, you create an array by writing a list of items separated by commas and wrapped in square brackets (**[** and **]**). So, you can create the previous MXML list of colors like this in ActionScript:

```
var colors:Array = [ "red","green","blue" ];
```

Now that you know how to create simple lists of data, you'll learn how to display that data in a list control. To populate a List control with data, you use the **dataProvider** property, passing it an Array. For example, to give a list of color names, you could bind the List's **dataProvider** property to an Array, such as the following:

```
<mx:List
width="150"
    dataProvider="{['Red','Orange','Yellow','Green','Blue','Indigo',
    'Violet']}" />
```

This would create a list that looks like Figure 10-1.

Figure 10-1. *A colorful list*

As you know, you can write a property for a component both as an XML attribute and as a child tag. So, you can create this same list with an array of items using just tags, populating its **dataProvider** by using the **<mx:dataProvider/>** child tag:

```
<mx:List
    width="150">

    <mx:dataProvider>

        <mx:Array>
            <mx:String>Red</mx:String>
            <mx:String>Orange</mx:String>
            <mx:String>Yellow</mx:String>
            <mx:String>Green</mx:String>
            <mx:String>Blue</mx:String>
```

NOTE

For any component in the Flex framework that uses a list of items, the property to remember is **dataProvider**.

```
            <mx:String>Indigo</mx:String>
            <mx:String>Violet</mx:String>
        </mx:Array>

    </mx:dataProvider>

</mx:List>
```

You set the **dataProvider** with a child tag, which you then fill with an array of colors, just like the array you created earlier in MXML.

Such a tag-based **dataProvider** is great for short lists of values, but it can get pretty verbose for more than a few items. Generally, you'll get larger sets of data from a separate file that you load in or from a data service on the web.

Lists of Complex Data

In the previous two examples, a list has taken an array of strings as a data provider. A list control can take an array of any arbitrary data. Consider a scenario in which you have a list of your favorite songs. Of course, you could list just the song names. However, you might want some additional information such as the artist or the album name that the song is on. In that case, you might want to use not an array of strings but an array of objects. An object is just a convenient container for multiple pieces of information, because it can have any properties you want. For this example, the properties **artist**, **album**, and **song** are useful:

```
<mx:List
    width="150">

    <mx:dataProvider>

        <mx:Array>

            <mx:Object
                song="In My Secret Life"
                album="Ten New Songs"
                artist="Leonard Cohen"/>
            <mx:Object
                song="Phantom Limb"
                album="Wincing the Night Away"
                artist="The Shins"/>
            <mx:Object
                song="Tinfoil"
                album="Live at Schuba's Tavern"
                artist="The Handsome Family"/>
            <mx:Object
                song="Highway 253"
                album="Extra Solar Sunrise"
                artist="The Saturn V"/>
            <mx:Object
                song="Junk Bond Trader"
                album="Figure 8"
                artist="Elliott Smith"/>
            <mx:Object
                song="Stalled"
```

NOTE

Notice that the `<mx:dataProvider/>` *tag must still use the* `mx` *namespace.*

NOTE

List controls also have the `rowCount` *property, which is a way to set the number of visible items.*

```
                        album="Through the Trees"
                        artist="The Handsome Family"/>
                <mx:Object
                        song="Every Dull Moment"
                        album="Bring on the Snakes"
                        artist="Crooked Fingers"/>

            </mx:Array>

        </mx:dataProvider>

    </mx:List>
```

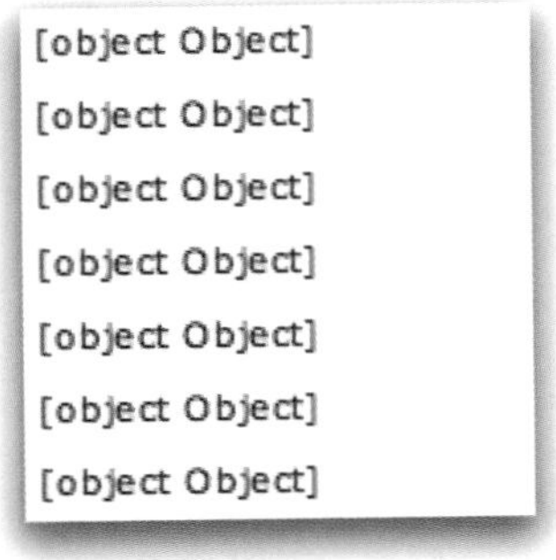

Figure 10-2. A list of objects, literally

Now you have a list populated by an array of objects, each with their own properties. But take a look at Figure 10-2 to see what this list looks like.

That's probably not the look you want. So, what happened? Because you had an array of objects instead of simple strings, the list wasn't sure which one to display. Because a regular object has a default string representation of "[object Object]," that's what the list displayed as its labels.

Custom label fields

Luckily, the List control has a property called **labelField**, which takes the name of the property you want displayed if your list is filled with complex data. Because you want to display the song names in the list, just set the List control's **labelField** to **song**. Figure 10-3 shows what the list looks like when displaying the **song** property as its **labelField**.

Figure 10-3. A list of objects, displaying the song names

A List control's default **labelField** is set to **label**, so there's another way you could accomplish the same thing—changing the **song** property on your array of objects to the property **label** would also cause the list to display correctly, because it looks for a **label** property. However, this isn't the recommended way to go: you don't need to modify your data to work with the list, because it should be the list's responsibility to work with your data!

Advanced lists

What if you wanted to display more than one property at a time? A great control that's built for just that is the DataGrid. It lets you specify multiple columns, each mapping to a property in the array of objects you passed to it. Essentially, it's a table, similar to a spreadsheet or HTML table.

An easy way to create a DataGrid is using Flex Builder's Design mode. When you drag and drop a DataGrid on the stage, Flex Builder writes the necessary code for you, which you can easily modify to suit your needs. Dropping a DataGrid onto the stage gives you the following MXML:

```
<mx:DataGrid>
    <mx:columns>
        <mx:DataGridColumn headerText="Column 1" dataField="col1"/>
        <mx:DataGridColumn headerText="Column 2" dataField="col2"/>
        <mx:DataGridColumn headerText="Column 3" dataField="col3"/>
    </mx:columns>
</mx:DataGrid>
```

Because a DataGrid can display multiple columns, you have to specify this via its **columns** property, which takes an array of DataGridColumns. It's on the individual DataGridColumn that you'll specify which property the column should display. You do this on the columns' **dataField** property. The **headerText** property specifies what to display as the column header. It's optional, because it will default to the name of the property specified in the **dataField**. However, you'll often want to modify it so you can display more descriptive text.

DataGrids, like all list controls, take a **dataProvider** to populate them. So, to create a DataGrid of songs, you could use the following code, pretty much copying and pasting the **dataProvider** property from the previous songs example:

```
<mx:DataGrid>

    <mx:columns>
        <mx:DataGridColumn headerText="Track Name" dataField="song"/>
        <mx:DataGridColumn headerText="Artist" dataField="artist"/>
        <mx:DataGridColumn headerText="Album Name" dataField="album"/>
    </mx:columns>

    <mx:dataProvider>
        <mx:Array>
            <mx:Object
                song="In My Secret Life"
                album="Ten New Songs"
                artist="Leonard Cohen"/>
            <mx:Object
                song="Phantom Limb"
                album="Wincing the Night Away"
                artist="The Shins"/>
            <mx:Object
                song="Tinfoil"
                album="Live at Schuba's Tavern"
                artist="The Handsome Family"/>
            <mx:Object
                song="Highway 253"
                album="Extra Solar Sunrise"
                artist="The Saturn V"/>
            <mx:Object
                song="Junk Bond Trader"
                album="Figure 8"
                artist="Elliott Smith"/>
            <mx:Object
                song="Stalled"
                album="Through the Trees"
                artist="The Handsome Family"/>
            <mx:Object
                song="Every Dull Moment"
                album="Bring on the Snakes"
                artist="Crooked Fingers"/>
        </mx:Array>
    </mx:dataProvider>

</mx:DataGrid>
```

This displays the list shown in Figure 10-4.

Track Name	Artist	Album Name
In My Secret Life	Leonard Cohen	Ten New Songs
Phantom Limb	The Shins	Wincing the Night Away
Tinfoil	The Handsome Family	Live at Schuba's Tavern
Highway 253	The Saturn V	Extra Solar Sunrise
Junk Bond Trader	Elliott Smith	Figure 8
Stalled	The Handsome Family	Through the Trees

Figure 10-4. A DataGrid displaying those same old songs

NOTE

The DataGridColumn has lots of other properties that help you customize a particular column. For instance, to set the width of a particular column, you use that DataGridColumn's **width** *property.*

Using XML Data

So, you've seen a few examples of using simple arrays and arrays of objects to populate list controls. But these controls can also handle another type of data: XML.

To help understand XML data, you'll jump back into the ContactManager application. You'll want to create a list of contacts in XML. To do so, you have to think about what fields you want to store. That's easy, because you've already created a UI expecting certain fields. A skeleton for the XML could be the following:

```
<contacts>
    <contact id="">
        <firstName/>
        <lastName/>
        <email/>
        <phone/>
        <phoneType/>
        <address/>
        <zip/>
        <birthday/>
        <color/>
        <company/>
    </contact>
</contacts>
```

NOTE

The **id** *attribute that's being placed on these XML tags has no relationship to the* **id** *attribute for Flex components. This is an arbitrary name you're using as an XML attribute, and you could use any name as a substitute, such as "name" or "number."*

This starts with a **<contacts/>** tag, which is the *root* of the XML document, the main tag that all valid XML needs to have. Then you can have any number of **<contact/>** tags, each of which has an attribute called **id** that can serve as a numerical identifier for that contact. Each **<contact/>** tag also has any number of child tags corresponding to the different properties of that contact. These properties could just as well be expressed as attributes, but it's always a safe bet to use child tags. That's because you may later decide to add properties to that child tag, or you may want to include other, more complex content in that child tag.

For the example, you're welcome to create your own list of contacts using this template or to use the list provided next.

One way to use XML data in your Flex applications is by using the `<mx:XML/>` tag. Inside that tag, try adding some contact data to your ContactManager application by adding the following MXML to it.

```
<mx:XML id="contactsXML" xmlns="" >
    <contacts>
        <contact id="0">
            <firstName>Alaric</firstName>
            <lastName>Cole</lastName>
            <email>alaric@oreilly.com</email>
            <phone>4155558273</phone>
            <phoneType>mobile</phoneType>
            <address>555 Green St</address>
            <zip>94001</zip>
            <birthday>07/20/1979</birthday>
            <color>0x00FF00</color>
            <company>false</company>
        </contact>
        <contact id="1">
            <firstName>O'Reilly</firstName>
            <lastName>Media</lastName>
            <email>booktech@oreilly.com</email>
            <phone>7078277000</phone>
            <phoneType>home</phoneType>
            <address>1005 Gravenstein Highway North, Sebastopol, CA
            </address>
            <zip>95472</zip>
            <birthday>07/20/1978</birthday>
            <color>0x009999</color>
            <company>true</company>
        </contact>
        <contact id="2">
            <firstName>Crystal</firstName>
            <lastName>Clear</lastName>
            <email>crystal4354@hotmail.com</email>
            <phone>5015556492</phone>
            <phoneType>mobile</phoneType>
            <address>555 Lakeview Dr</address>
            <zip>94001</zip>
            <birthday>3/6/1975</birthday>
            <color>0xFF66CC</color>
            <company>false</company>
        </contact>
        <contact id="3">
            <firstName>Google</firstName>
            <email>google@gmail.com</email>
            <phone>6502530000</phone>
            <phoneType>home</phoneType>
            <address>1600 Amphitheatre Parkway, Mountain View, CA
            </address>
            <zip>94043</zip>
            <color>0xFF0000</color>
            <company>true</company>
        </contact>
        <contact id="4">
            <firstName>Yahoo!</firstName>
            <email>yahoo@yahoo.com</email>
            <phone>4083493300</phone>
            <phoneType>home</phoneType>
            <address>701 First Avenue, Sunnyvale CA</address>
```

```
                        <zip>94089</zip>
                        <color>0x9900FF</color>
                        <company>true</company>
                    </contact>
                    <contact id="5">
                        <firstName>Whatcha</firstName>
                        <lastName>McCollum</lastName>
                        <email>w.mccollum@fakeemail.com</email>
                        <phone>3149884735</phone>
                        <phoneType>other</phoneType>
                        <color>0xFFFF00</color>
                        <company>false</company>
                    </contact>
                </contacts>
            </mx:XML>
```

NOTE

Remember that valid XML must always contain a root tag. Therefore, in this example, you must wrap the list of contacts in the root tag **<contacts></contacts>**. *You can actually call this tag anything you want, because it isn't going to be referenced anywhere—in the application, you simply reference the* **id** *of your* **<mx:XML/>** *tag, and that points to the root.*

In this code, you've given the **<mx:XML/>** tag an **id** of **contactsXML**, and you've additionally given it a blank namespace. When typing an **<mx:XML/>** tag in Flex Builder's Source mode, code completion may insert this blank namespace for you. It's not necessary for simple XML, but it doesn't hurt.

Now that you have the information available, you'll create a DataGrid to display it in your application. If you want, rearrange your application to give some space for the component, and then drag and drop a DataGrid onto your application in Design mode. Give it an **id** of **contactsDataGrid**. Then go into Source mode, and modify the **dataProvider** and columns to match the following:

```
<mx:DataGrid id="contactsDataGrid"
    dataProvider="{contactsXML.contact}">
    <mx:columns>
        <mx:DataGridColumn headerText="ID" dataField="@id"/>
        <mx:DataGridColumn headerText="First" dataField="firstName"/>
        <mx:DataGridColumn headerText="Last" dataField="lastName"/>
    </mx:columns>
</mx:DataGrid>
```

Again, you're using curly braces to bind the **dataProvider** of the DataGrid to the **contactsXML** XML you created. However, you'll notice that you don't bind to **contactsXML** directly but to **contactsXML.contact**. If you were to create a DataGrid like the following, it wouldn't display any data:

```
<mx:DataGrid id="contactsDataGrid"
    dataProvider="{contactsXML}"/>
```

That's because the XML itself isn't a list of data, and list controls want a list of items. In this case, **contactsXML** refers to the top-level node of the XML, **<contacts/>**. The DataGrid would think you were binding to that one node, which isn't a list of items but a single entity, and it would not display correctly. You get a list by using the expression **contactsXML.contact**, which points to the list of **<contact/>** tags you have.

Notice the first column in the DataGrid. There you've set the **dataField** to **@id**, not **id**. This is because the **id** is an attribute of the XML, not a child tag. Conversely, both **firstName** and **lastName** are child tags in the XML, so you can refer to them without the @ sign. The @ sign is a convenient way to show that you're wanting an attribute—because XML can have both

NOTE

Why the @ sign? Well, say it out loud: "the 'at' sign." We're dealing with "at"-tributes, so it made sense to use that symbol.

attributes and child tags, you want the ability to choose which. Figure 10-5 shows the results of the DataGrid using XML data.

ID	First	Last
0	Alaric	Cole
1	O'Reilly	Media
2	Crystal	Clear
3	Google	
4	Yahoo!	
5	Whatcha	McCollum

Figure 10-5. A DataGrid displaying a list of contacts from XML

You might not have realized you were doing it, but you've just learned a new technique, E4X. While it looks like the typical dot notation you're used to in ActionScript, it's actually not the same. E4X has a number of great features such as filtering and the ability to read and write XML through an improved API.

Actually, now that you've learned a bit about E4X, you can remove that first DataGridColumn, because it's not necessary to display the contact's **id** in the user interface. It just helps to know it's there and that you can access it with E4X.

NOTE

E4X stands for "ECMAScript for XML." ECMAScript is the language on which ActionScript is based. For details about its features and usage, consult the Flex documentation.

Loading External Data at Compile Time

Now you're using XML data within your Flex application, and you're starting to fill out this application. However, by looking at the source code, you might think it's a bit sloppy. That is to say, with all this XML data, the source code is long and more difficult to navigate and read. (Imagine if, instead of just a few, you had an XML list of 200 contacts.) That's why there's a convenient way to separate this XML into an external file and load it directly. The **<mx:XML/>** tag has a **source** property, and you can use that to point to a file.

First, create a blank XML file by choosing File→New→File. Choose the location corresponding to the source folder of this ContactManager project (the src folder), and enter a filename of **contacts.xml** (as shown in Figure 10-6). This creates a blank *.xml* file into which you can place the contents of the **<mx:XML/>** tag. (You can easily copy and paste everything between the **<mx:XML>** opening tag and the **</mx:XML>** closing tag into this new file.) Then, set the **source** property on the **<mx:XML/>** tag to point to that file:

```
<mx:XML id="contactsXML" xmlns="" source="contacts.xml" >

</mx:XML>
```

To save space and make your code cleaner, you can close the **<mx:XML/>** tag like this:

```
<mx:XML id="contactsXML" xmlns="" source="contacts.xml" />
```

Figure 10-6. The New File dialog box

HTTP

HTTP stands for Hypertext Transfer Protocol, and it's a standard for transferring information across the Internet. This protocol is used when opening a web page in a browser—it sends all the text and images you see displayed in your browser.

When you type an address in your browser to go to a web page, you may have typed *http://* at the beginning of the address. (If you didn't, the browser will automatically add *http://* to the front of the URL for you). The *http://* part simply means "use the HTTP protocol."

NOTE

For a Flex application deployed in a web browser, a relative URL is relative to the HTML page that loads the application.

Now the XML data is conveniently located outside the main source code. However, even though the XML file is pulled from another location, it is still compiled into the Flex application. It would be useful to pull such data at runtime, meaning you load the application and gather the XML after your application loads. This allows the file to be changed and ensures that you always load the latest version. To do so, you'll be using your first data service component, HTTPService.

Loading External Data at Runtime

The `<mx:HTTPService/>` tag is a quick and easy way to get text or XML content over the web using standard HTTP (see the "Into the Bin" box). This means you can load information from websites in HTML, or even sites created in PHP, ASP, or other web servers that generate HTML content.

The HTTPService component takes a `url` property, which points to the location of the file you want to load. If you've ever used HTML or dealt with HTTP in other ways, you know you can either specify an absolute URL, like *http://www.oreilly.com*, or specify a relative URL, which is relative to your server, like *images/someimage.jpg*.

Because you're going to be loading the XML file from within your project, you'll be using a relative URL in this example.

Into the Bin

When a Flex application is run in Flex Builder for a project deployed to the web, an HTML file is opened, and it has a compiled version of the application embedded within it. More is going on at compile time than simply a SWF file being created. Any files you have placed in your source folder are automatically copied to a folder called bin-debug. In the case of the *contacts.xml* file for ContactManager, a copy of that file is placed in bin-debug, as shown in Figure 10-7. That means when you run the application, it is the copy of the file in the bin-debug folder that gets pulled into the application. This works the same way with any media you may have in your Flex application, which I will talk about a little later in the book.

If you edit any of the files in the bin-debug folder, they will just get overwritten, so be sure to modify only the original version, located in the src folder.

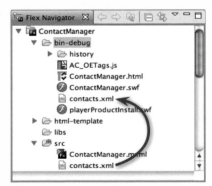

Figure 10-7. How extra files are copied to the bin-debug folder

Place the following code where your previous `<mx:XML/>` tag was:

```
<mx:HTTPService id="contactsService"
    resultFormat="e4x"
    url="contacts.xml"/>
```

This creates an HTTPService component, points it to the *contacts.xml* file you created earlier, and lets the service know you're loading XML data. If you don't set the **resultFormat** property, it will default to **object**, which makes the HTTPService component convert whatever data it receives into regular objects. This would make E4X unusable. To tell it you want to be able to use E4X and that the data you're loading is XML, set the **resultFormat** property to **e4x**.

The next step is to change your DataGrid's **dataProvider**. You're getting rid of the **<mx:XML/>** tag, so you need to update the DataGrid. To point it to the service's data, you use a property of the service called **lastResult** which holds the result of the most recent invocation of this service:

```
<mx:DataGrid id="contactsDataGrid"
     dataProvider="{contactsService.lastResult.contact}">
     <mx:columns>
         <mx:DataGridColumn headerText="First" dataField="firstName"/>
         <mx:DataGridColumn headerText="Last" dataField="lastName"/>
     </mx:columns>
</mx:DataGrid>
```

You know that **contactsService.lastResult** is the actual data that is returned from the service, which is going to be XML—but, again, you need to set the **dataProvider** to the list of contacts. So, the **dataProvider** should be **contactsService.lastResult.contact**.

However, there's one more step to getting this to work. The service component doesn't get invoked automatically. To invoke it, you call its **send()** method. So, set up a listener on your **<mx:Application/>** tag for the event called **applicationComplete**. This event fires when the application is fully loaded and ready and will then cause the **send()** method to be called. The start of your tag may now look like this:

```
<mx:Application
     xmlns:mx="http://www.adobe.com/2006/mxml"
     applicationComplete="contactsService.send()">
```

Now the service will be invoked when the application is opened, the data will be pulled in, and the binding will connect that data to your DataGrid. How's that for service?

NOTE

The method to invoke the service is called **send()** *because you're sending a request.*

It's Not Your Fault

When using an HTTPService, the data that is returned is reliant upon the remote server. Just like a web browser, it's using the HTTP protocol. Have you ever tried to go to a website and the page wouldn't load? This can happen with the HTTPService component as well.

When a web server has a problem, you may get what is called a *fault*. This means there's a problem: it may be that the information or file you're requesting no longer exists, or that the web server went down. If the server has such an error, the **lastResult** property will not be updated as expected. By default, Flex will pop up an alert informing you of the problem. If you'd like a custom response, you can listen for such errors by using the **fault** event. This event fires whenever a fault occurs.

NOTE

Remote data is not accessible to a Flex application unless the remote site has enabled access via special policy file. See the box "Playing Nice in the Sandbox" for more information.

Of course, you can take this skill of connecting to remote data and apply that to data elsewhere on the web. For a quick example, instead of using the local *contacts.xml* file, use an XML file residing on a remote web server, located at *http://greenlike.com/flex/learning/projects/contactmanager/contacts.xml*—in place of the *contacts.xml* file you're using locally. To do so, simply change the **url** property of the service to point to the remote file:

```
<mx:HTTPService id="contactsService"
    resultFormat="e4x"
    url="http://greenlike.com/flex/learning/projects/contactmanager/
    contacts.xml" />
```

NOTE

Notice that for an absolute URL, you must use the http:// protocol designation.

Now the application loads an XML file, not from your local disk, but across the web. You might notice a bit of latency when loading the application now, because this XML file is larger, and of course the file is traveling on the Internet. By default, Flex service components will display a pinwheel-style status indicator, or "busy cursor," to let you know that data is being downloaded. If you want to remove this, set the service's **showBusyCursor** to **false**.

Playing Nice in the Sandbox

When talking about Flash, or computer security in general, you're going to hear the term *sandbox* a lot. A sandbox is a secure spot for a program (such as Flash Player) to run in and do what it likes. It is a restrictive space in which the program isn't allowed to break away from and to which other programs may have limited access. You can think of a parent taking their kids to the park to play in an actual sandbox— a place where the child is free to play without the parents worrying too much about their safety.

In terms of Flash Player, a very secure sandbox can prevent Flash applications deployed on the web from accessing the user's filesystem, or gathering and manipulating data from a remote website that doesn't allow it. (However, for AIR applications, this sandbox is expanded.) The first and most prevalent of sandbox restrictions you're likely to encounter is when accessing remote data.

Simply put, a Flex application that will be deployed on the web isn't allowed to access data outside the domain to which the application is deployed—unless the owner of that website specifically allows it. Permission is given through the use of an *.xml* file called *crossdomain.xml*, placed on the root of the website.

This file lets the owner explicitly allow certain other domains to access the data or allow everyone access. To allow you to access the *contacts.xml* file on the website, I had to create a cross-domain file, granting access to everyone. You can view this cross-domain file at *http://greenlike.com/crossdomain.xml*. It looks like the following:

```
<?xml version="1.0"?>
<!DOCTYPE cross-domain-policy SYSTEM "http://www.adobe.com/xml/
    dtds/cross-domain-policy.dtd">
<cross-domain-policy>
    <site-control permitted-cross-domain-policies="all"/>
    <allow-access-from domain="*" />
    <allow-http-request-headers-from domain="*" headers="*"/>
</cross-domain-policy>
```

If the cross-domain file wasn't there or didn't allow everyone access, trying to download the *contacts.xml* file in your Flex application would result in an error, and you wouldn't get the data.

Now that you've learned how to connect to remote XML data and the `ContactManager` application is filled with actual contacts, you can continue building the interface.

Implementing List Selection

A List or list-based control not only shows a list of items but deals with selection as well. This means that items can be selected in the list and that information can be bound to the List control's **selectedItem** property.

You can take advantage of this as you continue with the `ContactManager` application. For now, remove what you have for the Contact Details section, and replace it with the following code:

```
<mx:Panel id="contactDetails"
    layout="vertical"
    x="400"
    y="10"
    paddingLeft="5"
    paddingRight="5"
    paddingTop="5"
    paddingBottom="5"
    width="400"
    title="Contact Details">

    <mx:HBox>
        <mx:Label id="nameLabel"
            text="{contactsDataGrid.selectedItem.firstName}
                {contactsDataGrid.selectedItem.lastName}"
            fontWeight="bold"
            fontSize="14"/>

    <mx:Label id="emailLabel"
        text="Email: {contactsDataGrid.selectedItem.email}"/>

    <mx:Label id="phoneLabel"
        text="{contactsDataGrid.selectedItem.phoneType}:
            {phoneFormatter.format(
            contactsDataGrid.selectedItem.phone)}" />

    <mx:Text id="addressText"
        text="Address: {contactsDataGrid.selectedItem.address}" />

    <mx:Label id="zipLabel"
        text="Zip Code: {contactsDataGrid.selectedItem.zip}" />

    <mx:Canvas
        width="60"
        height="60"
        backgroundColor="{contactsDataGrid.selectedItem.color}" />

</mx:Panel>
```

This code binds a few Label controls to the **selectedItem** property of the DataGrid. (Previously you had fields bound to the input controls, but you're going to create a view mode and an edit mode for your application, so for now you'll separate them.) The `selectedItem` is a specific item from the list of items that fills the DataGrid. You can bind to this via `contactsDataGrid.selectedItem`. For this example, the `selectedItem` is actually a `<contact/>` node and has properties such as `firstName`, `lastName`, `phone`, `phoneType`, and so on. In this case, you've bound Labels to specific properties of this `selectedItem`, as seen in Figure 10-8.

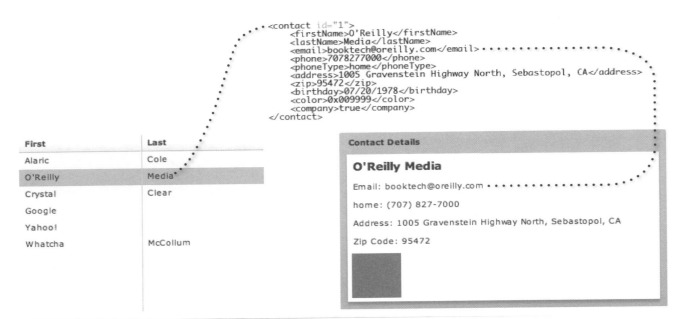

Figure 10-8. How a `selectedItem` *works*

NOTE

All list controls also have a property called `allowMultipleSelection` *which, when set to* `true`, *allows you to select more than one item at a time. To access the selected items, you use the* `selectedItems` *property instead, which is an Array of items.*

Another aspect to notice is the use of a control called Text. This control takes a **text** property and will resize itself to fit its contents. In a way, it works like a Label control, except it can render multiline text. It's a good control to use when you want to display a small chunk of text that you don't expect to need scrolling. For longer text that may need to be scrolled, a TextArea control is best.

Connecting to Search Results

Another, very powerful example of remote data is connecting to search results. For a nice real-world example I'll have you begin a new Flex project called Search. You can refer to Chapter 2 if you need a refresher on how to create a new project.

While Google also offers a public API that grants access to Flash and Flex applications, it requires the developer to know and parse the XML data it returns. I built an easy-to-use Yahoo! search component that makes it simple to place this data in a Flex application. To follow along with the next example, you need the ActionScript 3 Search API. Go to *http://developer.yahoo.com/flash/astra-webapis/*, and download the Yahoo! ASTRA Web APIs library.

You'll get a **.zip** file that, once extracted, will have a few folders that are pretty standard for Flex or ActionScript libraries: Build, Documentation, Examples, and Source. While the source code is available in the Source folder, look in the Build folder for a SWC file named *AstraWebAPIs.swc*.

Simply add this SWC file to the libs folder of your **Search** project, and you'll instantly have the SearchService component available in your application.

Now, how do you use this component? First, I'll recap the concept of namespaces. As you might remember, a *namespace*, in terms of Flex, is a way to distinguish groups of related components. You're going to be using a component called SearchService, but this component, of course, isn't part of the default Flex framework, and it's not going to use the namespace **mx**. Instead, it will be using a namespace called **yahoo**. However, as you've learned, typing the namespace in Flex Builder's Source mode isn't necessary if utilizing code completion, so when you want to add the **SearchService** component, you can start typing **<SearchService** and, if you allow code completion to complete your tag, the namespace will be inserted automatically. (If not, you can see how to add the namespace manually in the following example code.)

The SearchService component needs just one property to make it work: a string that is the criteria to search for, easily specified by the **query** attribute on the tag. You can bind this **query** property to a TextInput (**queryTextInput** is a good **id**), and clicking a Button can call the **send()** method of the **SearchService**.

While the SearchService component isn't related to the HTTPService component, it does have similar internals to make it work. It uses a method called **send()** and a property called **lastResult** as a way to make it easy for a Flex developer to get started.

You can build your very simple Search application with the following code:

```
<mx:Application
    layout="absolute"
    xmlns:mx="http://www.adobe.com/2006/mxml"
    xmlns:yahoo="http://www.yahoo.com/astra/2006/mxml">

    <yahoo:SearchService id="searchService"
        applicationId="YahooDemo"
        query="{queryTextInput.text}"/>

    <mx:HBox
        defaultButton="{searchButton}"
        y="10"
        x="10">

        <mx:FormItem
            label="Query:">
            <mx:TextInput id="queryTextInput"/>
        </mx:FormItem>

         <mx:Button id="searchButton"
            label="Search"
            click="searchService.send()"/>
```

SWC Files

A SWC file (usually pronounced "swik") is a compiled form for components and is convenient for three reasons. First, it's a single file that is easy to distribute compared to source code. Second, if you create components and don't want to distribute source code, a SWC gives you a certain degree of protection for your code, because it is highly inconvenient to get to the source code—it requires a decompilation tool. Third, because SWC files are precompiled, using them in your applications provides faster compile times.

In fact, the Flex framework you've been using is contained in a few separate SWC files.

```
        </mx:HBox>

        <!-- The results as a List -->
        <mx:List id="resultsList"
            dataProvider="{searchService.lastResult}"
            left="10"
            right="10"
            top="75"
            bottom="10"
            showDataTips="true"
            labelField="name"/>

    </mx:Application>
```

You might have noticed the use of a FormItem container in this code, outside a Form control. I personally use FormItem containers as a means of providing a label for form fields, although you could have just as easily accomplished this with a Label control inside an HBox.

You'll also see a new property of the HBox (and containers in general) called **defaultButton**. This property points to a Button control and makes it fire a **click** event when the Enter (Return on a Mac) key is pressed. Most people expect to be able to press the Enter (Return) key to submit a form, and this property takes care of that. It also provides a visual cue by highlighting the default button.

When you run the application, you can enter a search term, click the Button (or press the Enter/Return key), and submit your query. Assuming everything works as expected, data returns from Yahoo! search, and the results will appear in the list. By default, the list displays the title of the page (but I'll show you how to modify that in a moment). Running the application, you'll see something like Figure 10-9. Notice what happens when hovering

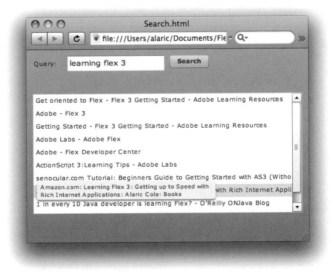

Figure 10-9. A simple but powerful search application

over an item in a list that has had its label clipped (from being too long to display in the available width of the list). A tooltip appears with the full text. This is called a *dataTip* in Flex, and it appears because you set the property `showDataTips` to `true` on the list.

How cool is that? You just built a powerful Yahoo! search application. Next, you'll learn how to make it even better.

Dragging and Dropping in Lists

Built into Flex's list controls is the ability to easily drag and drop data. No complex code is necessary to be able to drag an item from one list and drop it into another. All of this is built into the list controls, and you can turn it on by enabling two properties, `dragEnabled` and `dropEnabled`.

For an example, add another List control to the search application, setting its `labelField` to the same as the `resultsList`. Then, set this new List's `dropEnabled` property to `true`. This allows other List controls to drop items into it. Then, on the `resultsList`, set the property `dragEnabled` to `true`. This tells it to let people drag its items.

Now when you run the application, you can simply drag a favorite search result from the `resultsList` and drop it into the adjacent list! The following code shows the `dragEnabled` property added to the `resultsList` and adds a Panel and another List into which you can drop items. See Figure 10-10 for an example of how this works.

```
<mx:List id="resultsList"
    dataProvider="{searchService.lastResult}"
    left="10"
    right="318"
    top="74"
    bottom="47"
    showDataTips="true"
    labelField="name"
    dragEnabled="true" />

<mx:Panel
    layout="vertical"
    title="Favorites"
    right="10"
    top="74"
    bottom="47"
    width="300">
    <mx:List
        dropEnabled="true"
        labelField="name"
        width="100%"
        height="100%"/>
</mx:Panel>
```

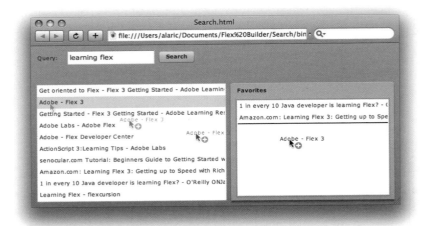

Figure 10-10. Dragging from one List into another

Why do you need to set the **labelField** on the new List (the one in which items can be dragged into)? Well, what is actually happening here is an item is being copied from the data provider of one List and is added to the data provider of another. If the new List did not have a **labelField** set, it would display **[object Object]** as its label, not knowing what to display.

Dragging and dropping works with other list controls as well, such as TileList and DataGrid. For example, you could replace the new List with a DataGrid; then if you dragged an item into the DataGrid, you would see every property of the search result item displayed as a column.

Using Inline Item Renderers

To easily customize the display of List controls, you're able to create your own content that the List will use to display its items. By default, the List creates a label field for each item, and the display (as you've learned) shows the property designated by a **labelField**. This label that a List control creates is called its **itemRenderer**, and you can create your own easily.

Consider the following code, which creates a special **itemRenderer** for the list in the **Search** example:

```
<mx:List id="resultsList"
    dataProvider="{searchService.lastResult}"
    left="10"
    right="10"
    top="74"
    bottom="10">

    <mx:itemRenderer>
        <mx:Component>
            <mx:Label
                text="{data.name}"
                fontWeight="bold"/>
        </mx:Component>
```

```
      </mx:itemRenderer>

  </mx:List>
```

This code forgoes the **labelField** property in lieu of a more custom display. You'll need to look at a few aspects of this code to understand what's happening. One is the **<mx:Component/>** tag. This tag wraps the MXML content for your **itemRenderer**; it tells Flex to create a component behind the scenes and reuse it for each item in the list. This is extremely powerful functionality, letting a developer create components right within the property of another component. That makes it quick to create item renderers, without having to create your own components. (However, creating your own component has a few benefits such as reusability.)

Inside the **<mx:Component/>** tag is the actual code for creating the **itemRenderer**. Notice that there is a single Label control. This will create a Label for each item in the List's data provider.

Instead of using a **labelField** property, you are telling the Label control what to display by a binding to the **data** property. The **data** property is a reference to a specific item in the List's **dataProvider**. Just as you specified **name** as the **labelField**, which told the list to use that property of each item, here you specify **data.name** to accomplish the same thing.

Because this List is populated with web search results, there is other information such as the textual summary of the page or the URL of the page that we can display. For instance, to show the summary of the page, you can instead bind to the **data.summary** property. However, this property may contain a lot of text, so a Label control isn't the most fitting. Instead, you can add a Text control, and bind its **text** property to **data.summary**. Text controls are great at displaying multiple lines of text. To allow both the Label and the Text control to be displayed, wrap them in a VBox, as displayed below.

NOTE

The content in an **<mx:itemRenderer/>** *tag isn't displayed in Design mode.*

NOTE

Each of these results is actually a class called WebSearchResult, which is included as part of the ASTRA Web APIs library. It contains properties such as **name**, **summary**, *and* **clickURL**. *If you would like to learn more about this class, consult the documentation that came with the Yahoo! ASTRA Web APIs library.*

```
<mx:List id="resultsList"
    dataProvider="{searchService.lastResult}"
    left="10"
    right="10"
    top="74"
    bottom="10">

    <mx:itemRenderer>
        <mx:Component>
            <mx:VBox
                width="100%" >
                <mx:Label
                    text="{data.name}"
                    fontWeight="bold"/>
                <mx:Text
                    width="100%"
                    text="{data.summary}"/>
            </mx:VBox>
        </mx:Component>
    </mx:itemRenderer>

</mx:List>
```

If you like, you can set the **variableRowHeight** property on the List. While a standard List control will make each of its rows the same height, setting this to **true** allows the list to vary in the row heights. With items such as the page summary being taller in one row than the next, the List can adjust accordingly and therefore maximize viewable content.

To see what your **Search** application looks like with a custom **itemRenderer**, see Figure 10-11.

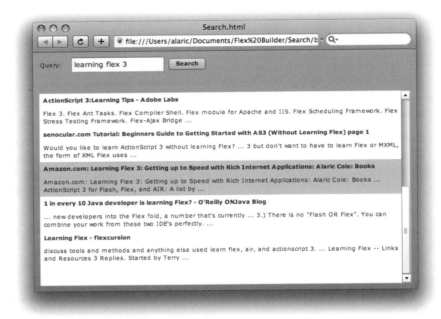

Figure 10-11. A custom itemRenderer *in use in the Search application*

Exploring Other Types of Service Components

It is outside the scope of this book to go over such services in detail, but I want to make sure you know what's available. While the **HTTPService** component is probably the most common service component you'll use, you may find the additional benefits of the **RemoteObject** component useful for your particular application, or you may need to access Web services, which you can do by using the **WebService** component.

WebService

The **HTTPService** component lets you access services that have a URL—data that presumably can be viewed in a browser such as HTML or XML. However, a number of Web services exist, which are accessible only through an XML standard called SOAP. While a bit heavier than other services, they are particularly prevalent in business-to-business applications, and you may find it necessary to connect to a SOAP Web service in Flex.

To easily access SOAP Web services, you can use the **WebService** component. You may also find a new feature of Flex Builder 3, the Import Web Services command, very useful. This command can point to a WSDL URL and create a good deal of code for you.

To access this command, select Data→Import Web Service (WSDL). From there you'll be prompted with a dialog box that asks you where you'd like to place the code that's generated, and for a URL to a WSDL description file. Flex Builder will generate the code needed to more easily access the Web service.

WARNING

SOAP Web services can be complex to use, and I recommend only using them if you have no other alternative.

NOTE

WSDL stands for Web Services Description Language, and is a common language model for describing Web services. It specifies what operations are available for a service and the format of the service's response.

NOTE

For a directory of Web services that you can use, check out www.xmethods.net.

RemoteObject

A very powerful data access component is the **RemoteObject** component, which lets you easily connect to server-side Java (Java EE or J2EE) or ColdFusion. You gain a number of benefits by using *remote objects*, which are maps to Java objects and ActionScript objects. This means actual data types such as Number or Date can be transferred across the wire intact. Another huge benefit of remote objects is that data can be compressed over the wire. That results in speedier access to large amounts of data. You also have the ability to use, among other benefits, data *push*, which allows you to listen for data changes on a remote server and get that new data automatically. (Think of an email application that didn't require you to manually get new mail, but would show you new mail as soon as it arrived.)

To use RemoteObject component, you must set up your application to use remote object access on a specific web server. This is typically done when creating a new Flex project. Under the New Flex Project dialog (Figure 10-12), the final section is called Server technology. Here you can choose a server type of ColdFusion or J2EE. You must select the "Use remote object access service" checkbox. If you are using ColdFusion, you may choose whether to use Flash Remoting or LiveCycle Data Services, while for J2EE applications you can only use LiveCycle Data Services.

NOTE

Java EE stands for Java Enterprise Edition, and is a version of the Java platform made for server-side processing. ColdFusion is actually a Java EE application, enabling you to create server code in a markup language.

Creating an Application from a Database

If you're using ColdFusion, PHP, J2EE, or ASP.NET, you're in luck. Flex Builder can actually generate server-side code for you, letting you easily connect to data in a database, and even modify that data. You supply the database, and all the necessary code for creating, reading, updating, and deleting records will be written for you, even the UI!

For PHP, J2EE, or ASP.NET applications, you must have a database and a web server set up using one of these technologies. Then, all you need to do is go to Data→Create Application from Database and follow the dialog boxes. An actual Flex application will be created, containing user interface elements and service methods for accessing this data. You can use this as a foundation for creating your application.

To use this functionality with ColdFusion, you'll first need to set up a ColdFusion server and install the ColdFusion extensions for Flex Builder. While you had the option to install these extensions when you installed Flex Builder, you can always add them later. See the article located at *http://livedocs. adobe.com/coldfusion/8/htmldocs/ othertechnologies_11.html* for instructions on how to install these extensions.

Figure 10-12. A new project being set up for ColdFusion Flash Remoting

To use this functionality, you'll also need to configure a web server based on one of these technologies. This requires more explanation than possible with this book. I recommend the Flex help article located at *http://livedocs.adobe.com/ flex/3/html/data_intro_2.html* to help get you started.

Summary

You've taken a giant leap in creating full-featured rich Internet applications and accessing data. In this chapter, you discovered how to use data that's created within your MXML code, or even data that's spread across the web. You learned some basics of working with XML data. You also learned a great deal about using list controls to display lists of data and even used an advanced list component, the DataGrid, within your **ContactManager** application.

Going much further, you saw how to add third-party components to supplement the standard Flex components, which opens up a huge number of excellent controls and containers you can take advantage of. You built a simple search application using Yahoo! search and used inline item renderers and a new Text control to create a rich display for the search data.

With these skills, you can take advantage of the incredible amount of data that exists on the web. In the next few chapters, you'll create richer, more powerful user interfaces that will really help your applications shine.

CONTROLLING FLOW AND VISIBILITY

One of the cool features of Flex is the ability to make a dynamic interface that is more reminiscent of desktop applications than most web-based applications. One of the tasks it can do out of the box is let you control the visibility of entire parts of your application. This is helpful when dealing with an application that may consist of different sections, not all of which should be visible at one time. With some of the standard Flex controls, you can partition your application into different views, even allowing people to customize the way they want to see a certain section.

Controlling Visibility

Every visual component in Flex has the ability to turn its visibility off and on. You control this with the **visible** property, which is **true** by default. This applies to all visual controls that Flex has, but it also applies to containers. As you have learned, containers are great tools not just for helping to align and lay out your application but also for structuring the different parts of your application. Because containers are visual components, they inherit such properties as visibility. This means you can set an entire container's visibility, and that property will propagate to the container's children.

Setting **visible** to **false** makes a component invisible, but it continues to take up its allotted space. For example, you may have a row of three buttons aligned horizontally inside an HBox. Turning the middle button's visibility off still allows it to take up space so that the first and third buttons are separated by the same distance as if it were visible. To make it so that the middle button doesn't take up space in its parent container, you set its **includeInLayout** property to **false**. See Figure 11-1 through Figure 11-4 for a visual explanation.

Figure 11-1. Three Button controls in an HBox, all visible

Figure 11-2. Three Button controls in an HBox; Button Two has `visible` *set to* `false`

Figure 11-3. Three Button controls in an HBox; Button Two has `includeInLayout` *set to* `false` *but* `visible` *set to* `true` *(Button Three overlays it)*

Figure 11-4. Three Button controls in an HBox; Button Two has both `visible` *and* `includeInLayout` *set to* `false` *(Button Three takes its place)*

Navigation Components

There may not be space on the screen for everything you want to display in your application. You might need to control what is visible at what time or provide a choice of views of a particular application. Consider preference dialog boxes in most desktop applications or the operating system's settings or control panel. These types of dialog boxes have a lot of options, and not all of them need to be visible at a time. Typically, they are organized in such a way that you can switch between groups of options—often with tabs that are suggestive of the way a group of files are organized in a file cabinet or the way a three-ring binder is divided into sections for each class, for instance.

Flex comes with a standard set of components that let you easily control the flow of your application or let you structure the visible elements into different views. These are referred to as *navigator containers*, and they provide a way to switch between their children. Instead of laying out their children in a vertical or horizontal (or other) fashion, the navigator containers show one child at a time, turning off the visibility of the others, and may provide controls like tabs that let you switch between the different views.

The TabNavigator is one of the most common navigator controls, so I'll talk about it first. The TabNavigator takes any number of child containers and provides a tab for each. Like all navigator containers, the TabNavigator's children must be containers. This is because containers, as stated earlier, provide a way of grouping other elements into a single entity. All containers also have a `label` property, and this is what is used to display the label of its corresponding tab. The TabNavigator doesn't want an array of labels or anything like that to display tabs; it simply wants a group of containers that have a `label` property. Consider the following code, which creates a set of three tabs that you can select to switch between three Canvas containers, each having a different background color. Figure 11-5 displays the output of this code.

```
<mx:TabNavigator id="view"
    width="200"
    height="200">

    <mx:Canvas id="redBox"
        label="Red"
        backgroundColor="#FF0000"/>
    <mx:Canvas id="greenBox"
        label="Green"
        backgroundColor="#00FF00"/>
    <mx:Canvas id="blueBox"
        label="Blue"
        backgroundColor="#0000FF"/>

</mx:TabNavigator>
```

NOTE

Remember that to change the label of any individual tab in a TabNavigator, you change the label of the corresponding container.

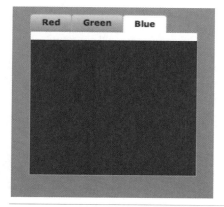

Figure 11-5. Three Canvas containers in a TabNavigator, creating three tabs

What is happening behind the scenes is the TabNavigator places the three containers (Canvas containers in this case) one on top of the other but sets only one to visible—the one whose tab is selected. When another tab is selected, only that particular container becomes visible, with the rest set to invisible. In this way, the TabNavigator, and all other navigator containers, provide a simple method of controlling the *view*, or a particular set of elements that should be visible.

The TabNavigator inherits its features from the aptly named ViewStack navigator container. The ViewStack is the workhorse behind the functionality of switching views, but it doesn't come with any visual means of switching views. For that, you can pair it with a navigation control such as a LinkBar, ToggleButtonBar, or TabBar. To implement similar functionality in a TabNavigator, you can use a ViewStack and connect it to a TabBar, placing both within a vertical layout:

NOTE

A Panel container's title property isn't the same as its label property. Its label property is, like all other containers, the text that displays in a navigator container, while its title is the text that displays in its title bar.

```
<mx:VBox>

    <mx:TabBar
        dataProvider="{view}"/>

    <mx:ViewStack
        id="view"
        width="200"
        height="200">
        <mx:Canvas id="redBox"
            label="Red"
            backgroundColor="#FF0000"/>
        <mx:Canvas id="greenBox"
            label="Green"
            backgroundColor="#00FF00"/>
        <mx:Canvas id="blueBox"
            label="Blue"
            backgroundColor="#0000FF"/>
    </mx:ViewStack>

</mx:VBox>
```

The TabBar, like other navigation controls, takes a **dataProvider** property, which you bind to an instance of a ViewStack. The TabBar looks at the child containers of the ViewStack and renders tabs with the proper labels, just like a TabNavigator would do on its own.

So, why would you ever want to use a ViewStack paired with a navigation control if there's a perfectly good TabNavigator you could use? Well, different navigation controls exist, so separating a ViewStack and its visual control gives you the ability to switch those navigation controls to your liking. For instance, you may want functionality similar to the tabs but don't want a "tab" look. In that case, you can use a ToggleButtonBar in place of the TabBar:

```
<mx:VBox>

    <mx:ToggleButtonBar
        dataProvider="{view}"/>

    <mx:ViewStack
        id="view"
        width="200"
        height="200">
        <mx:Canvas id="redBox""
            label="Red"
            backgroundColor="#FF0000"/>
        <mx:Canvas id="greenBox"
            label="Green"
            backgroundColor="#00FF00"/>
        <mx:Canvas id="blueBox"
            label="Blue"
            backgroundColor="#0000FF"/>
    </mx:ViewStack>

</mx:VBox>
```

This code takes the same **dataProvider** but gives a different look. Another choice is the LinkBar control, which creates a set of buttons with a special look and feel, reminiscent of hyperlinks.

Another reason to use a ViewStack is that you may not want the person using your application to directly control the view at all, instead choosing to control it yourself in code. Luckily, it's easy to control the currently selected view in a ViewStack or other navigator container. Each has a **selectedIndex** property, which you can set to an integer (zero-based) corresponding to a view. For example, to set the Green Canvas container in the previous code as the currently selected view, you could use the ActionScript **view.selectedIndex = 1**. For the Red one, you'd say **view.selectedIndex = 0**. Binding the **selectedIndex** properties of a List control and a navigator container, you could even allow a List to control the selected view of a ViewStack or other navigator container. Another way of setting the selected view is by using the **selectedChild** property. You can use this property to set a particular view by using the **id** of that container. In this way, you don't have to worry about the order of views, but you can concentrate on a particular view by its **id**. Consider the following code, which sets the Green view to visible when a Button control is clicked:

```
<mx:ViewStack
    id="view"
    width="200"
    height="200">
    <mx:Canvas id=""redBox"
        label="Red"
        backgroundColor="#FF0000"/>
    <mx:Canvas id="greenBox"
        label="Green"
        backgroundColor="#00FF00"/>
    <mx:Canvas id="blueBox"
        label="Blue"
        backgroundColor="#0000FF"/>
</mx:ViewStack>

<mx:Button
    label="Make Green"
    click="view.selectedChild = greenBox"/>
```

This ability can be useful in rich forms, where you have structured your forms by category and want only one visible at a time. In this way, you can direct the people using your application, providing them with a multistep process to fill out the forms, which can make them less daunting. Who wants to see a huge scrolling form? It's much better to partition it so that it not only looks smaller at first glance but also gives people a sense of direction—"I've finished parts one and two of three...nearly done!"

To do this, you can provide a Next button that, when clicked, sets the **selectedIndex** or **selectedChild** of a ViewStack that holds your various forms. See the "Using the Back Button: History Management" box later in this chapter for details on how you can even use the browser's forward and back buttons, letting people navigate the form in a way they're probably most familiar with.

NOTE

*It's good to know that navigation controls don't have to be tied to a ViewStack in order to work. If you want multiple ways of switching views in a TabNavigator (which already has a set of tabs to control it), you can connect a navigation control such as a LinkBar in the same way, by setting the LinkBar's **dataProvider** to the **id** of the TabNavigator. Both the TabNavigator's tabs and the LinkBar's buttons will be in sync with each other.*

NOTE

*For all navigator containers, the **selectedIndex** default value is **0**, and the **selectedChild** default is the first child.*

Creating a Photo Gallery Application

You'll now put some new navigation components to good use. One way in which you've probably used views is when looking at photos on a computer. Most modern programs that display photos allow them to be viewed in multiple ways, such as in a tile, a horizontal list, or a basic vertical list. You can create something like that very easily, and along the way, you'll learn how to display images in Flex. So, create a new project called **PhotoGallery** so you can get started creating a simple gallery of images, complete with multiple views.

Adding Multiple Views

For the first step, drag and drop a TabNavigator component onto the stage of your new application in Design mode in Flex Builder. This automatically creates a TabNavigator control with a single Canvas as its child.

When you select the TabNavigator, a pop-up toolbar will display at the top with a gripper or anchor handle and a plus and minus sign. The gripper provides a means of moving the TabNavigator around, while the plus and minus signs let you easily add and remove containers. Clicking the plus sign will open a dialog box asking you which type of container you want to add (Canvas, VBox, Panel, and so on), while also providing a quick way to add the label. So, using this dialog box or going into Source mode, make sure there are two Canvas children in the TabNavigator, with the labels "List View" and "Tile View."

> ### Selecting Navigator Containers in Design Mode
>
> When using navigation components, it can be challenging at first to understand whether you're selecting the navigation component or its children containers or the children. You may remember using Outline view or the Show Surrounding Containers option (as discussed in Chapter 8 in the "Visualizing the Structure of Your Application" section). These can be helpful when dealing with selection, but there's another way when using these components. To select the TabNavigator, you can click the gripper next to the plus and minus signs. This selects the TabNavigator, but it also allows you to move the navigator around by clicking and dragging this gripper. Double-clicking a tab also selects the parent TabNavigator.

Into the new containers, add a List control and TileList control, respectively, and set the sizes of the controls and the parent Canvas containers to take up all available space by setting their **width** and **height** properties to 100 percent. Your code should look like the following:

```
<mx:TabNavigator
    width="200"
    left="10"
    top="10"
    bottom="10" >
```

```
<mx:Canvas
    label="List View"
    width="100%"
    height="100%">
    <mx:List id="photosList"
        width="100%"
        height="100%"/>
</mx:Canvas>

<mx:Canvas
    label="Tile View"
    width="100%"
    height="100%">
    <mx:TileList id="photosTileList"
        width="100%"
        height="100%">
    </mx:TileList>
</mx:Canvas>

</mx:TabNavigator>
```

Populating the Gallery via XML

With your TabNavigator filled with a couple of views, each showing a different kind of list (a basic List control and a TileList control), you can now add some data to fill the lists. Because this is a photo gallery, it makes sense that your data will be a list of images. So, keep it simple and use some data via XML. I'll provide you with a simple list of images in XML. If you prefer to use another data source and feel comfortable designing the application that way, feel free to do so. Just make sure either you use the same structure as this or you modify your application accordingly to use a different structure (different attribute names, for example).

You can use the following XML, placing it in a file called *photos.xml* in your **PhotoGallery** application's source folder (usually named src—the same location as your *PhotoGallery.mxml* file). You will again use an HTTPService component to connect to this file.

```
<photos>
    <photo
        title="Yawning Camel"
        thumb="http://www.greenlike.com/photogallery/camel_thumb.jpg"
        image="http://www.greenlike.com/photogallery/camel.jpg" />
    <photo
        title="Crowdy Head Lighthouse"
        thumb="http://www.greenlike.com/photogallery/lighthouse_thumb.jpg"
        image="http://www.greenlike.com/photogallery/lighthouse.jpg" />
    <photo
        title="Sun Shade"
        thumb="http://www.greenlike.com/photogallery/sunshade_thumb.jpg"
        image="http://www.greenlike.com/photogallery/sunshade.jpg" />
    <photo
        title="Uluru"
        thumb="http://www.greenlike.com/photogallery/uluru_thumb.jpg"
        image="http://www.greenlike.com/photogallery/uluru.jpg" />
```

```
<photo
    title="Devil's Marbles"
    thumb="http://www.greenlike.com/photogallery/marble_thumb.jpg"
    image="http://www.greenlike.com/photogallery/marble.jpg" />
<photo
    title="Mother and Child"
    thumb="http://www.greenlike.com/photogallery/mother_thumb.jpg"
    image="http://www.greenlike.com/photogallery/mother.jpg" />
<photo
    title="Karnak Temple"
    thumb="http://www.greenlike.com/photogallery/temple_thumb.jpg"
    image="http://www.greenlike.com/photogallery/temple.jpg" />
<photo
    title="Contemplating the Purchase"
    thumb="http://www.greenlike.com/photogallery/purchase_thumb.jpg"
    image="http://www.greenlike.com/photogallery/purchase.jpg" />
</photos>
```

This code is a simple list of photo nodes, each having a **title** attribute, a **thumb** attribute, and an **image** attribute. The **title** attribute is the title of the image, while the **image** attribute contains a URL for the full image. The **thumb** attribute is a URL for a smaller, thumbnail representation of the image.

To connect to this file, add an **<mx:HTTPService/>** tag, giving it the following properties:

```
<mx:HTTPService id="service"
    url="photos.xml"
    resultFormat="e4x" />
```

NOTE

Alternatively, you can use the XML file on a server, located at http://greenlike. com/flex/learning/projects/photogallery/ photos.xml, pointing the HTTPService's URL to this instead.

*If you have your own images you want to use in this application, place them in the **PhotoGallery** application's source folder, and change the URLs in the XML file to point to your images. For instance, if you have an image named whitedog.jpg placed in a folder called myphotos, one of the photo node's **image** attributes could point to "myphotos/whitedog.jpg".*

As you saw in the previous chapter, any files you place in your source folder will be automatically copied to the output directory (called bin-debug *by default) when the application is built. So if you place a folder of images, they will be copied there, and your application will load the images from there when run.*

Be sure to call the service's **send()** method within the **applicationComplete** event listener in your Application so that the service is called when the application loads.

Now that you have data, you need to connect it to the two lists. If you remember from the previous chapter, when using XML data, the **dataProvider** of a List control needs a list of items. You're providing this here by binding it to **service.lastResult.photo**, because this points to the actual list of **<photo/>** nodes in the returned XML file. So, bind each of the List controls this way, and they will be populated at startup.

For the first List control (**photosList**), set its **labelField** to **@title**. Because the title of the image is placed as an attribute in XML, it must be accessed by the E4X expression **@title**, not simply **title**. So, you must change the **labelField** to reflect this, so that the List knows what to display.

Displaying External Images

The next step is to display the images. That's really easy to do, because the Image control was designed just for this purpose. Simply placing an Image control in your application and setting its **source** property to a URL will cause it to load the image. Any time its **source** property is changed, such as what occurs during a data binding, the image will reload.

So, place an Image control in your application, give it an **id** of **image**, and set its **source** property to the binding **photosList.selectedItem.@image**. This will bind the source to the **image** URL attribute of the particular XML node that is currently selected in the List control. Now, clicking the different items in the first List causes the Image control to load that image. Go ahead and run the application to see this. It should look like Figure 11-6.

Figure 11-6. The photo gallery in a List view

If no size is set on the Image control, it will resize itself to the actual size of the source image. So if the image or photo loaded is 300 pixels wide and 100 pixels tall, the Image will set its own width to 300 and its height to 100. While this may be the desired behavior in some applications, it's often best to know in advance the size of the Image control so you can plan your layout better. Setting an explicit size on the Image control will cause it to scale the loaded photo to fit within its bounds. So, you can set the Image control to an explicit height and width or, better yet, use constraints to anchor it to the edges of the application, letting the photo resize to take up available space. Doing so lets people resize their application, and the Image control scales its **source**.

You'll also want to set the **horizontalAlign** of the Image control to center, because this causes the source image to center itself within the Image control's bounds. This is useful when an image is loaded in portrait fashion—with the height being larger than the width—where the centering (or lack of) would be most noticeable.

Monitoring Loading Progress of Images

You may have noticed that it takes a moment to load the image. Especially if the connection is slow, this can be confusing to some people, because they may expect to click the item in the list and see the image load immediately. If it takes a while because of latency, someone may be tempted to click another item, assuming something is wrong. This, of course, only makes matters worse because the loading process has to begin all over again.

To provide better feedback in your application, you can use a ProgressBar control to monitor the loading process of these images. You can use the ProgressBar for many purposes, but it works surprisingly well with the Image control. All you have to do is set the **source** property of the ProgressBar to the **id** of the Image control you want to monitor, and it will just work.

So, to provide a better application, add a ProgressBar control with an **id** of **progressBar** to your application. Place it right on top of the Image control you just added, and set the ProgressBar's **source** to that image. Now, when an item is selected in the list, the image will begin loading, and the progress bar will display how much is remaining.

Browser Cache and Loading Progress

If you already loaded an image when you tried the PhotoGallery application or if you are using local images that you supplied yourself, you won't see the ProgressBar change from anything other than 100 percent. This is because that image is either local or has been *cached*, meaning a copy of the image file has been copied from its location to your machine for faster retrieval. It's therefore instantly loaded, and the ProgressBar doesn't display any progress because there isn't any—either it's loaded or it's not.

The browser is responsible for caching, and it does so in a similar fashion to when documents or images from an HTML page are loaded. In fact, the browser can cache *.swf* files. You'll notice this if you use Flex applications on the web—the first time you load the application, the default Flex application progress bar will show and it will take a moment to load, but the next time you visit the application it will load instantly.

Caching is usually the desired behavior, because it helps everything load more quickly. Most browsers provide a means of disabling or emptying the cache, which can be very helpful to developers. If you were to empty your cache and try loading the PhotoGallery images again, you would see the progress bar monitoring the loading process again.

Note that clearing your browser's cache may have adverse affects—you may see a noticeable decrease in speed when browsing sites you frequent, because the assets are no longer cached. When developing, you may find it most useful if you use one browser for daily activities and another browser for development, letting you clear the cache as necessary.

Once the image is fully loaded, the progress bar remains. That's not the desired behavior, because once the image loads, it's no longer necessary to see the progress bar. It would be best if the progress bar appeared when needed and disappeared when not. That's easy to do by using the **visible** property and a couple of events from the Image control.

The Image control has two events that are of interest, **open** and **complete**. The **open** event is fired when something begins to load, and the **complete** event fires when the loading is complete. Use those events to control the ProgressBar control's visibility.

First, set the ProgressBar to initially invisible by setting its **visible** property to **false** within the **ProgressBar** tag. Then, add a couple of event listeners to the Image control, toggling the ProgressBar's visibility. On the **open** event, set the ProgressBar to visible, and on **complete** set it to invisible. The code for these two controls may look like the following:

```
<mx:Image id="image"
    source="{photosList.selectedItem.@image}"
    left="270"
    top="10"
    bottom="10"
    right="10"
    horizontalAlign="center"
    open="progressBar.visible = true"
    complete="progressBar.visible = false"/>

<mx:ProgressBar id="progressBar"
    x="270"
    y="10"
    source="{image}"
    visible="false" />
```

Now you have a more responsive application, because it informs people that their clicks are actually doing something. A little feedback goes a long way when creating rich applications!

Customizing the TileList

Run the application and play around with it. You've probably noticed that Tile view is still incomplete. While for the List control, setting the **labelField** was enough to get it going, for the TileList you want to display more than the name of the image—a thumbnail representation would be great. To do that, you'll need to create an **itemRenderer** for the TileList and use another Image control.

For this Image control, you'll set its source to the **thumb** attribute of the data object it gets passed. You'll want to set the Image's **horizontalAlign** to center here again, because this will make the individual thumbnails look better, centering themselves in their spaces. (This centering is particularly important when a thumbnail is selected or hovered over, because of the highlight that the TileList creates; it won't look so good if the Image is aligned to the left of its space, because the highlight will be uneven on both sides.)

You can also use a **toolTip** on that Image to show the title of the loaded image. It will be the same property as what's used to set the other List's **label-Field**, but here you'll use it to create a pop-up tooltip when someone hovers the mouse over the image and pauses momentarily. Your TileList control code should now be the following:

```
<mx:TileList id="photosTileList"
    dataProvider="{service.lastResult.photo}"
    width="100%"
    height="100%"
    <mx:itemRenderer>
        <mx:Component>
            <mx:Image
```

> **NOTE**
>
> *If you're looking for a great way to connect to all kinds of photos, you can use the ActionScript 3.0 API available from Adobe that lets you interact with Flickr, the popular photo sharing site. This API includes features for not only searching for and displaying photos, but even uploading them and tagging them. This API requires a good deal of ActionScript knowledge to use it, but if you're interested in taking your* **PhotoGallery** *application to the next level, be sure to get the code at http://code.google.com/p/ as3flickrlib.*

```
                                    horizontalAlign="center"
                                    source="{data.@thumb}"
                                    toolTip="{data.@title}"
                                    width="100"
                                    height="60" />
                        </mx:Component>
                    </mx:itemRenderer>
                </mx:TileList>
```

Notice that the Image control has a width of 100 and a height of 60. This just ensures that, even if the thumbnail is very small or very large, it at least scales itself to be 100 pixels wide and 60 pixels tall. (This helps with the performance of the TileList as well, because it can rely on each item being a specific height and width instead of trying to calculate varying heights and widths.) Now when you run the application, the Tile View tab will display a nice tiled list of thumbnails. But, clicking the thumbnails won't do anything yet.

Syncing Two Lists

You can make the TileList set the larger Image control's source in a couple of ways. One option is to use `<mx:Binding/>` tags to create a multisource binding for the large Image control. Doing this, you could bind the Image to both list controls—then when either the **photosList** or **photosTileList** has a selection change, the Image will update itself. However, this isn't the best scenario, because when someone switches between the two views, each list might have a different selection. For example, if you clicked the third item in the TileList and that image loaded and then switched to List View, that list might have a different item selected. In other words, the two lists would be out of sync.

Instead of binding the large Image control to both lists, you can just leave it bound to the **photosList**. To sync the two lists, you can add an event listener to each of them for a **change** event. For the TileList, you tell it to update the List whenever the TileList changes, and you tell the List to change the TileList whenever the List changes. Now, when the TileList's selection changes, it will cause the other List to mimic that selection, and that will in turn cause the Image control to update its **source**.

NOTE

You should be able to simply bind the TileList's **selectedIndex** *to the List's* **selectedIndex**, *and vice versa, creating a two-way binding. However, doing so can create a recursion problem, causing your application's performance to degrade substantially.*

However, this method has one limitation because of the way navigator containers create their children. To make the application initialize more quickly, all views are not created all at once. That is to say, in the case of your two tabs, only the first tab's content is actually initialized at application startup, while the other tab's content isn't created until you navigate to that view. (This may seem unnecessary for your set of two views, but for an application with, say, 10 different views, the initial startup would be degraded without this feature.) For this application, this means the selections won't sync properly until the second view is initialized (by the person selecting that view). This is because the first list's **change** event would fire and attempt to update the TileList, but since the TileList isn't yet created, nothing would happen.

To get around this problem, navigator containers have a property that lets you modify when different views get created. The property is called creationPolicy, because it is a guideline set up to control the creation of controls. This property can accept one of four values: **all**, **auto**, **queued**, or **none**. The default is **auto**, which does as explained earlier, only creating the initial views. Setting **creationPolicy** to **all** creates all views at once, while setting it to **queued** creates all child containers and then the child containers' children in a sequence. The policy **none** simply prevents any views from being created—this is an advanced policy, requiring the developer to initialize views themselves. To fix the problem at hand, set the **creationPolicy** property of the TabNavigator to **all**. This makes sure both views are ready at startup and the selections sync as expected.

NOTE

The default creation policy setting of **auto** *is generally your best bet for performance reasons, as it creates its views as necessary.*

Your final application's code should look like the following code and may look like Figure 11-7:

```
<mx:Application xmlns:mx="http://www.adobe.com/2006/mxml"
    layout="absolute"
    applicationComplete="service.send()">

    <mx:HTTPService id="service"
        url="photos.xml"
        resultFormat="e4x" />

    <mx:TabNavigator
        width="250"
        left="10"
        top="10"
        bottom="10"
        creationPolicy="all">
        <mx:Canvas
            label="List View"
            width="100%"
            height="100%">
            <mx:List id="photosList"
                dataProvider="{service.lastResult.photo}"
                width="100%"
                height="100%"
                labelField="@title"
                change="photosTileList.selectedIndex=photosList.
                    selectedIndex"/>
        </mx:Canvas>

        <mx:Canvas
            label="Tile View"
            width="100%"
            height="100%">
            <mx:TileList id="photosTileList"
                dataProvider="{service.lastResult.photo}"
                width="100%"
                height="100%"
                change="photosList.selectedIndex=photosTileList.
                    selectedIndex" >
                <mx:itemRenderer>
                    <mx:Component>
                        <mx:Image
                            horizontalAlign="center"
                            source="{data.@thumb}"
                            toolTip="{data.@title}"
```

```
                                          width="100"
                                          height="60" />
                              </mx:Component>
                          </mx:itemRenderer>
                     </mx:TileList>
                </mx:Canvas>

        </mx:TabNavigator>

        <mx:Image id="image"
            source="{photosList.selectedItem.@image}"
            left="270"
            top="10"
            bottom="10"
            right="10"
            horizontalAlign="center"
            open="progressBar.visible = true"
            complete="progressBar.visible = false"/>

        <mx:ProgressBar id="progressBar"
            x="270"
            y="10"
            source="{image}"
            visible="false" />

    </mx:Application>
```

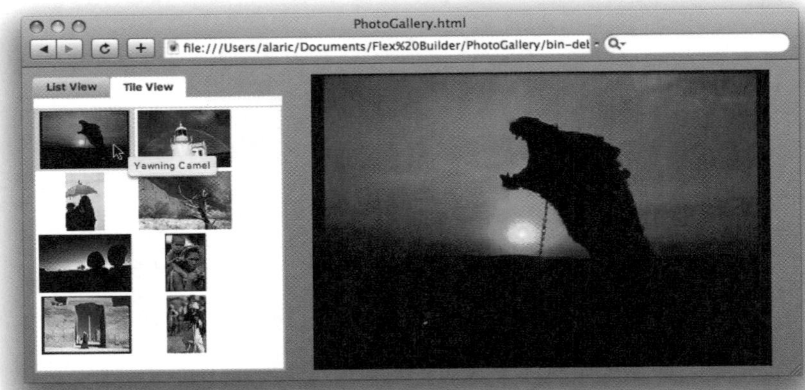

Figure 11-7. The photo gallery application in Tile View

Now that you've successfully created a simple photo gallery and learned about navigator containers, feel free to modify the application to try the different types of navigation controls and containers. For instance, try changing the tag from `<mx:TabNavigator/>` to `<mx:Accordion/>` and see how it looks. The Accordion component stacks its children vertically and is useful for multisection forms, because it can give people a sense of sequence and order—think of a checkout form where you have to enter shipping information and then enter your payment information. The Accordion also has a nice default effect when changing views. You'll learn how to easily add your own effects like this to other navigator containers in Chapter 13.

Using the Back Button: History Management

By default, the TabNavigator has a cool feature that just screams RIA: the ability to use the browser's back button. Actually, it can use the browser's forward button as well. The point is it can work with the browser's history. When you select, for instance, the second tab in the **PhotoGallery** application, notice that your browser's back button, when clicked, will change the view back to the first tab, as you can see in the sequence of screens in Figure 11-8. This is because this component is talking with JavaScript in the browser, letting it manipulate the function of the forward and back buttons. You might have noticed a history folder, containing some JavaScript and other files, in the bin-debug folder of your Flex applications. This folder contains the necessary files to allow history management to work.

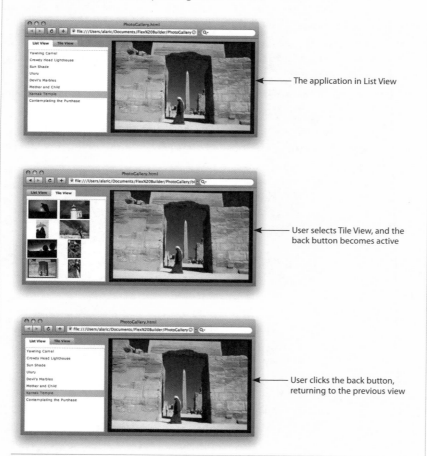

Figure 11-8. Using the back button to change the selected view

This is a useful feature, especially when working with rich forms or other applications, because it lets people do what they've learned they could do from experience with web pages. You can change this functionality via the **historyManagementEnabled** property of navigator containers. It's turned on by default with the TabNavigator and Accordion containers but is off by default with the ViewStack container.

In addition, you can use the class **mx.managers.BrowserManager** to provide custom history management for other controls—or any purpose, really. This requires some advanced scripting, so if you're interested, consult the Flex documentation.

Summary

In this chapter, you discovered how easy it is to structure your application by providing a set of user-selectable views. This lets you use your screen real estate in the most effective way. It can really help with organizing different parts of an application, such as rich forms or a dialog box with many options, because it prevents people from being overwhelmed. It also prevents having everything visible at once, which may cause the application to require scroll bars.

You used new navigation components to create customized views of a photo gallery application, providing both a simple text list and a tiled list of thumbnails to help people select their image. You also discovered how to load images from a local file or from the web and even found a way to monitor loading progress. This chapter also reaffirmed some important concepts, like using item renderers and loading external data, with an application that you can customize with your own photos.

While controlling visibility and using navigation controls is very powerful, there's another way to organize the views of your application that makes fluid interfaces very easy to implement called view states. In the following chapter, you'll see just how powerful Flex can be.

WORKING WITH VIEW STATES

View states are among the most powerful features for building a dynamic, flexible user interface. They allow you to specify different arrangements of your application at a specific time for a specific purpose. Consider a web application that has both a login page and a user preferences page—you can think of these two pages as the HTML equivalent of view states in Flex.

States provide a way to group a set of changes to the UI into understandable chunks—essentially, a *state* is a collection of changes to properties, styles, or behaviors of a component. While a developer could do this through sets of functions that make a batch of changes to the UI, the MXML that Flex states use is much more readable and easier to write—and with Flex Builder, it can all be created in a natural, visual way.

Scenarios for States

Think about the search application you built in Chapter 8. In that example, the person using your application sees a results list and a search field when they load the application. That's all fine and good, but it doesn't make sense to show a results list until there are actual results to view.

Of course, you could set the results list to initially invisible and then set it back to visible once there are results. However, you might want more changes to occur in the UI when results appear. For instance, it would be nice if when the application starts, the search fields are large and are the only user interface elements showing. To help direct the person using your application, it would make the most sense if the search fields appeared in the center of the application instead of on the top, drawing even more attention to themselves (see Figure 12-1). Then, once someone submits a search, the search fields can move to the top, making room for the list of results (see Figure 12-2). Not only would this scenario look cool and dynamic, but it would help guide people through the application, showing them only what is necessary at any given time.

Figure 12-1. The Search application in its initial state, showing only the search fields

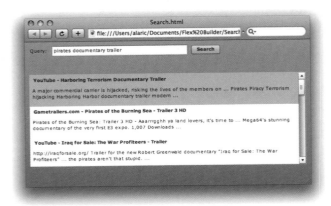

Figure 12-2. The Search application in an additional state; the search fields decrease in size and move to the top, while a list of results is added

States vs. Navigator Containers

States provide more flexibility than navigator containers in most cases. This is because, with states, different components can be reused between the states. That is to say, a Button control in one state can continue to exist in another state, just perhaps with modified properties. In fact, that same Button could even appear in a different part of the application, such as being moved from a Panel into a Form container. For navigator containers, you would have to re-create a different Button if you wanted it to appear in two different views.

You can also use states to build upon one another in a way that navigator containers cannot. Because of the way in which one state can be based upon another, you can provide your application with a cascading set of views, each dependent upon the other. For ViewStacks or other navigator containers, each view must be independent of the others.

However, this isn't to say that view states are always the right choice. As we have seen, ViewStacks, TabNavigators, and navigation controls have their uses. They're great for when part of the application needs to be structured into separate, independent parts. Also, navigation controls and the TabNavigator's tabbed interface provide easy and automatic switching between views, which would be more complicated to implement in states.

I'll start by explaining states hands-on, using Flex Builder's Design mode, and then I'll show you how to integrate this powerful functionality into your own applications. If you want to follow along, create a new project. In this example, you'll make an application with two states, one with a Button on the left of the screen and another with it placed on the right.

Figure 12-3. Creating a new state in the States panel

Creating New States

First, simply place a Button control on the stage on the left part of your application. Then, you'll use the States panel to create a new state. If the States panel isn't visible, you can show it by selecting Window→States. In the States panel, you'll see what is called a *base* state. All applications are considered to have a least one state, which is their base state. You can create a new state based upon this base state by clicking the first button in the States panel's toolbar, as shown in Figure 12-3.

Clicking the New State button prompts you with a dialog box asking for information about the new state, as shown in Figure 12-4. You can give the state any name you want, but it's best—as always—to be as descriptive as possible. For this simple example, just call the state stageRight because all this state will do is move a Button to the right.

Figure 12-4. The New State dialog box

Modifying State Properties, Styles, and Events

Now that you've created a new state, that new state will be selected in the States panel. This is your cue that whatever you modify in Design mode will be applied to this new state. Now you can simply drag the Button to the right of the stage. Once you've done that, switch between the two different states (the base state and this new stageRight state) in the States panel. You'll see that Design mode updates and shows the Button in its original location in the base state and moved to the right in the stageRight state. Note that you can also switch between different states using the States drop-down list in the Design mode toolbar (Figure 12-5).

State drop-down list

Figure 12-5. The Design mode State drop-down list

In the background, Design mode is generating some special MXML code for you. Every Flex application (and component, as you'll see later in the book) has a **states** property. This is its list of potential states, which are specified by the **<mx:State/>** tag. That tag takes a **name** property, which is the name of that particular state. Within that tag are a few different types of tags, each corresponding to different kinds of changes. Check out the code that might be created for this simple two-state example:

```
<mx:Application xmlns:mx="http://www.adobe.com/2006/mxml"
    layout="absolute">

    <mx:states>

        <mx:State name="stageRight">
            <mx:SetProperty
                target="{button1}"
                name="x"
                value="570"/>
        </mx:State>

    </mx:states>

    <mx:Button id="button1"
        x="10"
        y="10"
```

```
        label="Click to move"
        click="currentState='stageRight'"/>

    </mx:Application>
```

Notice the typical Button component near the bottom of the code—you can think of this as the component in its base state. Then within a **<mx:states> </mx:states>** tag, there's a single **<mx:State/>** tag with a name of **"stageRight"**. Within this tag are the actual changes that will occur. In this example, the change is a property change, modifying the Button's **x** property from its original 10 to a larger 570. This happens through the **<mx:SetProperty/>** tag, which takes three properties: a **target**, which is the **id** of the component that will be changed; a **name** property, which is the name of the property to change; and a **value** property, which is the new value it will have in this state.

NOTE

By default, the **currentState** *of an application is set to an empty String,* **""**, *and you can always switch back to the base state by setting* **currentState=""**.

To switch states, you use the **currentState** property of the application. In this case, the Button will change the application to the stageRight state when the Button is clicked.

Of course, different types of changes can occur in states other than simply modifying a component's properties. You can also set style properties and even change event listeners for a component. Take, for example, the old colored boxes routine from Chapter 8. The following code creates a single Canvas container with an initial background color of red. Then, two additional states are created called green and blue, which set the Canvas's **backgroundColor** to green and blue, respectively.

```
    <mx:Application xmlns:mx="http://www.adobe.com/2006/mxml"
        layout="absolute">

    <mx:states>

        <mx:State name="green">
            <mx:SetStyle
                target="{canvas}"
                name="backgroundColor"
                value="#00FF00"/>

        </mx:State>

        <mx:State name="blue">
            <mx:SetStyle
                target="{canvas}"
                name="backgroundColor"
                value="#0000FF"/>
        </mx:State>

    </mx:states>


    <mx:Canvas id="canvas"
        width="200"
        height="200"
        backgroundColor="#FF0000"/>

    </mx:Application>
```

Because a style property is different from a regular property, it requires the use of a `<mx:SetStyle/>` tag instead of a `<mx:SetProperty/>` tag. Besides this, however, its usage is the same.

For setting event handlers, one more type of tag exists, aptly named `<mx:SetEventHandler/>`. This is almost the same as the other two tags, except it takes a **handler** property instead of a **value** property. For the previous example that moved a Button to the right, you could change the **click** handler in the stageRight state so that clicking it returns the application to the base state.

```
<mx:Application xmlns:mx="http://www.adobe.com/2006/mxml"
    layout="absolute">

    <mx:states>
        <mx:State name="stageRight">

            <mx:SetProperty
                target="{button1}"
                name="x"
                value="570"/>

            <mx:SetEventHandler
                target="{button1}"
                name="click"
                handler=" currentState='' "/>

        </mx:State>
    </mx:states>

    <mx:Button id="button1"
        x="10"
        y="10"
        label="Click to move"
        click="currentState='stageRight'"/>

</mx:Application>
```

In this code, you'll now see a second child tag of the stageRight state that sets the **click** handler of the Button, making it return to the base state.

> **NOTE**
>
> *If you're using Flex Builder's Design mode, you may never have to write your own state code. Using the States panel, all the hard work is done for you. However, it always helps to understand what the code is doing in case you need to tweak it.*

Adding Components

You can also add or remove components within states. This means you can rework entire chunks of your application with simple MXML. Consider the example of a login form, common to many web applications. You may have often encountered a form on a website that asks for your username and password. However, if you don't have a username and password for that site, you might click a link taking you to a different page—a registration page. And on that registration page, you'll be prompted for information such as your full name—and of course your choice of username and password. Wouldn't it be nice if you could stay on the same page with the extra fields popping up as needed? I'll show you how in the following example, which you can see working in Figure 12-6.

Figure 12-6. A login form in its original state

This first bit of code shows a Form container inside a Panel, populated with a username field and a password field. This is pretty standard stuff for you. See Figure 12-6 for how this looks.

```
<mx:Application xmlns:mx="http://www.adobe.com/2006/mxml"
    verticalAlign="middle">

    <mx:Panel id="loginPanel"
        title="Returning Users Sign In"
        horizontalAlign="right"
        paddingLeft="5"
        paddingRight="5"
        paddingTop="5"
        paddingBottom="5">

        <mx:Form id="loginForm">
            <mx:FormItem id="usernameFormItem"
                label="Username:" >
                <mx:TextInput/>
            </mx:FormItem>

            <mx:FormItem id="passwordFormItem"
                label="Password:" >
                <mx:TextInput
                    displayAsPassword="true"/>
            </mx:FormItem>
        </mx:Form>

        <mx:Button id="submitButton"
            label="Sign in"/>

        <mx:ControlBar
            horizontalAlign="right">

            <!-- This LinkButton will change the state when clicked -->
            <mx:LinkButton id="registerLink"
```

```
            label="Don't have an account yet?"
            color="#1B337B"
            click="currentState='registration'" />

        </mx:ControlBar>

    </mx:Panel>

</mx:Application>
```

However, you could then create a "registration" state, adding a couple of fields to the Form and changing a few properties to reflect this registration state. That would allow you to reuse existing components, building upon the UI in subsequent states. You could add the following code to the application, creating this additional state with extra fields, as seen in Figure 12-7.

```
<mx:states>

    <mx:State name="registration">
        <!-- Set properties on the Panel container -->
        <mx:SetProperty
            target="{loginPanel}"
            name="title"
            value="New User Registration"/>

        <!-- Set properties on the Button -->
        <mx:SetProperty
            target="{submitButton}"
            name="label"
            value="Register"/>

        <!-- Modify the LinkButton control's label -->
        <mx:SetProperty
            target="{registerLink}"
            name="label"
            value="Already have an account with us?"/>

        <!-- Modify the LinkButton to change back to the sign in
             form -->
        <mx:SetEventHandler
            target="{registerLink}"
            name="click"
            handler="currentState=''"/>

        <!-- Add a Full Name field to the Form -->
        <mx:AddChild
            relativeTo="{loginForm}"
            position="firstChild">
            <mx:FormItem id="fullNameFormItem"
                label="Full Name:">
            <mx:TextInput/>
            </mx:FormItem>
        </mx:AddChild>

        <!-- Add a password confirmation field to the Form -->
        <mx:AddChild
            relativeTo="{loginForm}"
            position="lastChild">
            <mx:FormItem id="confirmPasswordFormItem"
```

```
                                    label="Confirm Password:">
                          <mx:TextInput
                              displayAsPassword="true"/>
                          </mx:FormItem>
                      </mx:AddChild>

                  </mx:State>

              </mx:states>
```

The first four nodes of the **<mx:State/>** tag in the code change properties of the application, but the final two are different. They are **<mx:AddChild/>** tags, and they're used to add components.

The **<mx:AddChild/>** tag simply takes as child tags the regular old MXML you're used to using. It also takes a couple of important properties that tell it where to place the new component. The property **relativeTo** takes an instance of another existing component. In the previous example, **relativeTo** is set to the **loginForm** through the use of curly braces. The other property is **position**, which stipulates where to place the new component in relation to the component specified by the **relativeTo** property.

In the example above, **position** is set to **firstChild** for the **fullNameFormItem** component; this means that the added component should be made as the first child of the container **loginForm**, meaning it is at the bottom of the display list of that container, and the first item created within it. For **confirmPasswordFormItem**, its **position** is set to **lastChild**, meaning it will be created as the last child of the **loginForm** container. (Other possible values are **before** and **after**, and these let you create a component relative to a sibling component instead of a parent—either right *before* it on the display list or right *after* it.)

Figure 12-7. A login form in an additional state, with two new fields, a different title for the Panel, and a different label for the Button

Putting States to the Test

Now that you understand a few things about states, you can take advantage of them in your projects.

The Search Application

Return to the **Search** application you created in Chapter 10. Open that project so you can make a few changes to the UI to take advantage of states, like I mentioned earlier in this chapter. While it would be great to have planned the application around states and to have developed it with them in mind, you won't have to rebuild it from scratch. You'll want your initial state to have only a search field, which means the results list shouldn't be there. But it's already there in the base state. Luckily, you can take advantage of the ability to both add and remove components via states, and I'll show you how.

Removing components

Open the main application (*Search.mxml*) in Design mode, and add a new state called search. You're going to be working backward in a sense, because the "results" state will actually be the base state you've already created—the application as is. Making sure you've selected this search state, you can now select and then delete the **resultsList** List control. Don't worry, it's still there in the base state—you can switch back, and you'll see it. You're just removing it in the search state, because you don't want it taking up space when it's not populated with anything. Now, since your application has all this free space, you can adjust the placement of the search fields, putting them more in the center. Using constraints, you can set the **horizontalCenter** and **verticalCenter** style properties of the HBox, letting it place itself in the center of the application. You may also want to change the font size of the fields, making them more prominent and easier to read. The code that Design mode generates for the states may look like this:

```
<mx:states>
    <mx:State name="search">
        <mx:RemoveChild
            target="{resultsList}"/>
        <mx:SetProperty
            target="{hbox1}"
            name="x"/>
        <mx:SetProperty
            target="{hbox1}"
            name="y"/>
        <mx:SetStyle
            target="{hbox1}"
            name="horizontalCenter"
            value="0"/>
        <mx:SetStyle
            target="{hbox1}"
            name="verticalCenter"
            value="-30"/>
        <mx:SetStyle
```

```
                                             target="{hbox1}"
                                             name="fontSize"
                                             value="18"/>
                            </mx:State>
```

NOTE

If you want to find and replace the **hbox1** *id and all references to it in your code, you can use the Find and Replace feature of Flex Builder. Select Edit→Find/ Replace to open a Find/Replace dialog box, where you can easily search for and replace text. Especially useful is that the text you have selected in your code when you invoke this dialog box will automatically populate the Find field in the dialog box.*

Note the tag **<mx:RemoveChild/>**. This tag takes a target (the results list in this case) and removes it. In the previous examples, you were always adding components, but in this example, because the base state contains a results list that you don't want, you simply remove it with this tag. Also notice a few properties and styles are set on a component called **hbox1**. This is actually the HBox that contains the search field and search Button. An **id** wasn't set on it, so Flex Builder generated one so it could reference the instance in the state's code. (It's not a particularly descriptive name, so that's another reason to always give your components an **id**.) Because you want to place the HBox in the center of the application, it makes sense that the **horizontalCenter** and **verticalCenter** styles are set here. However, you may notice that the first two **<mx:SetProperty/>** tags contain a **target** property and a **name** property, but not a value. This is because they aren't setting new values but instead actually removing that property from the component. (In ActionScript, the equivalent would be setting the properties to **null**.)

Setting the initial state

Now you've created this new state, but if you run the application, it will of course remain in the base state, which contains the results list and the previous layout. In this case, you want to set the initial state of your application to something other than the base state. To do so, double-click the search state in the States panel. This opens the Edit State Properties dialog box, which looks a lot like the New State dialog box. In this dialog box, you'll see a "Set as start state" checkbox. Checking this box sets the search state to the initial state when the application runs. What it actually does is set the **currentState** attribute on the **<mx:Application/>** tag.

The final task you'll want to do is to set the **currentState** back to the base state, showing the results list, once you have results to display. One way to do this would be by adding a **click** event handler to the search Button. Another, better way would be to listen for the **result** event of the **searchService**:

```
<yahoo:SearchService id="searchService"
    query="{queryTextInput.text}"
    result="currentState = ''" />
```

Now, when the **searchService** component gets a result, it fires the **result** event, which sets the application back to its base state. The full code for the **Search** application follows, and the results should look like Figures 12-1 and 12-2.

```
<mx:Application
    xmlns:mx="http://www.adobe.com/2006/mxml"
    xmlns:yahoo="http://www.yahoo.com/astra/2006/mxml"
    layout="absolute"
    currentState="search">
```

```
<mx:states>
    <mx:State name="search">
        <mx:RemoveChild
            target="{resultsList}"/>
        <mx:SetProperty
            target="{hbox1}"
            name="x"/>
        <mx:SetProperty
            target="{hbox1}"
            name="y"/>
        <mx:SetStyle
            target="{hbox1}"
            name="horizontalCenter"
            value="0"/>
        <mx:SetStyle
            target="{hbox1}"
            name="verticalCenter"
            value="-30"/>
        <mx:SetStyle
            target="{hbox1}"
            name="fontSize"
            value="18"/>
    </mx:State>
</mx:states>

<yahoo:SearchService id="searchService"
    query="{queryTextInput.text}"
    result="currentState = ''" />

<mx:HBox id="hbox1"
    verticalAlign="middle"
    defaultButton="{searchButton}"
    y="10"
    x="10" >

    <mx:FormItem
        label="Query:">
        <mx:TextInput id="queryTextInput"/>
    </mx:FormItem>

    <mx:Button id="searchButton"
        label="Search"
        click="searchService.send()"/>

</mx:HBox>

<!-- The results as a List -->
<mx:List id="resultsList"
    dataProvider="{searchService.lastResult}"
    left="10"
    right="10"
    top="74"
    bottom="10"
    variableRowHeight="true">

    <mx:itemRenderer>
        <mx:Component>
            <mx:VBox
                width="100%" >
                <mx:Label
```

```
                    text="{data.name}"
                    fontWeight="bold"/>
                <mx:Text
                    width="100%"
                    text="{data.summary}"/>
            </mx:VBox>
        </mx:Component>
    </mx:itemRenderer>

    </mx:List>
</mx:Application>
```

The ContactManager Application

To really understand how powerful states can be, let's return to the tried-and-true **ContactManager** application you last worked on in Chapter 10. As it currently stands, you'll see a list of contacts, the read-only view of the contact details (the Contact Details panel), and an editable view of the contact details (the Contact Editor panel). Obviously, this could stand to be enhanced, and states are the way to go.

For this application, consider two possible states:

- A read-only view of the contact details, shown when a contact is selected

- An editable view of the contact details, shown when someone edits a contact

You could implement this by creating a couple of states in the **ContactManager** application. However, you can create these states in another way—not in the application itself but in a custom component. In the following pages, you'll learn how to modularize this application by creating your first component. While it may sound difficult, it's really easy using MXML.

Making the application modular

Creating a component can be as simple as placing your current MXML code into a separate file. In Flex, it's easy to create *composite components*, which just means you're creating one component by mixing others together. This is typically done by creating a separate *.mxml* file, using a container, and placing the desired components within it. Then you reference this component in your main application using an MXML tag, just like the default Flex components you're used to using or the Yahoo! Search component you've used in the **Search** application.

If you look at it one way, the Contact Details panel and the Contact Editor form are almost the same, but one uses Labels to just display the information, while the other uses TextInput and other controls to let you manipulate the information. It might have occurred to you that they could just be two different views of the same data. To do this, you could create a component called ContactViewer that will have two states, a base state and an edit state.

To create a component in Flex Builder, you can use the New MXML Component dialog box. So, to start creating your custom component, select your project in the Flex Navigator and then select File→New→MXML Component. This opens the dialog box shown in Figure 12-8.

Figure 12-8. The New MXML Component dialog box

Here you can give the component a descriptive filename and choose what the component is based on. The filename will actually be the name of the component—and therefore the name of the MXML tag you'll use in your application—so it can't contain any spaces or start with anything other than a letter. Like all components, it's good to use *camel case*, which means separating words using an initial capital letter (presumably like the humps of a camel), and starting the name with a capital letter.

The component it's "based on" means the other component that this will *extend*, or inherit the properties and methods of another component and build upon them. When creating custom MXML components, you'll typically extend another visual component, adding features to it. It's usually a container, because containers let you easily add controls to them and provide a simple way to encapsulate functionality. Your component's name should be ContactViewer, and the component it should be based on is Panel.

Once you create the file, you should see it open in either Design mode or Source mode, and the code should be as follows:

```
<?xml version="1.0" encoding="utf-8"?>
<mx:Panel xmlns:mx="http://www.adobe.com/2006/mxml"
    layout="verical"
    width="400"
    height="300">
</mx:Panel>
```

Notice the namespace that is placed here, just as it is for the `<mx:Application/>` tag. That's a necessary part of making this a component. Now whatever you place inside this tag will be part of the component. That's what you'll be doing next: cutting and pasting some of the code from your `ContactManager` application and placing it in here.

Cutting and pasting code

First, go to the `ContactManager` application and, while in Source mode, select the contents of the Contact Details panel. In other words, select everything between the opening and closing `<mx:Panel></mx:Panel>` tags. Then, select Edit→Cut to cut this code. Next, you will paste it inside the new ContactViewer component. So, switch to ContactViewer, and in Source mode paste this code in the component (Edit→Paste) between the opening and closing `<mx:Panel>` `</mx:Panel>` tags.

You'll also want to copy any attributes you've placed on the Contact Details panel and place them on the new ContactView component. However, you won't want to place the `id` attribute. That's because an MXML component cannot have an `id` placed within its definition. An `id` is something you give to a specific reference to a component, not within the definition.

Now you have the UI for the base state of this ContactViewer component. Next, create a new state within it called edit. Then, while in this new state in Design mode, delete the contents of the component—all the controls inside it will be deleted. This will remove all of these "read-only" components from the edit state, though they'll still exist in the base state. You'll replace them with the Form from the Contact Details panel in the `ContactManager` application. Simply cut and paste this Form into the empty ContactViewer Panel in its edit state. The easiest way is to select the Form while in Design mode in your main application and cut it from there. Then, in Design mode in the ContactViewer component, simply paste it. Alternatively, you could cut the code in Source view, add your own `<mx:AddChild/>` tag, and paste it within this tag.

After that, change the title of the Panel from Contact Details to Contact Editor in the edit state. Now you'll have the two modes you need, all within a single component.

However, you have to do a bit more to make this work. You'll notice that the new component has references to properties of the `contactsDataGrid`, as well as references to functions that don't exist in this component. Though it's in the same project, it doesn't actually know anything about any of the code in the `ContactManager` application. So, you'll have to do two things: give it the code it needs to work, and pass it the information it needs to display. I'll focus on the former now, and once I show you a new trick, I'll return to the latter.

First, cut the entire `<mx:Script/>` tag from the `ContactManager` application and all the ActionScript code within it. Then paste this into the ContactViewer component, right after the opening `<mx:Panel/>` tag. Just like an Application, an MXML component can have an `<mx:Script/>` tag and ActionScript code. Because this code is all for validation and data massaging, it makes sense to have it encapsulated within this component and not in the main application.

Creating component properties

Now, you'll want to create a variable in the ContactViewer component called **contact** and make it of type Object. You can create it in ActionScript or with an `<mx:Object/>` tag. It will need to be bindable, so if you use ActionScript, be sure to place a `[Bindable]` metadata tag above the variable declaration (as discussed in Chapter 7). This creates a property on the ContactViewer component called **contact**. This **contact** property will be the data for this component, and you will pass it the **selectedItem** of the **contactsDataGrid** in the main application in a moment. First, however, replace all references to **contactsDataGrid.selectedItem** with this **contact** property. For instance, you would want to replace this:

```
<mx:Label id="emailLabel"
    text="Email: {contactsDataGrid.selectedItem.email}"/>
```

with this:

```
<mx:Label id="emailLabel"
    text="Email: {contact.email}"/>
```

An easy way to do this is by using Find and Replace (Edit→Find/Replace). After replacing these references, save the component, and make sure there aren't any errors. If there are, it should be easy to find out what is wrong and fix the problem. It may be that you forgot to close a tag or you pasted the code in the wrong place. Flex Builder has great error checking and will usually give you a detailed explanation of what it thinks is wrong.

Using custom components

After saving your new component, it's now time to put it to use. In the **ContactManager** application, remove any references to Contact Editor or Contact Details. Then, add your new ContactViewer component. You can do this easily in Design mode by using the Components panel. At the very top of this panel you'll see a Custom item, as shown in Figure 12-9. This is where your custom components for this project are placed. Under this item you should see your ContactViewer component. You can drag and drop it onto the application, just like any other component.

Organizing custom components with packages

Once you've placed the custom component in your application in Design mode, check out the code created by switching back to Source mode. You'll probably see something like this:

```
<ns1:ContactViewer
    x="318"
    y="10">
</ns1:ContactViewer>
```

NOTE

While you can't do so in a component in an application, you can place `<mx:Script/>` *tags in a custom component's source file. This is how you give your custom component scripting functionality.*

NOTE

While it's frustrating if you save the ContactViewer component and see all the errors that occur, it's a good thing to make this component free from any references to a specific application. Having accomplished this bit of work, you can even reuse it in other applications without worry.

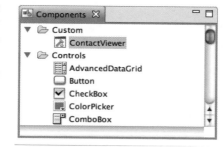

Figure 12-9. A custom component in the Components panel

That's your component, in its own namespace, **ns1**. Because your component isn't part of the Flex SDK (it's just using it and extending it), it needs its own namespace to distinguish itself. Flex Builder adds this automatically for you—look back at the `<mx:Application/>` tag to see the namespace definition that was added to it:

```
xmlns:ns1="*"
```

This means, "Create a namespace named **ns1** and make it point to the application's source directory." The asterisk (*) character means the namespace is referring to everything in the current project directory.

You might find the name of the namespace to be a bit vague. As usual, Flex Builder will name things for you with an index-based name, as in **ns1**, **ns2**, **ns3**, and so on. You can easily change this (as discussed in Chapter 4), and you'll do that in a moment.

The standard practice is to place components into a folder or subfolder to organize them. Up until now you've placed your component without any organization for the sake of brevity, but it's usually best to organize them. This is because as you continue developing in Flex, you'll probably find yourself creating a number of components, and organization is key as your library grows. Placing your components in different *packages*, or folders and subfolders, based on what they do, is a great way to accomplish this. For instance, you may have a few controls that you've created and want to place them in a folder called controls; you may also have created some layout container components and might place them in a folder called containers. This helps you differentiate various components based on what they do.

The standard naming scheme for packages is using what is called *reverse domain* naming. A domain is something like *adobe.com* or *oreilly.com*, so a reverse domain would be *com.adobe* or *com.oreilly*. Say you work at O'Reilly, and you created a new Flex control. You could place that control in the com.oreilly.controls package. What this actually means is that you would place your component in a directory with the structure com/oreilly/controls. If you have a website, you can use your domain name for your package structure. If you don't, you can simply use your name or nickname to create the package.

Placing components in particular folder is called *packaging* because it groups related components, like the way you might package similar items in boxes when you're moving into a new home. You could label your boxes "dishes" or "toys" so that you know what they contain at a glance. The same works for components—keeping them organized by their types lets you quickly know how they're used. Also, as mentioned, organizing your code like this prevents naming collisions, letting you more freely name your components without worrying that a name is already taken by another component. This is because a component's package can become its namespace. If you create a component called Button, placing it in a package will distinguish it from the default Flex Button when you use it in your code.

To understand this, you'll create a package for your ContactViewer component. This is really easy to do. First, you can just remove the `<ns1:ContactViewer/>` tag from your application and remove its namespace declaration from the `<mx:Application/>` tag, because you'll be replacing them.

Next, you'll need to create the package by creating an empty set of folders in your project. Go to the Flex Navigator panel, and select your **ContactManager** project's source folder (ContactManager/src). Then select File→New→Folder to create the folders. You're free to create any package structure you desire, but for this example you could use the structure com/oreilly/view, because the component is used as a way to view part of the application. While you can create one folder at a time, the New Folder dialog box lets you create a hierarchical structure of folders by entering a path with folders separated by forward slashes (/). So, the easiest way is to enter **com/oreilly/view** in the Folder name field and click Finish (see Figure 12-10).

NOTE

If you've just placed the component in Design mode, you can probably undo the addition of both the component tag and the namespace declaration by selecting Edit→Undo.

NOTE

It's best to keep package names in lowercase, as this is a commonly accepted standard. Because class names are typically capitalized, keeping package names in lowercase helps to distinguish them. Also, be sure not to use any special characters in the package names, because these are not allowed.

Figure 12-10. The New Folder dialog box

Once the folders are created, making your ContactViewer component part of the com.oreilly.view package is as easy as dragging and dropping it into the view folder.

Alternatively, you can create the folders using your operating system's file system, such as Windows Explorer or Mac's Finder. Navigate to where your projects files are stored, which is usually /Users/yourusername/Documents/ Flex Builder 3/ on a Mac and C:\Documents and Settings\yourusername\ My Documents\Flex Builder 3\ in Windows. From there, you can add folders. Once you return to Flex Builder, the new folders should show automatically. If they don't, you can select your project in the Flex Navigator and select File→Refresh to refresh the folder list.

Figure 12-11. The package structure of a custom component

Figure 12-11 shows the way your project's folders should be structured, with the ContactViewer component placed in the new package.

Now that you have the component in its new location, you can drag the new version onto your application in Design mode, just like you did by using the Components panel. Switching to Source mode to view the code, the new namespace created in the **<mx:Application/>** tag now looks like this:

```
xmlns:ns1="com.oreilly.view.*"
```

Previously the ContactViewer component was in the base directory (*), it's now located under this new namespace. You might want to give the namespace a more descriptive name, such as view:

```
xmlns:view="com.oreilly.view.*"
```

Of course, if you change the name of the namespace, you'll need to update it for the component's tag as well:

```
<view:ContactViewer
    x="318"
    y="10">
</view:ContactViewer>
```

Getting to the Source (Files)

You might have wondered why your custom components get placed in a namespace like **com.oreilly.view**, while the default Flex components have a namespace like **http://www.adobe.com/2006/mxml**. Adobe does this when it distributes the Flex components by bundling them into a *.swc* file through a special process.

Actually, all Flex components are organized into packages. You can see this by viewing the source for the components, which is located in a special directory on your file system. If you've installed Flex Builder, the source files for most of the Flex framework is shown as follows (assuming you've installed in the default locations):

- Mac: */Applications/Adobe Flex Builder 3/sdks/3.0.0/frameworks/projects/ framework/src/mx*

- Windows: *C:\Program Files\Adobe\Flex Builder 3\sdks\3.0.0\frameworks\projects\ framework\src\mx*

There you'll see a number of folders such as controls, core, effects, utils, and so on. Adobe's process creates a more complex namespace that actually aggregates these various packages. This is because a namespace isn't limited to a single package but can actually span multiple packages.

For general development, pointing a namespace to a single package is sufficient. If you find that you're creating a large library and want to create your own unique namespace for all your custom components, you can create your own SWC using a Flex Library project, which is a special type of project just for creating compiled libraries of custom components. The process requires the use of a file called *manifest.xml*, which stipulates each of your components and registers them with a namespace of your choice. To learn more about this advanced process, check the Flex documentation for *component libraries*.

Using custom component properties

Now that you have your component all packaged up, the next step is to hook it into the **selectedItem** of the **contactsDataGrid** so that it can become populated with contact data again. You'll be able to easily do this by setting its **contact** property with a binding:

```
<view:ContactViewer
    contact="{contactsDataGrid.selectedItem}"
    x="318"
    y="10">
</view:ContactViewer>
```

Now, whenever the **selectedItem** changes, that information will be passed to this **contact** object that you created, updating the view accordingly.

While you'll be able to see the different states of the ContactViewer by switching between them in Flex Builder's States panel, the application doesn't have a way to switch those states yet. Now you'll need to set up controls for allowing people to switch between the base state and the edit state at runtime.

To do so, you'll use a Button. First, however, add a new container called ControlBar to the bottom of the ContactViewer in its base state. ControlBar is a special container that works only with Panel (and TitleWindow, which is an extension of Panel). It attaches itself to the very bottom of the Panel, giving it a new look. The ControlBar container works essentially like an HBox, laying out controls in a horizontal fashion. It's just a nice way to add Buttons and other controls to the bottom of Panel, as it will automatically attach itself to the bottom of the Panel, and give it a rounded look. Now, within this ControlBar, place a single Button and give it the label "Edit." Also, give it an **id** of **editAndSaveButton**. (As you might notice from its **id**, this Button is going to be used for multiple purposes, changing its functionality based on the state.) Finally, set a **click** handler for the Button that changes the **currentState** to edit.

Next, switch to the edit state in Design mode and select this same Button. Change the label of the Button to "Save," and change its **click** handler to revert to the base state via the ActionScript **currentState=""**. This way, the person using your application will first see an Edit button; once clicked, the button will change the details panel to an edit panel. The Edit button will in turn change into a Save button that returns this component to its base state when clicked. (Note that the Save button does not actually save the changes to the contacts.)

As a final touch, you'll want to set the **contactsDataGrid** to have its first item selected. This is because right now the ContactViewer will display itself whether or not it has any contact data, and if it doesn't have any, it just displays an ugly blank panel. This is an easy one to fix, because you can just set the DataGrid's **selectedIndex** to **0**. Once the contact data loads and populates this grid, the initial item will be selected, and it will display in the ContactViewer.

NOTE

When using Flex Builder's Design mode for modifying view states, pay particular attention to which state you're working in. If you don't, you may inadvertently modify a property of a component within a different state than you had planned—and this could cause you a lot of frustration trying to trace down your error. For instance, if you were in the edit state when adding a Button, it would not be created in the base state—and because this is the Button that makes the application switch to the edit state, it would never show up when the application was run.

NOTE

The `contactsDataGrid.selectedItem` *property, which is an Object, can be evaluated to a Boolean (true/false) in a binding. The rules is: If the Object is* `null`, *convert to* `false`, *otherwise, convert to* `true`. *So, if the* `contactsDataGrid` *does not have a* `selectedItem` *set, that* `selectedItem` *is considered* `null` *and evaluates to* `false` *in the binding to the* `visible` *property.*

If you prefer not to have the first item in the DataGrid selected and instead prefer to hide the ContactViewer until someone selects an item, that's easy to accomplish as well. Simply set the ContactViewer's **visible** property to the **selectedItem** of the **contactsDataGrid**:

```
visible="{ contactsDataGrid.selectedItem }"
```

What this means is "If the **contactsDataGrid** has an item selected, set the **visible** property to **true**, otherwise make it **false**." This way, when the application loads, only the DataGrid of contacts will display. Upon selecting an item in the DataGrid, the contact details will appear. (Then, after clicking the Edit button, the Contact Editor will show up as usual.)

That's all there is to the core functionality of the **ContactManager** application, as you can see in Figure 12-12 and Figure 12-13. Now, the complete code for the ContactsViewer component is a bit large, so you'll want to check out the source code by downloading it from the companion site. Because most of the logic of this application is now in the ContactViewer component, the main application is now very small:

```
<mx:Application
    xmlns:mx="http://www.adobe.com/2006/mxml"
    xmlns:view="com.oreilly.view.*"
    layout="absolute"
    applicationComplete="contactsService.send()" >

    <mx:HTTPService id="contactsService"
        resultFormat="e4x"
        url="contacts.xml" />

    <mx:DataGrid id="contactsDataGrid"
        dataProvider="{contactsService.lastResult.contact}"
        selectedIndex="0"
        left="10"
        top="10"
        bottom="10"
        width="300">
        <mx:columns>
            <mx:DataGridColumn headerText="First"
                dataField="firstName"/>
            <mx:DataGridColumn headerText="Last" dataField="lastName"/>
        </mx:columns>
    </mx:DataGrid>

    <view:ContactViewer
        contact="{contactsDataGrid.selectedItem}"
        x="318" y="10">
    </view:ContactViewer>

</mx:Application>
```

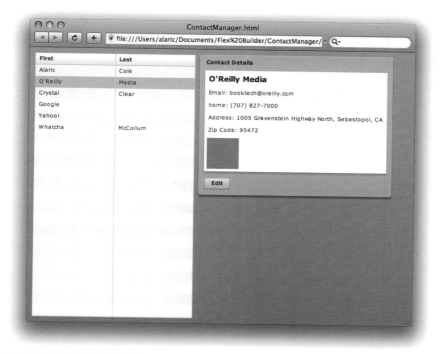

Figure 12-12. The ContactManager *application, with ContactViewer in its base state*

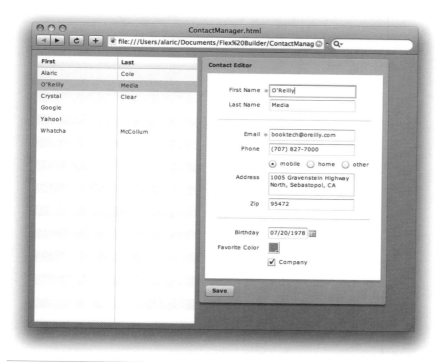

Figure 12-13. The ContactManager *application, with ContactViewer in its edit state*

Deep Linking

Another great feature that you can use with states or navigator containers—but one that requires a good knowledge of ActionScript and a little JavaScript—is *deep linking*. This lets you save the state of your application, or a currently selected tab in a TabNavigator, in the URL of the deployed Flex application. This means people can bookmark a specific view of your application, and you can share a link that takes people to a specific state in your application.

Deep linking provides a way for you to specify a parameter of a URL that points to a particular state. You have probably encountered these URL parameters if you've ever paid attention to the address bar of your browser when visiting websites—they're the part after the main address, and they give additional information to the server. If you've ever used Yahoo! search, you might have seen a URL in your address bar like the following:

http://search.yahoo.com/search?p=flex

In this case, *http://search.yahoo.com/search* is the base URL, and *p=flex* is a single parameter *p* set to *flex*. (The question mark [?] is simply a cue to the server that whatever comes after it is a parameter.)

Sometimes on a website you'll see a hyperlink that links to another part of the same HTML document. This is accomplished through an *anchor*, a special hyperlink that contains a hash (**#**) followed by the name of the section of that document, like the following:

http://en.wikipedia.org/wiki/Anchor_tag#Links_and_anchors

In the previous URL, *#Links_and_anchors* is the anchor, and it points to a specific part of the page at *http://en.wikipedia.org/wiki/Anchor_tag*.

Deep linking in Flex uses a similar paradigm, where you can create anchors or URL parameters that will link to specific points in your application.

Check out the Flex documentation on deep linking for more information on how to use this powerful feature.

Summary

Now you've encountered the most common features of Flex development, empowering you to create your own rich Internet applications. In this chapter, you discovered the concept of view states, which let you easily design the flow of your applications. Adding this to your knowledge of navigator containers and navigation components, you're ready to build advanced interfaces for any type of application. In fact, you've already used these concepts in applications that you built yourself—a search application, a photo gallery, and a contact manager application.

You also learned a very important concept: how to use MXML components. Creating your own component, you made the `ContactManager` application more modular and cleaner. This simple exercise has given you the information you need to create your own reusable MXML components that you can share across your own applications and even share with other developers.

You've made it far, and have just finished one of the more technical parts of the book. To celebrate, I'll cover what may be the most fun and expressive part of Flex in the next chapter, adding effects and filters.

CHAPTER 13

APPLYING BEHAVIORS, TRANSITIONS, AND FILTERS

Now that you've learned all of the most important skills for building applications in Flex, it's time to have some fun. All Flex visual components have a standard set of graphic filters and effects that let you create really expressive applications with minimal effort. *Effects* are auditory or visual changes to components, typically an animation of some form. *Filters* are static visual changes such as blurring or drop-shadows. In this chapter, you'll discover how incredibly easy it is to apply visual effects to your components with simple MXML.

Behaviors

All Flex visual components have a special set of behaviors built in. These behaviors let you easily add effects to your components, making really expressive applications quick and easy. They're essentially limitless, but the most common effects create functionality like fading a component's visibility in or out or showing the movement of a component from one place to another with an animation. Other common effects are sound effects, which are noises that can be played for certain events or actions.

Behaviors are really just an effect paired with a *trigger*, or an action that occurs in the application. This is typically from an event such as a mouse click, a mouse rollover, or some other event that a component dispatches, like when it's created for the first time or when it's hidden or shown.

Using Common Effects

To show how behaviors are implemented, let's start with the `PhotoGallery` application you last worked with in Chapter 11. Open that project's main application file, because you'll be working on it, adding some cool new effects to it.

In this application, photos are loaded in response to items being selected in a list. Also, a ProgressBar shows up when needed and becomes invisible when not in use. Effects can be used to make these actions—changing photos and hiding and showing a ProgressBar—smoother and more elegant.

Because behaviors are effects matched with triggers, if you're familiar with the events that a component fires, chances are that there's an effect that is triggered by that event. (See Table 13-1 for a list of common behaviors and their corresponding events.)

Table 13-1. The most common behaviors and associated trigger events

Behavior Name	Corresponding Name of the Event Trigger	Description of the Event Trigger
addedEffect	add	The component is added to the display list.
removedEffect	remove	The component is removed from the display list.
creationCompleteEffect	creationComplete	The component is created.
focusInEffect	focusIn	The component gains keyboard focus.
focusOutEffect	focusOut	The component loses keyboard focus.
showEffect	show	The component's **visible** property is changed from **false** to **true**.
hideEffect	hide	The component's **visible** property is changed from **true** to **false**.
moveEffect	move	The component's **x** and/or **y** properties are modified.
resizeEffect	resize	The component's **width** or **height** is changed.
mouseDownEffect	show	The mouse button is pressed while the mouse pointer is over the component.
mouseUpEffect	mouseUp	The mouse button is released while the mouse pointer is over the component.
rollOverEffect	rollOver	The mouse pointer rolls over the component.
rollOutEffect	rollOut	The mouse pointer rolls off the component.

NOTE

While the behaviors listed in Table 13-1 are the most common ones in visual components, other component-specific effects also exist, such as the **completeEffect** *of the Image control. To check the possible effects for a component, either check its documentation or use the Category view of the Flex Properties panel to see potential effects.*

Consider the case of the Image component used in the **PhotoGallery** application. It fires a **complete** event when its source finishes loading. You've already used this event to change the visibility of the ProgressBar. It also has a style property called **completeEffect**, which lets you specify an effect that will play when the **complete** event fires.

To see what happens, add a Fade effect to the large Image component that loads the photos. The quickest way to do this is by setting the value of **completeEffect** to **Fade**, which tells Flex to create a standard fade effect:

```
<mx:Image id="image"
    source="{photosList.selectedItem.@image}"
    left="270"
    top="10"
    bottom="10"
    right="10"
    horizontalAlign="center"
    open="progressBar.visible = true"
    complete="progressBar.visible = false"
    completeEffect="Fade"/>
```

Now, when you run the application and load a photo, the Image component will slowly fade in. What is happening is that once the **complete** event occurs and before the Image is shown, the Fade effect sets the Image's **alpha** value to **0** and then progressively increases it until it becomes fully opaque. This is called, in Flash terminology, a *tween*, because it's an animation in be*tween* two properties or states. Most of the common visual effects are using a tween-ing mechanism of some kind.

The addition of this effect makes the appearance of the photo less startling and can be very pleasant for anyone using your application. Instead of the photos immediately changing, the Fade effect creates an obvious visual cue that a new image is appearing, and it just looks great.

The ProgressBar could use an effect to show its appearance and disappear-ance, because it tends to show and hide itself suddenly. Luckily, all visual components have both a **showEffect** and a **hideEffect**, which are behaviors that can play an effect when the component is shown or hidden. You'll use both of them, providing a fade-in when the ProgressBar shows and a fade-out when it's hidden.

```
<mx:ProgressBar id="progressBar"
    x="270"
    y="10"
    source="{image}"
    visible="false"
    showEffect="Fade"
    hideEffect="Fade"/>
```

Now when the ProgressBar shows up, it will fade in nicely, and when it's hid-den, it will fade out. This is much preferable to the way it was before, suddenly appearing and disappearing.

However, you might notice that after running the application, the default **label** of the ProgressBar isn't fading with the rest of it. While the graphics of the ProgressBar fade in and out nicely, this text doesn't seem to follow along. This is because in the default setup of a Flex application, you are using *device fonts*, or fonts that are loaded from the user's system, to display text. Because of a current Flash Player limitation, device fonts aren't able to have an alpha value of less than 1, which means fade effects don't work with them. They are also not able to be rotated or changed by any other graphical manipulation, which does limit the types of effects that can be used with them.

To get around this issue, you have a couple of options. One is to *embed* fonts, which is a special way to include specific fonts of your choice compiled in the application (more on this in the next chapter). This allows the alpha value to be set on the text, which means the fades will work properly. Another option

> **NOTE**
>
> *Setting an effect has no impact on the effect's corresponding events. For instance, the* **completeEffect** *uses the* **complete** *event to trigger its playing, but it doesn't matter whether you've specified a listener for the* **complete** *event. They will work independently of one another.*

> **NOTE**
>
> *To see a list of common effects, see the section "Common Effects and Their Properties" later in this chapter.*

> **NOTE**
>
> *By setting a show or hide effect to a Fade, the proper animation will automatically display. When the component is shown, it will fade in, and when it is hidden, it will fade out.*

> **NOTE**
>
> *While effects that manipulate alpha (Fades) or rotation (Rotate) cannot be used with device fonts, other effects will work fine.*

is to just get rid of the label altogether. Because the ProgressBar shows up only temporarily and already gives its information without a label, you can just remove the label by setting it to an empty string:

```
<mx:ProgressBar id="progressBar"
    x="270"
    y="10"
    source="{image}"
    visible="false"
    showEffect="Fade"
    hideEffect="Fade"
    label=""/>
```

Applying Effects to Navigator Containers

Because navigator containers set the visibility of their children, **hideEffect** and **showEffect** will work for their children. In the **PhotoGallery** application, we have a TabNavigator with two Canvas containers, each holding a different type of list control. Instead of the views switching abruptly as they currently do, you could add some of these fade effects to the Canvas containers. Simply add a **showEffect** of **Fade** to each of the two Canvas containers, and when the views are switched, they will fade in nicely—that is, except for the first one.

You might notice that while the fade works great for the Tile view, which has a TileList filled with image thumbnails, the first List view doesn't show the fade properly. Again, the problem is with device fonts being used by the List control's labels. However, you can easily fix this with an alternative effect called Dissolve. The Dissolve effect gets around the issue by drawing a white rectangle layered over the List control and then applying a fade-out on that rectangle. The result is what appears to be a perfect fade-in for the List control. So, just replace the **showEffect** of the List view Canvas with a Dissolve, and it will work fine:

```
<mx:TabNavigator
    width="250"
    left="10"
    top="10"
    bottom="10"
    creationPolicy="all">
    <mx:Canvas
        label="List View"
        width="100%"
        height="100%"
        showEffect="Dissolve">
        <mx:List id="photosList"
            dataProvider="{service.lastResult.photo}"
            width="100%"
            height="100%"
            labelField="@title"
            change="photosTileList.selectedIndex = photosList.
selectedIndex">
        </mx:List>
    </mx:Canvas>
```

```
<mx:Canvas
    label="Tile View"
    width="100%"
    height="100%"
    showEffect="Fade">
    <mx:TileList id="photosTileList"
        dataProvider="{service.lastResult.photo}"
        width="100%"
        height="100%"
        change="photosList.selectedIndex =
            photosTileList.selectedIndex" >
        <mx:itemRenderer>
            <mx:Component>
                <mx:Image
                    horizontalAlign="center"
                    source="{data.@thumb}"
                    toolTip="{data.@title}"
                    width="100"
                    height="60"/>
            </mx:Component>
        </mx:itemRenderer>
    </mx:TileList>
</mx:Canvas>

    </mx:TabNavigator>
```

NOTE

Another common behavior you can implement for this application is **creationCompleteEffect**. *This effect plays when a component is first created.*

Now your **PhotoGallery** application has a much nicer look and feel, and all it took was a few minutes and a few lines of MXML to make it happen!

Exploring More Effects

Another common effect is Resize, which animates a component's size change. One of your applications, **ContactManager**, could benefit from a Resize effect. In this application, the ContactViewer component changes its size based upon its contents and its state. While the component's size change is obvious, a Resize effect could really make the abrupt change smoother. Even more important, at the bottom of this component is a Button control that works as either an edit button or a save button. When the ContactViewer's size changes, this Button's location is changed quickly. A Resize effect could help to ease the size change and keep this Button from changing its position too quickly.

Open the **ContactManager** application, and add a **resizeEffect** of **Resize** to the ContactViewer instance:

```
<view:ContactViewer id="contactViewer"
    contact="{contactsDataGrid.selectedItem}"
    x="318"
    y="10"
    resizeEffect="Resize">
</view:ContactViewer>
```

Now, when you run the application, you will see that the size change is animated nicely. Clicking the edit button, the ContactViewer switches to its edit state, adjusting its size to accommodate the extra controls inside, so this transition is more obvious thanks to a nice animation.

NOTE

While setting `horizontalScrollPolicy` *and* `verticalScrollPolicy` *to* `off` *solves a little Resize effect glitch, it prevents scroll bars from showing if they are really needed.*

However, the scroll bars appearing and disappearing during the size change causes a bit of an issue. You might notice this when the application loads and the first resize occurs. This is because as the component goes from small to larger, its animation clips the contents momentarily, and the container decides to add scroll bars. This isn't a big deal, but if you want to get rid of this, it's easy to do. Every component has two properties that control the appearance of scroll bars: `horizontalScrollPolicy` and `verticalScrollPolicy`. These two properties help the component decide whether scroll bars appear horizontally or vertically, respectively. By default the properties are set to `auto`, meaning they will appear when needed. You can set this to `on` if you want scroll bars to always appear, or in this case you can set them both to `off`. This prevents them from ever showing up.

```
<view:ContactViewer id="contactViewer"
    contact="{contactsDataGrid.selectedItem}"
    x="318" y="10"
    resizeEffect="Resize"
    horizontalScrollPolicy="off"
    verticalScrollPolicy="off">
</view:ContactViewer>
```

NOTE

While I'm showing you real-world uses of the more common effects, you can experiment with a number of others. Feel free to create a new project and just have fun with them.

So far you've use a Fade effect for when a component changes its visibility and a Resize effect for the `resizeEffect` behavior. However, it's good to note that a behavior and an effect are interchangeable. That is to say, a `resizeEffect` behavior doesn't always have to use a Resize effect—it can use any other effect, such as a Fade or a Wipe. However, in many cases, each behavior has one effect that is the most useful.

Customizing Effects

So far you've set behaviors using a default effect. That is, you've named an effect class such as Fade or Resize as the value of a behavior. This is very convenient, but you may find that you want more control over your effect properties. To do this, you can declare an effect instance using the corresponding MXML tag somewhere in your application. This lets you specify, for example, multiple types of Fade effects from which you can choose.

NOTE

Like with all nonvisual components, you shouldn't place effects inside a container tag other than the top-level `<mx:Application/>` *tag (or within a custom component's root tag). It's best to place the tags somewhere at the top of your application or component.*

Add an `<mx:Resize/>` tag to your **ContactManager** application, and give it an `id` of **fastResize**. This creates a specific instance of a Resize, which you can customize. Give this instance a **duration** of **300**. The **duration** property is a standard property of all effects and lets you stipulate the length of time, in milliseconds, that the effect should play. Three hundred milliseconds is about a third of a second, so this effect will be pretty zippy:

```
<mx:Resize id="fastResize" duration="300"/>
```

Now you've declared a Resize effect and given it an `id` that lets you refer to it in your code. Next, you can replace the current `resizeEffect` of the ContactViewer with this particular instance. Instead of passing in **Resize**, giving it a standard Resize effect, you can pass in a custom effect, **fastResize**:

```
<view:ContactViewer id="contactViewer"
    contact="{contactsDataGrid.selectedItem}"
    x="318"
    y="10"
    resizeEffect="{fastResize}"
    horizontalScrollPolicy="off"
    verticalScrollPolicy="off">
</view:ContactViewer>
```

Run this application again to see the customized the effect. Notice how it changes the feel of the application because the Resize effect happens a bit more quickly.

NOTE

When using custom effect instances, you need to use curly braces to signify a binding.

Using Composite Effects

This Resize effect works great when the ContactViewer grows as a result of changing from its details mode to its edit mode. However, you could do even more to show the change than just animating a resize. One way to accomplish this is by using a Dissolve effect on the ContactViewer, which could create a nice fade from one mode to the next. But you've already set up a Resize effect to occur, so how can you make this happen?

Parallel

You don't have to replace your existing Resize effect, because you can actually just add a Dissolve. You can play multiple effects at once using a special effect tag called Parallel. The `<mx:Parallel/>` tag wraps other effect tags, grouping them and letting them play simultaneously. This lets you create custom composite effects.

Because you want both a Dissolve effect and a Resize effect to play simultaneously, replace your previous Resize effect with the following code:

```
<mx:Parallel id="fadeAndResize">

    <mx:Dissolve/>

    <mx:Resize id="fastResize" duration="300"/>

</mx:Parallel>
```

Now you can replace the **resizeEffect** of your ContactViewer with a binding to **fadeAndResize**. This causes the new composite effect to play whenever the component changes its size. Both a Dissolve and a Resize will play at the same time, preventing the ugly clipping that occurs with a typical Resize effect. This fade-and-resize effect will look great and inform people of the mode change that is occurring.

NOTE

*Setting a **duration** on a Parallel effect will typically set the duration on the internal effects, if they don't already have a duration set.*

Sequence

Another special type of effects tag is `<mx:Sequence/>`. This tag lets you specify effects that will play in sequence. Like Parallel, Sequence lets you group multiple effects together. However, unlike Parallel, it plays each effect one after

NOTE

*When using Sequence effects, a useful tag to know is `<mx:Pause/>`. This tag has a **duration** property that lets you specify a period of time to pause the sequence.*

the other instead of all at once. You could try replacing the `<mx:Parallel/>` tag in the previous code with an `<mx:Sequence/>` tag to see the difference.

Common Effects and Their Properties

In addition to **duration**, all effects have special properties that you can use to configure them. They have properties that define starting and ending information for the target of the effect, allowing you to customize it. For a Resize, this would be the starting and ending values for **width** and **height**, while for a Move effect this would be starting and ending values for **x** and **y**.

It's not usually necessary to stipulate such properties, because Flex can set the values for you based upon the starting and ending values of a component's changed properties. For instance, if you change a Panel's **x** from **0** to **100** and you specify a Move effect for that Panel, Flex will automatically place the Move's **xFrom** property to **0** and its **xTo** property to **100**.

If no explicit values are set for an effect and Flex can't determine the proper ones from the starting or ending property of a component, the effect will use its own default values.

The following sections discuss the standard effects and their most important properties.

NOTE

To see live examples of each of these effects, point your browser to the Flex 3 Component Explorer at http://examples. adobe.com/flex3/componentexplorer/ explorer.html. Here you'll find a section called "Effects, View States, and Transitions" that will give you real-world examples of every effect, complete with code you can use in your own applications.

Blur

A Blur effect softens the details of an image, like an unfocused lens.

The Blur effect has the following properties that you can adjust:

blurXFrom

> Sets the initial amount of horizontal blurring.

blurXTo

> Sets the final amount of horizontal blurring.

blurYFrom

> Sets the initial amount of vertical blurring.

blurYTo

> Sets the final amount of vertical blurring.

Blurs are useful for showing movement and can be coupled with Move effects. A very strong Blur effect (a property value of 20 or greater) can produce an interesting morphing look.

Dissolve

A Dissolve effect modifies the **alpha** property of a rectangular overlay, letting the target component under it appear or disappear gradually.

The Dissolve effect has the following properties that you can adjust:

alphaFrom

> Sets the initial alpha value.

alphaTo

> Sets the final alpha value.

color

> Sets the color of the overlay rectangle that the effect will display over the target component. The default value is the color specified by the target component's **backgroundColor** style property, so you won't usually need to set this. If no **backgroundColor** is set, it defaults to white (0xFFFFFF).

Dissolves are a great substitute for Fade effects when using device fonts.

NOTE

For a Dissolve effect, if the target is a container, only the children of the container will be affected by the fade. In the case of a Panel container, the borders and title bar of the Panel will not fade; just its contents will fade.

Fade

This effect animates the **alpha** property of a component, letting it change gradually from transparent to opaque or from opaque to transparent.

The Fade effect has the following properties that you can adjust:

alphaFrom

> Sets the initial alpha value.

alphaTo

> Sets the final alpha value.

Glow

This effect applies a glow to a component, animating a lighting effect that makes it look like light is coming from inside the component.

The Glow effect has the following properties that you can adjust:

alphaFrom

> Sets the initial alpha value.

alphaTo

> Sets the final alpha value.

blurXFrom

> Sets the initial amount of horizontal blurring for the glow.

blurXTo

> Sets the final amount of horizontal blurring for the glow.

blurYFrom

> Sets the initial amount of vertical blurring for the glow.

blurYTo

Sets the final amount of vertical blurring for the glow.

color

Sets the color of the glow.

inner

Specifies whether the glow is an inner glow or an outer glow. The default is **false**, giving it an outer glow.

knockout

Specifies whether the object has a knockout effect, making its fill color more transparent and revealing the background color of the target. The default value is **false**.

Iris

This effect animates an expanding or contracting rectangular mask centered on the target, like the iris of a camera lens. The effect can be used to expose the target or to hide the component. Think of old movies that use this effect at the end.

The Iris effect has the following properties that you can adjust:

showTarget

Specifies whether the Iris exposes the target (**true**) or hides it (**false**, which is the default)

Move

This effect gradually changes the position of a component.

The Move effect has the following properties that you can adjust:

xFrom

Sets the initial horizontal position of the component.

xTo

Sets the final horizontal position of the component.

yFrom

Sets the initial vertical position of the component.

yTo

Sets the final vertical position of the component.

xBy

Sets the number of pixels to move the component in the horizontal direction. You can use this instead of an **xFrom** or **xTo** to specify the *amount* to

NOTE

If you apply a Move effect to a target inside a container with a relative layout, such as a VBox or Panel with a layout other than **absolute***, the effect will not work properly. This is because while a Move will occur, the position of the target will immediately be changed back by the container.*

move instead of the initial or final **x** position. This property is ignored if both **xFrom** and **xTo** are specified.

yBy

Sets the number of pixels to move the component in the vertical direction. You can use this instead of a **yFrom** or **yTo** to specify the *amount* to move instead of the initial or final **y** position. This property is ignored if both **yFrom** and **yTo** are specified.

Resize

This effect changes the width and height of a component over a specified time interval, animating the change in size.

The Resize effect has the following properties that you can adjust:

widthFrom

Sets the initial width of the component.

widthTo

Sets the final width of the component.

heightFrom

Sets the initial height of the component.

heightTo

Sets the final height of the component.

widthBy

Sets the number of pixels to change the component's width. You can use this instead of a **widthFrom** or **widthTo** to specify the *amount* to resize instead of the initial or final width. This property is ignored if both **widthFrom** and **widthTo** are specified.

heightBy

Sets the number of pixels to change the component's height. You can use this instead of a **heightFrom** or **heightTo** to specify the *amount* to resize instead of the initial or final height. This property is ignored if both **heightFrom** and **heightTo** are specified.

hideChildrenTargets

This property is used just with Panel containers, hiding the contents of the Panel while the Resize in taking place. This property takes an array of Panels.

When you apply a Resize effect on a component when other components base their size on that component, their size will appear to animate as well. This happens when other components use constraints based on the size of the affected target or are sharing the space of a relative layout container.

Rotate

This effect rotates a component around a point, which is by default the top-left corner. You specify the origin of the rotation so that a component can rotate around a different point, such as its center. You also set the starting and ending angles of rotation, based on 360 degrees. If a number is greater than 360, this effect will set it to 360.

The Resize effect has the following properties:

angleFrom

> Sets the initial rotation.

angleTo

> Sets the final rotation.

originX

> Sets the center point of the rotation horizontally, in regard to the component to which the effect is applied. The default is 0.

originY

> Sets the center point of the rotation vertically, in regard to the component to which the effect is applied. The default is 0.

WipeLeft, WipeRight, WipeUp, and WipeDown

The wipe effects are used to set the visibility of components, exposing or hiding the component as if an invisible rectangle were moving over it.

These effects have the following property that you can adjust:

showTarget

> Specifies whether the wipe exposes the target (**true**) or hides it (**false**, which is the default)

Zoom

This effect zooms a component in or out, like a camera lens. This can make the component appear to be either farther away or closer, scaling its target.

The Zoom effect has the following properties that you can adjust:

zoomHeightFrom

> Sets the initial scale of the component vertically. The default is 1. Setting this to 2 doubles the component's size, scaling accordingly. Setting this to 3 triples the size, and so on.

zoomHeightTo

> Sets the final scale of the component vertically.

zoomWidthFrom

Sets the initial scale of the component horizontally.

zoomWidthTo

Sets the final scale of the component horizontally.

originX

Sets the center point of the zoom horizontally. The default is the center of the component.

originY

Sets the center point of the zoom vertically. The default is the center of the component.

AnimateProperty

The AnimateProperty effect is a very customizable effect. It lets you animate (create a tween for) any numeric property of a component.

The AnimateProperty effect has the following properties that you can adjust:

property

Sets the name of the property you want you modify. You set this as a string.

fromValue

Sets the initial value of the property.

toValue

Sets the final value of the property.

For instance, to simulate a Resize effect just for the height of a Panel, you could specify **height** for **property** and give the effect a **fromValue** and a **toValue**.

Sound Effects

Just like you can add visual effects, you can add sound effects to your applications. Such sound effects can be useful for notifying people when a dialog box pops up, like an alarm sound in a calendaring application. If you find yourself developing games in Flex, sound effects can be an easy way to add sounds based upon some triggering event in your game.

To create a sound effect, you must use the `<mx:SoundEffect/>` tag. The `SoundEffect` class takes a `source` property, which you can set to an MP3 file. Then, once you have an instance of a `SoundEffect` with an `id`, you can refer to this effect through any of the component behaviors, like `showEffect`, `resizeEffect`, `mouseDownEffect`, and so on. Although it's not a visual effect, you use it just like the other effects you've learned.

NOTE

Flex doesn't come with any sounds built in, so you must provide your own.

For example, imagine you have an MP3 of the clicking of a camera shutter and you want to play this sound in your **PhotoGallery** application every time a photo loads. Using the **completeEffect** of the Image control, you could attach this sound effect.

Your effect tag may look like this, placed somewhere at the top level of your application:

```
<mx:SoundEffect id="shutterSound"
    source="camera_shutter.mp3"/>
```

And your Image control may use the effect as follows:

```
<mx:Image id="image"
    source="{photosList.selectedItem.@image}"
    left="270"
    top="10"
    bottom="10"
    right="10"
    horizontalAlign="center"
    open="progressBar.visible = true"
    complete="progressBar.visible = false"
    completeEffect="{shutterSound}"/>
```

NOTE

You will need to use very small sound files when using them as sound effects. This is because the sound must be downloaded before it becomes available for use, and this may cause unwanted latency with large files. I'll discuss an alternative to downloading sounds at runtime in the next chapter when I show you how to embed assets in your compiled application.

Keeping Effects Effective

When starting out with effects and behaviors, it's easy to get carried away. Effects are so easy to add and so much fun that you may want to add them in every possible situation. You should have fun with effects, of course. But when you're adding an effect, it's good to think about why you're adding it. Is it just because it looks cool, or is it because it serves a purpose? Looking cool can definitely be a purpose—and after all, this *is* Flash—but overusing effects can become tiring for people using your application, especially if it slows them down. The old adage "less is more" is good advice to follow when it comes to using effects and behaviors.

Think about the duration of the effect, because this can really change the way someone perceives the speed of the application. An effect with a very long duration may make the application feel sluggish, while a slightly shorter one makes it feel snappy. Try adjusting the duration of your effects to see what feeling it imparts. Remember that the first time someone sees an effect, it may be perfect—but if they have to see the same one a dozen times, it might not be so great.

When using sound effects, you must be careful. Some people enjoy the additional feedback that sound can give, but many prefer not to have their computer make any sounds at all. If your application uses sound effects, it's good practice to provide people with a choice, letting them turn sound effects on or off.

It's usually best to use an effect when it provides information about the application. For instance, when a Panel is moved from one part of the application to another, people may not notice the movement if the Panel simply disappears from one place and pops up in another immediately ("Hey, where'd that Panel go?"). Using a Move effect would make the change more obvious, saying that the Panel has moved. Effects can make the experience of an application more human, and that's always a great thing.

States Made More Interesting

While you can always apply behaviors to specific component instances, you can specify particular effects when changing view states. Using *transitions*, you specify an effect or group of effects to play on multiple components whenever state changes occur.

Let's return to the **Search** application you built using view states in the last chapter. In this application, a search field is first made large and placed in the center, and once search results are retrieved, the field shrinks and moves to the top left of the screen. Currently, this movement is immediate and jumpy, and it may take someone a moment to realize that the search fields were moved. You can add a transition that will make this movement more natural and understandable.

You apply transitions via the **transitions** property of an Application or custom component. Typically you'll set these using a child tag of the **<mx:Application/>** tag, because it will hold complex content. Just as the **states** property of the Application accepts an array of **<mx:State/>** tags, the **transitions** property accepts one or more **<mx:Transition/>** tags. Each of these **<mx:Transition/>** tags accepts an effect instance. In this case, you want to specify one transition: a Parallel effect that will both move and resize.

So, open your **Search** project, and place the following MMXL code somewhere under the root **<mx:Application/>** tag in the *Search.mxml* application. (I like to place my transitions code next to my view state code.)

```
<mx:transitions>
    <mx:Transition>

        <mx:Parallel target="{hbox1}">
            <mx:Move />
            <mx:Resize />
        </mx:Parallel>

    </mx:Transition>
</mx:transitions>
```

Notice in this code that a single transition with a Parallel effect targets **hbox1**, which is the HBox container that holds the search input fields for this application. Because the HBox doesn't have any behaviors applied, such as **moveEffect** or **resizeEffect**, the **target** property is the way to tell the effect what to attach itself to.

This code stipulates that whenever a state change occurs, a Parallel effect should play for the **hbox1** component.

This begs the question, why not just apply a **moveEffect** and a **resizeEffect** to the HBox? That would be fine, of course, but transitions let you set effects to play based upon state changes. Applying a **moveEffect** and **resizeEffect**

NOTE

*You use a binding to specify the instance name (***id***) of the component you want the effect to target. If you want to specify more than one target, you can use the* **targets** *property, which takes an array. For example, to specify a Move effect that targets two Buttons named* **submitButton** *and* **resetButton***, you'd use the following code:*

```
<mx:Move targets="{ [submitButton,
    resetButton] }" />
```

NOTE

You can also declare effects and play them programmatically. Instead of relying on state transitions or behaviors to play the effects, you can call the **play()** *method of any effect (visual or sound) to have complete control. For this to work, either the effect must have a* **target** *set already or you can specify a target in the* **play()** *method. For instance, to play a Dissolve effect you declared called* **fastDissolve** *on a List called* **shortList**, *you would call* **fastDissolve,play(shortList)**.

to the HBox would have it play the effects any time it's moved or resized, while transitions let you to specify an effect to play only upon certain state changes.

If you run this code, you'll notice that the HBox (with its search input fields and Button) will fly in from the top left at first. This is because the application actually has a starting state different from its base state—the original position of the HBox is the top left of the screen, but you've specified that its **currentState** should change when the application begins. Because the HBox is therefore considered to have changed its size and location, the effects play. That's probably not what you had planned to occur, so I'll show you how to fix it.

One of the huge benefits of transitions is that they let you easily specify which state changes should play them. You can change your transition's code to the following to cause the effect to play when only changing from the search state:

```
<mx:transitions>
    <mx:Transition fromState="search">

        <mx:Parallel target="{hbox1}">
            <mx:Move />
            <mx:Resize />
        </mx:Parallel>

    </mx:Transition>
</mx:transitions>
```

NOTE

The **Transition** *class also has a property called* **toState**, *which lets you tell it to play when changing to certain states. Depending upon your requirements, you can set a* **fromState**, *a* **toState**, *or both. By default, a transition will play for all state changes unless they are specified.*

The transition has a property called **fromState**, and this code uses this property to tell it to play the effect only when changing from the search state to another state. Now when you run the application, the effect doesn't play when the **Search** application first loads, but only when a search is invoked. This is because, at first, the application switches from the base state to the search state; then, once a search is invoked, it switches back to the base state from the search state.

Using Action Effects

You're close to finishing up this transition, but you may have noticed it doesn't work perfectly yet. Because of the **resultsList** being added back to the display list when you have search results (and therefore the state is changed back to the base state), it interrupts the Move and Resize effects on the HBox. What you want it to do is finish playing the effects and *then* add the List.

The way to do this is using an **<mx:Sequence/>** tag coupled with another special effect tag called **<mx:AddChildAction/>**. Wrap your previous **<mx:Parallel/>** tag in an **<mx:Sequence/>** tag, and then add the **<mx:AddChildAction/>** tag to the end:

```
<mx:transitions>
    <mx:Transition fromState="search">

        <mx:Sequence>
            <mx:Parallel target="{hbox1}">
                <mx:Move />
                <mx:Resize />
            </mx:Parallel>

            <mx:AddChildAction target="{resultsList}"/>
        </mx:Sequence>

    </mx:Transition>
</mx:transitions>
```

The `<mx:AddChildAction/>` tag is a way to specify *when* you want a child added to the display list. Because you want to play the Move/Resize effect for the HBox first and then add the `resultsList`, you place this special `<mx:AddChildAction/>` tag after the `<mx:Parallel/>` tag within the Sequence. Then, once the Move/Resize effect finishes, the `resultsList` will be added, and your effect will look and work as expected.

This is called an *action effect*, because it doesn't actually draw any animation but applies the change specified by a corresponding state tag. You can use four different action effects, which correspond to a state change tag with a similar name:

SetPropertyAction

Sets a property on a component. This corresponds to an `<mx:SetProperty/>` tag within a state.

SetStyleAction

Sets a style property on a component. This corresponds to an `<mx:SetStyle/>` tag within a state.

AddChildAction

Adds a component to the display list. This corresponds to an `<mx:AddChild/>` tag within a state.

RemoveChildAction

Removes a component from the display list. This corresponds to an `<mx:RemoveChild/>` tag within a state.

You can never be too sure when an action will occur in a state change, so it's good practice to use these special action effects when you can. To be sure that an action occurs at the right time, you'll typically use these action effects inside a Sequence right before the visual effect tag, giving you complete control over when properties are assigned or children are added and removed and ensuring the effect works as desired.

More on Action Effects

Using action effects properly can take a little experience. Having such control over your transitions may require you to really think about what you want to happen. It can be useful for you to create a simple timeline of any transition, helping you to decide on what should happen when. Once you do that, you can place action effect tags as necessary, ensuring your effects always work perfectly.

For another example of action effects, in your applications you may want to use a Dissolve effect on a component that is added to an application via an **<mx:AddChild/>** tag in a state. In this case, you want to place an **<mx:AddChildAction/>** tag right before the **<mx:Dissolve/>** tag within a Sequence. This will ensure that first the child is added and available, and then the Dissolve effect will play. Without this, the effect might play first, making your component fade in. Then the component would immediately disappear until a moment later, when the "AddChild" happens. This would result in an untimely Dissolve and a funky blinking component.

The following code fades in two Button components, one after the other. The Button named **button1** is faded in before the Button named **button2**:

```
<mx:Sequence targets="{[button1, button2]}">

    <mx:AddChildAction target="{button1}"/>
    <mx:Dissolve target="{button1}"/>

    <mx:AddChildAction target="{button2}"/>
    <mx:Dissolve target="{button2}"/>

</mx:Sequence>
```

Filtering Effect Targets

When using transitions, you can apply effects conditionally. Using something called *target filters*, you can specify that an effect play for certain components that meet the criteria. To use these filters, you must first specify all the possible targets you think you'll want to play the effect on. Then, you specify the filter criteria using the filter property of the effect.

The following are the possible criteria filters:

add

Plays the effect on any component that is added to the display list

remove

Plays the effect on components that are removed from the display list

show

Plays the effect on components whose **visible** property changes from **false** to **true**

hide

>   Plays the effect on components whose **visible** property changes from **true** to **false**

move

>   Plays the effect on components whose **x** or **y** property changes

resize

>   Plays the effect on components whose **width** or **height** changes

Using target filters, you could change the transition in your **Search** application to the following:

```
<mx:transitions>
    <mx:Transition fromState="search">

        <mx:Sequence targets="{[hbox1, resultsList]}">
            <mx:Parallel>
                <mx:Move filter="move" />
                <mx:Resize filter="resize" />
            </mx:Parallel>

            <mx:AddChildAction filter="add" />

        </mx:Sequence>

    </mx:Transition>
</mx:transitions>
```

Now, instead of specifying a target for each effect instance, you can list all possible targets for the transition as a whole and then filter each particular effect by type. In the previous example, the search fields and the list of results are both specified as potential targets for the transition. Then any of the targets that are moving will have a Move effect applied, and any that resize will have a Resize applied; finally, any components that are set to be added will then be added.

Filters

Have you ever used Photoshop or a similar graphics application to create interesting visual effects on your photos? Using what are commonly known as *filters*, you can manipulate static images in many fun ways.

Because many of the effects actually use these filters, you may already have a good idea of what each accomplishes. Also, the properties of these filters are closely matched with the available properties of their corresponding effects, so if you know one, you can easily learn the other.

The following list discusses the most common filters.

NOTE

*Setting a container as the **target** of an effect doesn't set that container's children as a target of the effect for the purposes of effect filters. While targeting a Dissolve effect on a Panel will of course affect that Panel's children, trying to dissolve a specific TextInput within that container will not.*

Figure 13-1. A BevelFilter applied to a gray box

Figure 13-2. A BlurFilter applied to a gray box

Figure 13-3. A red GlowFilter applied to a gray box

BevelFilter and GradientBevelFilter

Bevels are commonly used to give a three-dimensional, chiseled look to a component (see Figure 13-1). The GradientBevelFilter uses a gradient color on its bevel, which improves the realism of the filter.

BlurFilter

Like the Blur effect that uses this filter, a blur provides an out-of-focus look to a component. See Figure 13-2 for an example.

DropShadowFilter

This filter lets you easily add a drop shadow to any component, giving your application more depth with the illusion that the component is raised up off the application. See Figure 13-4 for an example.

GlowFilter and GradientGlowFilter

These two filters provide an edge glowing effect on any component to which they are applied. See Figure 13-3 for an example.

ColorMatrixFilter, ConvolutionFilter, and DisplacementMapFilter

These three filters are much more complex than the other filters in the way their properties are set. If you want to learn more about them, check out the documentation for ColorMatrixFilter, ConvolutionFilter, and DisplacementMapFilter. These are very powerful filters that can dramatically change the look of your components. The DisplacementMapFilter could even be used to warp your entire application into a sphere!

NOTE

While filters can be used to give your components a custom appearance, they're also useful as a convenient way to get a certain user interface look. For instance, to give a Button a more classic look, you can apply a bevel filter to it. To give it a more pronounced highlight, you could apply a GlowFilter on `rollOver` *(and remove it on* `rollOut`*).*

Applying Filters

To apply filters, you use the `filters` property of a component. This accepts an array of filters, meaning you can apply multiple filters at a time to get the look you want. The easiest way to add filters is by using an `<mx:filters/>` tag for your component and placing individual filter tags within that tag.

To try filters, open the **PhotoGallery** application again. Here, you could apply a DropShadowFilter to the main Image, giving it more depth:

```
<mx:Image id="image"
    source="{photosList.selectedItem.@image}"
    left="270"
    top="10"
    bottom="10"
    right="10"
    horizontalAlign="center"
    open="progressBar.visible = true"
    complete="progressBar.visible = false"
    completeEffect="Fade" >
    <mx:filters>
        <mx:DropShadowFilter distance="10"/>
    </mx:filters>
</mx:Image>
```

Figure 13-4 shows how the **PhotoGallery** looks after applying this filter.

Like everything else in Flex, you can apply filters both in MXML and in ActionScript. For instance, to create the previous DropShadowFilter and apply it to the Image control in ActionScript instead of MXML, the syntax would be as follows, placed in a function that is called some time after the Image control is available, such as on its **creationComplete** event:

```
var dropShadowFilter:DropShadowFilter = new DropShadowFilter();
dropShadowFilter.distance = 10;

image.filters = [dropShadowFilter];
```

Using ActionScript and filters, you can apply filters dynamically at runtime. In fact, with a little work, you could turn the **PhotoGallery** application into a little photo-editing application, letting people apply their own filters to the images.

NOTE

Some controls and containers, such as Panel, have a **dropShadowEnabled** *property. This lets you quickly apply a drop shadow without having to use the DropShadowFilter.*

NOTE

For a great example of the power of Flex, take a look at www.photoshop.com/ express. This is a free version of Adobe Photoshop, which uses (among other things) filters to apply effects to images.

Figure 13-4. The **PhotoGallery**, *with a DropShadowFilter applied to the photo*

Tricks of the Trade

While it's true that many effects will not display correctly because of the way device fonts are rendered, you can use a cool trick to get around this issue. All you have to do is apply a filter to a component, and it will render device fonts in a way that effects will work. What actually happens is that text with a filter applied is rendered by Flash Player as a graphic, which then allows even device fonts to be manipulated with effects.

If you don't want the filter to actually manipulate the way your components display, you can simply set the values of that filter in a way that it won't show. For instance, I often set a BlurFilter with a **blurX** and **blurY** of **0** on text components if their effects don't render properly. This applies a filter for the purposes of making the effect work but doesn't actually change the look of the component, because the actual blurring is 0.

```
<mx:Button
    label="Fancy Button Text" >
    <mx:filters>
        <mx:BlurFilter blurX="0" blurY="0"/>
    </mx:filters>
</mx:Button>
```

With this simple trick, you can apply any effect you want without worrying about device fonts getting in the way.

Summary

In this chapter, you discovered that Flex provides a number of great ways to create interesting audible and visual effects for your application, right out of the box. You enhanced your applications to use some of these new effects, providing a rich user experience with very little code. Feel free to have fun with the applications you've built, because they're yours. Up next, you'll discover how to customize every visual aspect of your Flex applications, making your applications truly custom and unique.

CHAPTER 14

STYLING APPLICATIONS

Flex comes with a powerful and extensible framework of components. The framework isn't bound to any one style or look. The Flex components do come with a default look and feel, but you can easily change them using styles. You have the ability to quickly modify specific style properties of individual components or even create styles that can be applied to all components. Using Cascading Style Sheets (CSS), you can create reusable styles that let you make major changes to the look of your applications. You can even use custom graphics such as *.jpg* and *.gif* files to entirely replace the look of components.

Using Inline Styles

You can apply styles to a component in a couple of ways. You've already been using a few style properties in the applications you've built. You've used properties like `fontWeight`, `fontSize`, and `backgroundColor` in the `ContactManager` application to customize controls. You applied them using *inline styles*, meaning you applied the styles inside the MXML tag of a component.

The easiest way to apply these styles is by using Flex Builder's Design mode. In this mode, the Standard view in the Flex Properties panel gives you the most common style properties for a particular component. For applying complex styles like gradient fills, this panel is a lifesaver. You don't have to worry about the specifics; you simply select colors with the drop-down color picker or apply font styles and other properties with simple text input fields and drop-down lists. Remember that style properties, while set the same way in MXML, are inherently different than regular properties. You must use the `setStyle()` and `getStyle()` methods to apply them in ActionScript.

Take a look at Figure 14-1 for an overview of the most common style properties. While these are different for each component, getting acquainted with these basic styles will take you a long way.

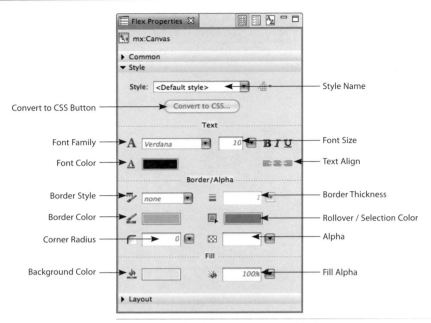

Figure 14-1. The Flex Properties panel Style section

You'll use the **PhotoGallery** application you've been working on to give an application a new look. Open the main **PhotoGallery** application file, and go to Flex Builder's Design mode where you can quickly modify styles.

You'll be giving this application a darker look. The first step is to change the background color of the Application. While the Application does have a **backgroundColor** style property, it also has a **backgroundGradientColors** property, which lets you create a *gradient*, or smooth transition between multiple colors, instead of a flat color. You can set this most easily by using the Fill section of the Flex Properties panel. You can choose a couple of colors using the drop-down color pickers, and Flex will create an array of the proper colors for you in code.

Use the Fill color fields to apply a gradient going from black (#000000) to dark gray (#999999). Doing so will create the proper **backgroundGradientColors** attribute for the **<mx:Application/>** tag. Also included is a setting called **backgroundGradientAlphas**, which sets the alpha transparency values on the gradients. This is useful if you want to have one part of the gradient with a different transparency value from the other. You can adjust this setting using the Fill alpha pop-up sliders in this same Fill section.

Your **<mx:Application/>** tag should look like the following code, and you can see the result in Figure 14-2:

```
<mx:Application xmlns:mx="http://www.adobe.com/2006/mxml"
    layout="absolute"
    applicationComplete="service.send()"
    backgroundGradientAlphas="[1.0, 1.0]"
    backgroundGradientColors="[#000000, #999999]">
```

Figure 14-2. The `PhotoGallery`, *with a dark gradient background*

The next step is to make the TabNavigator and its lists match this new color scheme. Using the Background color picker in the Flex Properties panel, apply a black (#000000) background color to the TabNavigator and both list controls. These components do not accept gradients, only a flat color. You'll need to set the background color to black for both the controls and the TabNavigator, because they both have a default **backgroundColor** of white.

Once you've applied this dark background color, you'll quickly notice that the color of the text is still dark, making it now difficult to read. To fix this, you'll want to lighten the color of the text. You can set the color of text on most controls by using the Font color field in the Flex Properties panel, which has an icon that looks like a letter *A* with a bar of colors beneath it. Setting the color through this sets the style property called **color**.

Now your **PhotoGallery** application has a very different look, just by changing a few colors, as shown in Figure 14-3.

> ## Cascading Styles
>
> The style **color**, as well as many other styles, will "cascade" down to child components. This is called CSS *inheritance*, and it means that if you set this style on a container tag (or the Application), it will propagate to the children of that container, setting their text to that same color. So, taking advantage of this, you can easily set the text color of most components by setting the **color** style on the Application.

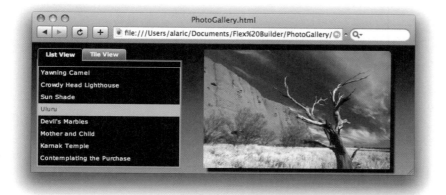

Figure 14-3. The `PhotoGallery`, *getting darker*

> **NOTE**
>
> *To find out whether a style property cascades to the child component, check the documentation for the particular style in the Flex Adobe Flex 3 Language Reference.*

The highlight colors of the list and the focus colors of the application components are still the default blue. You can change this to your liking as well.

While the list controls could have their **selectionColor** styles changed, which affects the color of just the selected items, you can create a more efficient change using the **themeColor** style of the Application. The **themeColor** property accepts any color and can dramatically change the look and feel of your application. This property will set the **selectionColor** of list controls as well as the focus and highlight color of all components. This property cascades so many levels, it will even change the color of the ProgressBar's fill. So for this one, choose your color wisely, and enjoy. You can see a **themeColor** of green in Figure 14-4.

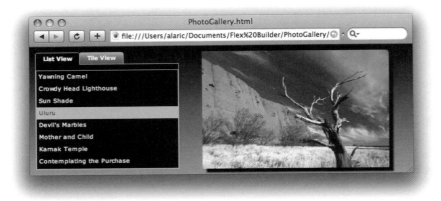

Figure 14-4. The PhotoGallery *with a green theme color*

Color Names

You know that usually you must specify colors using a hexadecimal value, but you can use an actual color name instead in the case of a few colors. For instance, when setting **backgroundColor** as an attribute of an MXML tag, you could specify black in either of two ways:

    backgroundColor="0x000000"

or

    backgroundColor="black"

While this can be convenient for basic colors such as red, green, blue, white, and black—okay, so maybe black isn't a color—unless you're very good with colors, using a color picker and specifying a hexadecimal value is best. The possible color name values you can use in Flex are **"black"**, **"blue"**, **"green"**, **"gray"**, **"silver"**, **"lime"**, **"olive"**, **"white"**, **"yellow"**, **"maroon"**, **"navy"**, **"red"**, **"purple"**, **"teal"**, **"fuchsia"**, **"aqua"**, **"magenta"**, and **"cyan"**.

In addition to these, there are four special colors in Flex, called **"haloOrange"**, **"haloBlue"**, **"haloSilver"**, and **"haloGreen"**.

Using Style Sheets

You can apply styles in another way: by using an `<mx:Style/>` tag. The `<mx:Style/>` tag lets you store your styles into a central location. Instead of setting a style for each component inline, you can use CSS to create style definitions that can be reused across multiple components. This is akin to using styles in word processing programs—instead of having to set, for example, the font size and color of each heading in a document individually, you can create a style that applies to all headings. If you've used styling in word processing programs, you also know that it can save you a lot of time if you ever decide to change a particular style, because you can change it once, and all text that uses that style is automatically updated. For Flex, this means you can define style properties such as font color, background color, font size, corner radius, and others in one place and reuse them across your application.

You can define CSS in an application by placing it within an `<mx:Style/>` tag. Alternatively, you can place it in an external *.css* file (discussed in the "External Style Sheets" section).

NOTE

CSS is a separate language from MXML and ActionScript and is a standard way to create style sheets. It isn't the goal of this book to make you an expert in CSS, but I will go over some basics so you can get going with it in your applications.

CSS Syntax

CSS syntax is, at its most basic, a style rule using a style name followed by opening and closing curly braces, between which are placed individual declarations for that style rule. You make the declarations by specifying a style property followed by a colon, after which you place the value for that property. You separate each declaration with a semicolon, and typically you make only one declaration per line, as shown in Figure 14-5.

NOTE

While the use of curly braces may look similar to ActionScript, CSS is an entirely different language (for one, it's declarative like MXML, not procedural like ActionScript). Note, for instance, the use of a colon (:) instead of an equal sign (=) to assign a property to a value.

```
            style rule
               ↓
.someStyleRule
{                    property        value
                        ↓              ↓
    someColorProperty : #FFFFFF;
    someNumberProperty : 18;

}
```

Figure 14-5. CSS syntax

You can create style declarations in CSS using three major methods: *class selectors*, *type selectors*, and *global styles*.

Class selector styles

Class selectors are style rules that are created by name, which can then be used by any component. This lets you group style properties and assign them to components all at once. For instance, you could create a style rule with a font color of white and a font size of 18 and call it `greatWhite`. For class selector rules in CSS, you use a period to precede the name. The CSS for this rule would look like the following:

```
<mx:Style>
.greatWhite
{
    color: #FFFFFF;
    fontSize: 18;
}
</mx:Style>
```

NOTE

If you've been using CSS in HTML, you may have noticed that the HTML attribute to apply class selector styles is called **class***, while in Flex it's known as* **styleName***.*

To use this style on a component, you would set that component's **styleName** property to the name of the style, but without the preceding period. For example, to apply the **greatWhite** style to a Button instance, you could use the following MXML:

```
<mx:Button styleName="greatWhite" />
```

When a style sheet is defined for an application, you can easily set the **styleName** property of a component in Design mode using the Style drop-down list, located in the Style section of the Flex Properties panel, as shown in Figure 14-1.

Style Property Names in CSS

In this chapter, you're seeing CSS style names that match the inline style property names of components. For instance, you can set the style for font size for a Button inline with the attribute **fontSize="14"** or with the following CSS:

```
Button
{
    fontSize: 14;
}
```

However, actually two naming schemes are used in Flex CSS. The one used in this chapter uses camel case, such as the previous code. However, standard CSS, such as that used in web pages, has a different naming scheme, which separates words via hyphens instead of capital letters.

Thus, the following CSS is also valid:

```
Button
{
    font-size: 14;
    font-weight: bold;
    corner-radius: 7;
}
```

You can use either naming scheme in your CSS style sheets, but you must use camel case for inline style attributes.

Type selector styles

Type selectors work differently than class selectors. Type selectors let you actually set all instances of a component to a specific style. This means, for example, that you could specify a set of styles that you want on all instances of a Button, or all instances of a Panel, in your application. To use type selectors, you create a style definition using the component's name:

```
<mx:Style>
Button
{
    color: #FFFFFF;
    fontSize: 18;
}
</mx:Style>
```

This code would make all Button components be white with a font size of 18, without the need to specify any style properties on the Buttons themselves.

Global styles

Global styles are a way to apply certain styles to everything in your application. While applying type selector styles to the Application means components can inherit many styles (see the box "Cascading Styles" for more information), not all of them will. Using a global style will ensure that the style propagates to everything in your application.

To use global styles, you use the word **global** as the name of the style rule. The following code shows a font color and font size that will affect everything:

```
<mx:Style>
global
{
    color: #FFFFFF;
    fontSize: 18;
}
</mx:Style>
```

External Style Sheets

You can create an external style sheet (CSS) file and include it with your Flex application. You do this by using the **source** property of an **<mx:Style/>** tag. This lets you separate your styles from the main application, which helps with two things. First, it lets you quickly switch out *.css* files, enabling you to change the entire look and feel of your applications with one file. This means you can create one or more external style sheets and easily change them, enabling you to change your entire application with one line of MXML. Second, if you're working in a team environment, separating the styles into a separate file allows a designer to keep their work apart from yours. A designer can work with the *.css* file, while a developer works on the main application.

Using this new concept, you can change your **ContactManager** application to take advantage of the **<mx:Style/>** tag and CSS.

I've created a *.css* file that you can use with this application to drop in a new look. You can get this file at *www.greenlike.com/flex/learning/projects/contactmanager/styles.css* and place it in the **ContactManager**'s source folder.

NOTE

Because Flex inherits many (but not all) of the CSS attributes that HTML can use, you can even reuse style sheets that were created for web pages in your Flex applications.

Once you've done this, you can add an `<mx:Style/>` tag to the main application that will import this style sheet:

```
<mx:Style source="styles.css"/>
```

The *.css* file loaded via an `<mx:Style/>` tag is actually compiled into the Flex application at build time. This is different from HTML, which loads its external *.css* files when the page loads. In other words, when you deploy your Flex application, changing the *.css* file with another on the server won't make any difference—if you make changes to the *.css* file, you need to recompile your Flex application. However, Flex does come with the ability to load styles at runtime by compiling style sheets into a *.swf* file and loading it at runtime. For more information on this feature, search the Flex documentation for *runtime styles*.

Creating a Blank CSS File

If you're handy with CSS or feel like starting from scratch, you can create a blank *.css* file and have it immediately available for your Flex application. You can create a new *.css* file by first selecting the project in Flex Navigator and then selecting File→New→CSS File. A dialog box will appear that lets you input a filename. (See Figure 14-6.)

Figure 14-6. The New CSS File dialog box

Once you click Finish, this blank *.css* file will open in Flex Builder, where you can edit the CSS directly or use the advanced Design mode features to change it visually.

Add the `<mx:Style/>` tag somewhere in the top-level tag, like you would do with `<mx:Script/>` tags and effect tags. This will cause the application to import this *.css* file. You can see this change directly in Design mode. Running the **ContactManager**, it should now look like Figure 14-7.

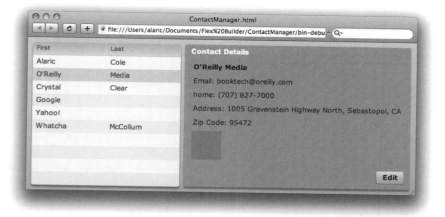

Figure 14-7. The ContactManager *application with a new style sheet*

Now you've witnessed the power of using external CSS style sheets, because you changed the entire look of the application with essentially a single line of code. You can use this concept over and over again, switching this style sheet with another that you've found on the Web or one you've created yourself.

The contents of the *styles.css* file are as follows:

```
global
{
    backgroundAlpha: .7;
    fontSize: 14;
}

Application
{
    backgroundColor: haloSilver;
    themeColor: #69a6fa;
}

DataGrid
{
    alternatingItemColors: #F7F7F7, #E2E8F4;
    backgroundDisabledColor: #C4DFF4;
    dropShadowEnabled: true;
    headerColors: #96BEF4, #C7DCF9;
    headerStyleName: dataGridHeader;
    horizontalGridLines: false;
    verticalGridLines: false;
}

.dataGridHeader
{
    fontSize: 12;
    color: #474545;
}

Panel
{
    backgroundAlpha: 1.0;
    backgroundColor: #6B9BC8;
```

```
        borderAlpha: 1.0;
        borderColor: #6B9BC8;
        controlBarStyleName: panelControlBar;
        cornerRadius: 3;
        dropShadowEnabled: true;
        titleStyleName: panelTitle;
}

.panelControlBar
{
        horizontalAlign: right;
}

.panelTitle
{
        color: #FFFFFF;
        fontWeight: bold;
        fontSize: 18;
}

TextInput
{
        cornerRadius: 7;
        borderStyle: solid;
        backgroundAlpha: 0.8;
}
```

The *styles.css* style sheet uses both class and type selectors to apply its styles. Type selectors are the most prevalent, because the purpose of this style sheet is to change the application as a whole without any changes required in the MXML code other than attaching the style sheet. However, class selectors are there as well. They're used for certain style properties of components, because these properties require complex styles. For instance, the Panel has a style property called **titleStyleName**, which controls the style of the text in the title bar. Because the title's style may need multiple style definitions such as font size and color, a class selector style rule named **.panelTitle** is created, and the **titleStyleName** points to this style.

Now that you have an external style sheet, you can take advantage of a great feature of Flex Builder. A *.css* file, like an *.mxml* file, can be modified visually in Flex Builder's Design mode. Try it—open the *styles.css* file, and make sure you're in Design mode. In the toolbar next to the Source/Design mode button and the Design mode Refresh button, you'll see a few new buttons, as shown in Figure 14-8.

Figure 14-8. The toolbar for a .css file in Design mode

With these buttons, you can select, create, and remove styles. Try selecting the Panel rule from the Style drop-down list, and notice how it displays an example Panel graphic. This graphic will update automatically when its styles are changed, allowing you to quickly make the right style changes visually.

The Flex Properties panel for style sheets is similar to the one for *.mxml* files, just much more complete. In Standard view, nearly every available style property is at your fingertips. For some styles that require their own style rule, such as a Panel's `titleStyleName` style, an Edit button is available that will let you modify that particular rule.

Using CSS Design mode, you don't need to know much about CSS at all, because you can accomplish a great deal visually. Have fun with this style sheet, modifying properties to your liking. Then switch back to Source mode to see the CSS that is written for your changes; this is a great way to learn CSS.

NOTE

To create a new style rule, you can use the toolbar button New Style (see Figure 14-8). This will prompt you with the New Style Rule dialog box. Creating new style rules is discussed in the box "Converting Inline Styles to CSS."

Converting Inline Styles to CSS

If you're using inline styles with an application, you always have the option of converting the styles to an external style sheet. Just select a styled component in Design mode, and within the Style section of the Flex Properties panel you will see a Convert to CSS button (see Figure 14-1). Clicking this button will prompt you with a New Style Rule dialog box (see Figure 14-9), which lets you attach a new style sheet and add style rules to it. (If Flex Builder prompts you to save the application before continuing, go ahead and save it.)

Figure 14-9. The New Style Rule dialog box, asking for a CSS file

If you don't have an external *.css* style sheet defined for this application, the dialog box will have a warning that "A CSS file must be specified." No problem, because you

can create one here using the New button on the top right.

Clicking the New button will open the New CSS File dialog box, which lets you create a *.css* file, as shown in Figure 14-6. Once you've created a new *.css* file, the New Style Rule dialog box will be populated with this file, as shown in Figure 14-10.

Figure 14-10. The New Style Rule dialog box, creating a type selector for the Button component

You have a few choices here for the type of style you want to create. For instance, to create a type selector to modify all Buttons that use this style sheet, choose "Specific component" as the selector type. To create a class selector, choose "All Components with style name." Clicking Finish will create the CSS rule and open the new *.css* file.

Style Precedence

You can apply styles in many ways, and some take precedence over others (see Figure 14-11). Inline styles take the lead, so even if a style is set for a component using a class or type selector, the inline style will always override them. As for class and type selectors, class selectors will take precedence. This means that if a Button's style has been set using a type selector, applying a style to all Button instances, a specific Button that has a **styleName** property set will override the type selector.

Figure 14-11. Style precedence in Flex

The easiest way to remember this is that setting styles on a specific instance of a component will always prevail and that specific style properties will always beat a more generic **styleName**.

Embedding Assets

NOTE

For a quick and fun way to get CSS code for your components by using a visual tool, check out the Flex Style Explorer online at http://examples.adobe.com/flex3/consulting/styleexplorer/Flex3StyleExplorer.html. While Flex Builder has the most extensive toolset, this can be a real time-saver and a useful tool if you're not using Flex Builder.

Next, you'll open the Search application to learn about embedding assets, and you'll apply some new styles to this application as well. Open the *Search. mxml* file in Design mode, and switch to the base state. Once you're there, select the Application (by clicking the background in Design mode), and modify its styles using the Flex Properties panel, giving it a new background gradient. For this application, a grayscale look might be nice, so you could give it a background gradient of white to gray. (0xFFFFFF to 0xA1A1A1 would work nicely.) Also, setting the **themeColor** of the application to a gray or silver color would be a suitable look.

Embedding Icons

One of the styles that some Flex components can use is displaying an icon. Buttons use the **icon** style property to display an icon inside of them, which by default is on their left side. However, to apply an icon to a Button control or other component that uses them, you must embed the graphic in your application, because the icon isn't downloaded at runtime. Embedding assets requires a special compiler command, and the easiest way to do this is by using the Flex Properties panel in Design mode.

Because adding an icon requires a graphic file, you can either find your own favorite icon or get one from my website. I've created a magnifying glass icon that you can download from *www.greenlike.com/flex/learning/projects/search/ search_icon.png*. Whether you use mine or your own, be sure to place the graphic in the **Search** project's source folder.

With the search Button selected, the Flex Properties panel will display an Icon field under the Common section, where you can modify the most common properties. To easily add the proper code for embedding the icon, click the folder icon to the right of this field. This displays an Open dialog box, where you can point to a graphic to embed. Navigate the folder structure to select *search_icon.png* or your preferred graphic. Once you've finished with the dialog box, Flex Builder refreshes and should display the icon on the Button in Design mode (see Figure 14-12).

NOTE

The TabNavigator can also display icons on its tabs. To add icons there, you actually set the **icon** *property of the container inside the TabNavigator. This is the same concept as setting the container's* **label** *for display in the tab.*

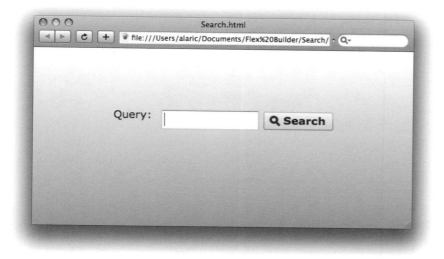

Figure 14-12. The Search *application, showing an icon*

Looking at the code that was generated by adding the icon in Design mode, you should see a new statement, **@Embed**, followed by parentheses and the source for the embedded icon:

```
icon="@Embed(source='search_icon.png')"
```

This is the way you can embed assets inline in MXML, and you can use this same syntax to embed other media assets.

Embedding Sounds

Just as you can embed graphics to make them immediately available for use for such things as icons, you can embed sounds in your applications. In the previous chapter, I showed you how to use sound effects, and I mentioned that some latency may occur when downloading large sound files at runtime. To get around this issue, you can embed your MP3s in the Flex application.

For an example of how to embed sounds for a sound effect, you can add one to the **Search** application. Go into Source mode to see the code for the transitions that you created earlier. In this code you'll see a Parallel effect that has a Move effect and a Resize effect. You can add a sound effect here to play a sound as the other two visual effects play.

To do so, you'll need an *.mp3* file. Again, you can use your own favorite or get one from my site at *www.greenlike.com/flex/learning/projects/search/whoosh. mp3*. Place the *.mp3* file in the project's source folder. The **<mx:SoundEffect/>** tag takes a **source** property, which you can use to place a similar **@Embed** statement to a Button's icon property. You can give it a sound using the following code:

```
<mx:Transition fromState="search">

    <mx:Sequence targets="{[frm, queryTextInput, searchButton,hbox1,
        resultsList]}">
        <mx:Parallel>
            <mx:Move filter="move" />
            <mx:Resize filter="resize" />
            <mx:SoundEffect source="@Embed(source='whoosh.mp3')"/>
        </mx:Parallel>

        <mx:AddChildAction filter="add"/>

    </mx:Sequence>

</mx:Transition>
```

This should play the sound effect while moving the search fields in the transition from the search state back to the base state.

Embedding Fonts

In the previous chapter, I mentioned the concept of embedding fonts. While Flex uses system (or device) fonts by default, it's possible to include your own fonts. The easiest way to embed fonts is by using a CSS declaration, and the simplest way to do this is by using Design mode. If you want to embed a font, I recommend creating an external style sheet and using Design mode to create the code for you.

The embed code that would be created for the Arial font might be like the following code, using an **@font-face** declaration inside a style sheet:

```
@font-face
{
        src:local("Arial");
        fontFamily: myEmbeddedFont;
}
```

This code embeds the Arial font from the developer's system and makes it available for use via the myEmbeddedFont font name. This font name can then be used as the **fontFamily** style for a component. The following CSS would use this embedded font and make it the default font for the entire application:

```
Application
{
        fontFamily: myEmbeddedFont;
}
```

Skinning

The Flex style system is very powerful and customizable, but you may find that it just isn't enough. For instance, if you want a CheckBox control to look like a light switch or you want a Button to have an irregular shape, styling won't cut it. You may find that you have graphical assets and you want to use them for your components.

Every Flex visual component has the ability to accept a graphic to modify its appearance. This is called *skinning*, because it's just replacing the *skin* of a component—the core functionality remains intact. Graphical skinning lets you drop in graphics to change the outward appearance of a component.

Most components have more than one skin, representing the different parts of the component or different states that a component can be in. These are specified as style properties, usually with the word *Skin* at the end of the property name. For example, a Panel has both a **borderSkin** that accepts a graphic for the display of its border and a **titleBackgroundSkin** that shows as its title bar. A Button control has an **upSkin** for its normal up state, as well as a **downSkin** for when it's pressed, an **overSkin** for when the mouse rolls over it, and a **disabledSkin** to display when its **enabled** property is set to **false**.

For example, a Button could be skinned with four *.png* graphics for four of its states. If you had four *.png* files named *up.png*, *over.png*, *down.png*, and *disabled.png*, you could skin a Button control like the following:

```
<mx:Button
    upSkin="@Embed(source='up.png')"
    overSkin="@Embed(source='over.png')"
    downSkin="@Embed(source='down.png')"
    disabledSkin="@Embed(source='disabled.png')" />
```

This code uses the same **@Embed** statement that is used to embed other media, such as sounds and icons.

When you skin a component, it's a good idea to set skins for each of these states so that you can customize each aspect of the component. If you were to set only the **upSkin** of a Button to a custom graphic, then once someone rolled the mouse over the Button, the default Button look would appear, and this wouldn't look very nice if the two graphics didn't match.

You can easily get a list of the available skin properties by looking at the Category view of the Flex Properties panel for a particular component. However, the easiest way to skin components is by using an external style sheet, because you can take advantage of the additional features of the Skin section of the CSS Design mode. When you've selected a style rule in CSS

NOTE

*The Button control also has a **skin** property, which applies the same graphic skin to all states of the Button.*

Design mode, notice the Style/Skin toggle bar in the upper-right section of the Flex Properties panel (shown in Figure 14-13). This will show a Skin section, where you can easily embed graphic assets via a Skin drop-down list.

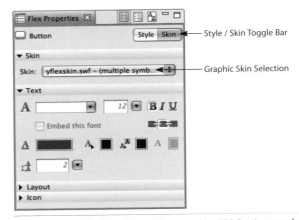

Figure 14-13. The Flex Properties panel in CSS Design mode

You can choose whether to import graphics from a typical file, such as a *.png*, *.gif*, or *.jpg*. You also have the option of using assets from a compiled *.swf* or *.swc* file. This way, you can use graphics you've created from a variety of sources. When you choose a type of graphic from the list, you will see a dialog box with a list of all the possible skins. From this dialog box, you can point to a file or Flash symbol that you want to import, and all the embed code will be written for you. You will also be able to see the skins displayed in Design mode. For components such as Button, which have multiple skin states, you will see them as well, as shown in Figure 14-14.

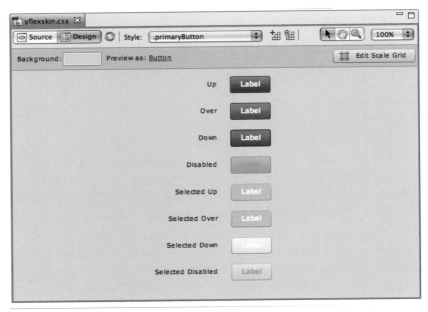

Figure 14-14. A skinned Button in CSS Design mode

Scaling Skins

Design mode for CSS has another great feature, which lets you edit the scaling grid for your components. The scaling grid is an invisible grid that controls which parts of a graphic skin should scale when the component is resized and which parts should not. For instance, if you have a Button skin with rounded corners, you wouldn't want the corners to scale themselves when the Button was resized to a larger width; you would just want the skin's interior to scale. That's what the scale grid allows (see Figure 14-15 and Figure 14-16). Everything within the square that is created by four imaginary lines will scale, and everything outside it will not. See Figure 14-17 for a screen shot of the scale grid editor.

Figure 14-15. A button skin, resized horizontally (without a scale grid set)

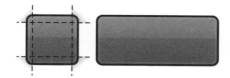

Figure 14-16. A button skin, resized horizontally (with a scale grid set)

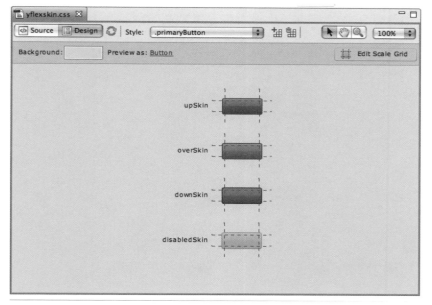

Figure 14-17. The scale grid editor for a Button skins

NOTE

*Just as you can set a skin for each state of a Button control, you can set a different icon for each state. While setting the **icon** style property will apply a single icon for all states, you can use CSS Design mode to specify icons for the up, over, and disabled states of a Button, for instance.*

Using Themes

You have the ability to not only change certain parts of your application, but the application as a whole using CSS. You can achieve this through style properties, the skinning of components, or often both. When you group styles and/or skins in a separate style sheet, you are creating an application *theme*.

Once you create such themes, you can share them among your projects or distribute them on the Web for others. You may also find some useful themes for your applications online. Because such themes use external assets, they often include both a *.css* file as well as graphics such as a *.png* file or a *.swf* file. To use them in your application, you would copy the files to your project's source folder and add an `<mx:Style/>` tag to your application, pointing its **source** to the *.css* file for that theme.

For ease of distribution, some themes are packaged as a single *.swc* file, which is a compiled file that includes both the necessary *.css* file and the external assets inside it. To use these theme files in your application, you must use a special compiler option. To do so, select your project, and select Project→Properties. From there, choose the Flex Compiler item in the list at the left of the dialog box, which will take you to the options for the Flex compiler. In this section, you'll see a field labeled "Additional compiler arguments," and in this field you can place the argument **–theme** followed by the name of your theme *.swc* file (see Figure 14-18).

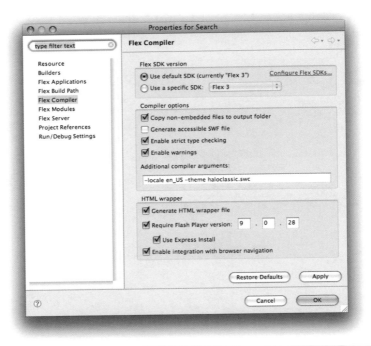

Figure 14-18. The Flex compiler options dialog box

For instance, Flex Builder comes with a theme called Halo Classic, which is available at the following locations:

Mac:

/Mac/Applications/Adobe Flex Builder 3/sdks/3.0.0/frameworks/themes/ HaloClassic/haloclassic.swc

Windows:

C:\Program Files\Adobe Flex Builder 3\sdks\3.0.0\frameworks\themes\ HaloClassic\haloclassic.swc

You can copy this SWC into your project and point the compiler **–theme** argument to this file, and your applications will use this theme.

The Default Theme

Flex comes with a built-in theme called Halo Aeon. This theme is built using programmatic skinning, which means the skins are created from drawing in ActionScript, not from graphics files like *.jpg* or *.png* files. This is actually what enables the standard Flex components to support many style properties like **cornerRadius**, **borderStyle**, and **backgroundColor**. Because the programmatic skinning draws in script, these style properties can work.

Flex applications actually use a *.css* file to apply the default theme, and you can find it at the following locations for a typical Flex Builder installation:

Mac

/Mac/Applications/Adobe Flex Builder 3/sdks/3.0.0/frameworks/projects/
framework/defaults.css

Windows

C:\Program Files\Adobe Flex Builder 3\sdks\3.0.0\frameworks\projects\framework\
defaults.css

If you're interested, you should take a look at this file to understand how CSS is used for Flex components.

Also, your Flex Builder installation comes with an alternative, graphical default theme. It uses a *.css* file to apply graphic skins, which are available as a *.fla* (Flash IDE) file. If you have a copy of the Flash IDE and want to take a look, you can find the graphical theme at the following locations:

Mac

/Mac/Applications/Adobe Flex Builder 3/sdks/3.0.0/frameworks/themes/
AeonGraphical/src

Windows

C:\Program Files\Adobe Flex Builder 3\sdks\3.0.0\frameworks\themes\
AeonGraphical\src

NOTE

To learn the basics of drawing in Flash Player, check out the documentation for the Drawing API. This will let you draw anything you like using vector commands and can even give you the skills to create your own programmatic skins.

For an example of how applications can change their look with a new theme, see Figure 14-19, Figure 14-20, and Figure 14-21.

NOTE

If you want to easily change your applications to a completely new look, grab some themes online at www.scalenine.com.

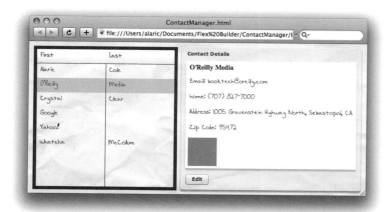

Figure 14-19. The ContactManager *application with the Flekscribble theme (authored by Ralf Sczepan) applied*

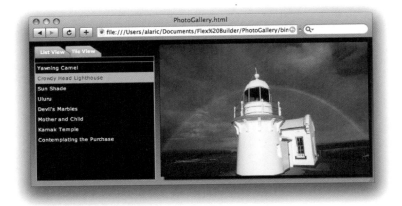

Figure 14-20. The PhotoGallery *application with an overlapping tabs theme (authored by Juan Sanchez) applied*

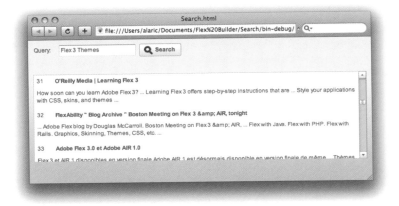

Figure 14-21. The Search *application with Yahoo! theme applied, available at http://developer.yahoo.com/flash/articles/yahoo-flex-skin.html*

Summary

In this chapter, you went beyond building Flex applications to customizing the look and feel of them. You learned that you can change the styles of your components in a few ways, by using inline style properties or CSS style sheets and even by dropping in external graphics. While you can master CSS yourself, you can also rely on the power of Flex Builder to visually design your components.

You may find that you need to tweak the look of only a few components, or you may decide that you want an entirely new look that you create yourself. The look and feel of your Flex application is limited only by your imagination.

This chapter took you through the final set of skills for developing applications in Flex. In the next, final chapter, you will learn how you can take your applications and show them to the world.

CHAPTER 15

DEPLOYING YOUR APPLICATION

In this final chapter, I'll cover the required steps for sharing your application with the world. Whether you choose to deploy your application on the Web, on the desktop, or on both, I'll show you how.

Each deployment has its pros and cons. Web applications are accessible by going to a web page that hosts the application. This is very convenient to many people, because the application can be used on any computer and is available as long as the computer has access to the Internet. However, some people may not have an Internet connection available at all times or may want to use the application offline.

Desktop applications are always available, because they are installed on each person's computer. Such applications are more traditional, opened by going to the Windows Start menu, to the Mac OS X Dock, or by other means. They are available without using a browser, because they run in their own window. Desktop applications also provide the ability to drag and drop from other applications, and they can read and write to a computer's filesystem. However, they also must be installed on each computer on which they're going to be used.

Whichever method you choose, you can be assured that your application will work on any major operating system. This means you can write a Flex application once and make it available to anyone, regardless of what operating system they prefer.

Deploying to the Web

You've primarily been developing and testing the Flex applications in this book in a browser. When you created the **ContactManager**, **PhotoGallery**, and **Search** applications, you specified in the New Flex Project dialog box that you planned to deploy each one as a web application. This doesn't limit your application to being deployed on the Web only, though, because you can always migrate a web application to the desktop. While I'll show you how to do just that in the later section "Deploying to the Desktop," in this section, I'll cover the process of deploying to the Web.

The first step in deploying your web application is building a release version. When you've been developing your application, you've seen that the compiled version is placed in an output directory called bin-debug by default. This is a build that contains debugging information for use with the debug version of Flash Player. This is what Flex Builder uses for its Debugger and Profiler (you'll learn more about Profiler in the box "Tweaking Performance"). This is great for when you're developing, but when you're ready to deploy, it's good to create a release build that doesn't include this debugging information, because the resulting *.swf* file will be smaller.

I'll show you how to create a release build for the **PhotoGallery** application, so open that project now. Before you create the build, it's a good idea to check your settings for your build. This will actually affect the release build as well as the debug build, so it's a good idea to be familiar with this process.

Modifying Build Settings

You can check your build settings by selecting the project in the Flex navigator and selecting Project→Properties. In the Properties dialog box, select the Flex Compiler item from the list at the left (see Figure 15-1). This opens the Flex Compiler properties, allowing you to modify options for your build.

Figure 15-1. The Flex Compiler Properties dialog

Flex SDK version

The first section of options in this dialog box sets the Flex SDK version. By default, the Flex 3 SDK is used, so you don't have to worry about this one unless you want to develop for an older version of the SDK. For instance, if you've ever used previous versions of Flex, you may have code that uses an older SDK (such as Flex 2.0). Because some of the API will change from one version to the next, the "Use a specific SDK" option lets you set which you'll use. For this application, you can leave the default.

Non-embedded files

The setting, "Copy non-embedded files to output folder," specifies whether to include extra files such as *.xml* files or graphical assets in the build. Leave this item turned on to copy the necessary files such as *photos.xml* which the `PhotoGallery` application needs to run. If you prefer to manually copy the necessary files, you can turn off this item—but beware, any time you change a source file, you'll need to manually copy the file to the output directory.

Accessibility

The next item concerns accessibility. *Accessibility* is everyone's "ability to access" your application, and the term typically applies to users with impaired vision, hearing impairments, or mobility or cognitive impairments. The option "Generate accessible SWF file" is referring specifically to the use of a *screen reader*, a special application that can read the contents of a computer screen to a user with impaired vision. This option is turned off by default, because a bit of extra code will be included in the compiled version of your application to enable it to communicate with a screen reader. Unless you never expect your users to require a screen reader—such as when you're developing an application for a specific known group of users—it's a good idea to turn on this checkbox. (For example, if you turn on accessibility for the compiled *.swf* file for the `PhotoGallery` application, you'll see the file is 318KB. Compare this to the compiled version without accessibility enabled, which is 328KB.) However, there is much more to creating accessible applications than simply turning on a checkbox. For more information on this, see the box "Designing Accessible Applications."

NOTE

When a public building is erected, it must have ramps and other structures to make accessing the building possible for everyone. So too should a public application be made accessible to all.

Designing Accessible Applications

While turning on the compiler option "Generate accessible SWF file" is a great step toward making your applications more accessible, it's not a complete solution. You may not have thought about it at this point, but lots of folks with impairments or disabilities exist who probably want to use your application.

Often, users who have low or no vision would like to access your application. While this may not seem to make sense with an application used to view photos, accessibility does apply to these applications. For instance, a user may not be blind but simply have color-blindness or low vision. In this case, it's important to make sure your application doesn't rely on color differentiation and that the colors of your application don't interfere with readability. Also, make sure your application can be viewed at lower screen resolutions, because many users with vision impairments will use lower resolutions. Even for those who can't see at all, they should—at the very least—be able to interact with your application enough to know that it's a photo-viewing application. While blind users will not be able to see the images, they may still want to know about the photos, such as their descriptions or other content.

To help keep your applications accessible, be careful using audio. A user may find that sounds interfere with their ability to understand their screen reader, so always provide an easy way to turn off sounds or music, if your application includes them. Also, make sure that any audio content you have has captioning available.

In addition, always ensure that the components you use don't require the use of a mouse—in other words, the full use of the application should be possible through keyboard navigation alone. Some people may not be able to use a mouse, but this shouldn't keep them from being able to experience your application. All standard Flex components have keyboard navigation built-in, so this is not usually a problem. However, there may be other aspects of your application that require a mouse, such as a context menu or command that is available only through a double-click action. A good rule of thumb is to provide multiple ways to accomplish a task, so if you have something accessible through the mouse, also provide an obvious way to access this through the keyboard.

Further, pay attention to the *tab index*, or the order in which the focus changes when the Tab key is pressed. Typically Flex will provide a logical tab index based on the placement of controls on the screen. However, it's a good idea to always test the tab index with the keyboard, especially if you're using a custom tab index. In fact, one of the best ways to ensure you've designed an accessible application is to test it with a keyboard alone. Drop the mouse for a few minutes, and see how well you can use your own application.

Finally, make certain your application is easy to understand and navigate. Also, provide icons and other graphics that enhance the application, but don't rely on icons alone to convey meaning. For instance, in the **Search** application, you'll see a magnifying glass icon on the search button that helps to communicate that clicking the button will begin a search. However, a label on that button still reads "Search," because the icon alone doesn't suffice. (Such an icon could also mean "zoom in," for instance.)

Making your applications accessible often makes your applications cleaner, simpler, and easier to use for all your users, not just those with impairments. So, follow these simple rules every time, and you'll ensure you're creating not only accessible applications but also *well-designed* applications. Making your application easier to understand and use is always a good thing.

Compiler warnings

The next couple of options are whether to enable strict type checking and warnings. It's a good idea to leave both of these turned on, because this will output useful notifications in the Problems panel, which will help to keep your applications performing well.

HTML wrapper

The HTML wrapper is the *.html* file that is generated for your Flex application. This file will be output to *PhotoGallery.html* in the output directories, and it includes code to embed the *PhotoGallery.swf* file in a web page. Unless you have written your own, leave Generate HTML wrapper file turned on so you'll have a page that will load in web browsers. (For more information on the generated *.html* file and how to customize it, see the box "Customizing the HTML Wrapper.")

Customizing the HTML Wrapper

While the generated HTML file may be fine for many developers, you may want to modify the template for the HTML wrapper or even create your own HTML file. If you want to customize it, it helps to understand what's going on inside the file.

The HTML template is located under your project's root folder in a folder called html-template. This directory contains additional files that may be copied into your output folder, but the main file is called *index.template.html*. This is not the final *.html* file that will be output, but a template that is read by the Flex compiler. After adding certain information, a final *.html* file is output that embeds the Flex application.

The template contains variables, or *tokens*, such as **${title}**, which are special placeholders that the Flex compiler will replace with actual text values. Table 15-1 lists the available tokens. While the default value of these tokens is generally fine, you may need to modify some of them, such as **${title}**, which is the text that displays as the HTML page's title.

You can also modify other parts of this file, such as the content that displays if a user doesn't have Flash Player installed. You can find this content by looking through the file for a variable called **alternateContent**.

Table 15-1. HTML wrapper token list

Token Name	Description
${application}	This option sets the **id** of the embedded SWF file. This allows it to be accessed by JavaScript or other browser scripting languages.
${bgcolor}	This is the background color of the HTML file. While a Flex application typically takes up the entire browser window and therefore doesn't display this color, it's viewable when the user resizes the application or when the Flex application doesn't take up the entire window. Note that you can also set this using the SWF metadata tag as described in Chapter 14, "Styling Applications."
${height}	This is the height of the application, set by the **<mx:Application/>** tag's **height** property.
${swf}	This token sets the full path of the compiled application's *.swf* file.
${title}	This is the title of the HTML page, which displays in the title bar of the browser. By default, this is the name of the Flex application, such as **PhotoGallery**.
${version_major}	This is the required major version number of Flash Player, for example, 9. This token appears only in wrappers with Flash Player version detection code, as set in the HTML wrapper compiler options.
${version_minor}	This is the required minor version number of Flash Player, as set in the HTML wrapper compiler options.
${version_revision}	This is the required revision version number of Flash Player, as set in the HTML wrapper compiler options.
${width}	This is the width of the application, set by the **<mx:Application/>** tag's **width** property.

Flash Player version

The next item in the Flex Compiler options is whether to include code in this HTML wrapper for checking the version of the Flash Player plug-in. Because different versions of Flex components, or your own ActionScript code, may require specific versions of Flash Player, you can leave the defaults here. The option Use Express Install will enable the application to request that people update their versions of Flash Player if they don't currently have the required version. Turning on this box will include a *.swf* file called *playerProductInstall.swf*, along with some extra code in the HTML wrapper, in the output directory for your application.

Browser navigation integration

The final item in this dialog box is "Enable integration with browser navigation." Turning on this item outputs the necessary files (in the history folder of your project) that make history management work for your application, such as the ability to use the browser's Back and Forward buttons. (This was explained in more detail in Chapter 11.) The PhotoGallery application doesn't use history management, so it's fine to turn off this feature.

Exporting a Release Build

Now that you've finalized the options for your build, it's time to create a release version. You can create a release version by selecting the project in the Flex Navigator and selecting Project→Export Release Build. This will display the dialog box shown in Figure 15-2.

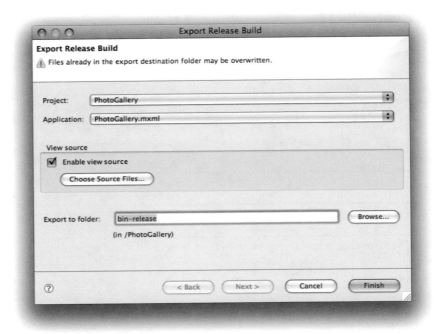

Figure 15-2. The Export Release Build dialog box

NOTE

You may have multiple applications in a single project. This can be useful if you require the same assets, components, and/or settings for multiple applications and would like to keep them in the same project.

Because you selected the project in the Flex Navigator, the first option for this dialog box, Project, is filled in for you. The next option, Application, lets you export a release build for different applications, if you have more than one in a project. For the PhotoGallery project, as well as the other projects you've created using this book, you have only one application per project, so you don't need to worry about this one.

Sharing Source Code

The next section in the Export Release Build dialog box is the "View source" section. Turning on the "Enable view source" checkbox will create a folder in the final build that contains a web page with your source code. This page will contain a list of the individual files for your application and a custom viewer that lets users instantly view your source code (see Figure 15-5 for an example). The page will also contain a link to download the source code as a .zip file. If you feel comfortable sharing your code with the world, turn on this checkbox. Sharing source code is a great way to help others learn Flex. It's also a way to give tech-savvy users access to the internals of your application so that if they find problems, they can give you specific information about what went wrong.

If you choose to turn on the ability to view the source files, you may not want to include all of the files. If you want to pick and choose certain files, click the Choose Source Files button. This opens a dialog box shown in Figure 15-3, which contains a tree list of your source files. In this case, I've chosen to include only the code under the src directory, and not to include files from the HTML wrapper source (the html-template folder) or the empty libs folder. You can also change the name of the directory to which the source code will be output.

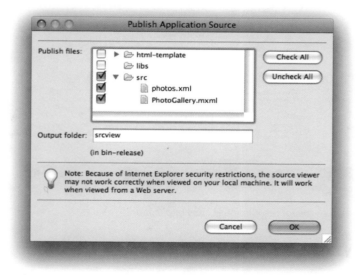

Figure 15-3. The Publish Application Source dialog box

If you've enabled the ability to view the source files, the `<mx:Application/>` tag for your *PhotoGallery.mxml* application will have a new attribute added called **viewSourceURL** that points to the directory for your source code. This attribute causes the Application to create a context menu item called View Source, which users of your application will see when they right-click the

If you're developing an application for a company that doesn't want to release its source code, be sure to disable the ability to view source for the application. Also, be certain if you've previously turned on "Enable view source" that the source files don't remain in the output directory. Even if you disable source view for the application, if you have uploaded the source output files to a web server, they are still accessible.

application in a web browser (see Figure 15-4). Selecting this menu item will open the source view, as shown in Figure 15-5.

Figure 15-4. The **PhotoGallery** *application, showing the context menu*

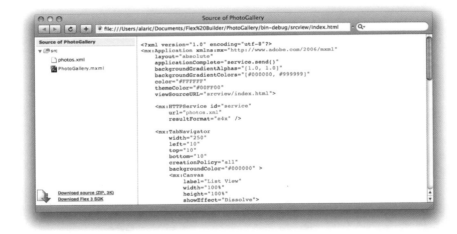

Figure 15-5. The source view for the **PhotoGallery** *application*

Setting Where to Export Files

The final option of the Export Release Build dialog box is the "Export to folder" option, which lets you modify the location and name of the folder that will contain the files for the release build. Accepting the default is fine, unless you prefer a different name or want to automatically place the build in another directory on your computer or on a networked drive. For now, just accept the default of bin-release and then click the Finish button. A release build will be placed in a new folder in the **PhotoGallery** project called bin-release, as shown in Figure 15-6. This folder contains only the files necessary for the application to run in a web browser.

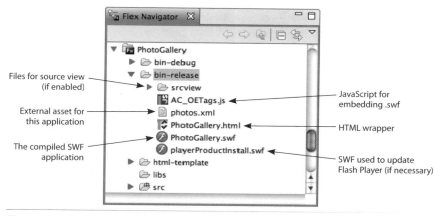

Files for source view (if enabled)

External asset for this application

The compiled SWF application

JavaScript for embedding .swf

HTML wrapper

SWF used to update Flash Player (if necessary)

Figure 15-6. The release build folder structure for PhotoGallery

Decreasing Download Time

Flex applications are incredibly small considering their rich features. The final size of your application is determined by a few factors, such as the amount of code the application contains and the number of components used. Because only the code necessary for the application to run is included in the final compiled *.swf* file, the more components you use in your application, the larger it will be. Because applications deployed on the Web will be accessed in a web browser and must be downloaded in order to be viewed, it makes sense to want to keep your applications as small as possible, because this will decrease the amount of time people have to wait to view and access it.

A typical Flex application, using a few standard components such as Button controls, List controls, and a few containers, is about 300KB. However, you can decrease the impact of the Flex components on the size of your application. One of the very cool features of Flex is the ability to dramatically decrease application size by keeping the standard Flex component framework cached on people's machines so they don't have to download it for each Flex application they view.

Flex separates the framework code into a separate file. When someone first views a Flex application, they will download this framework and cache the file on their machine. The next time they view that Flex application, or any other Flex application that enables this *framework caching*, they won't have to download the framework again—they'll be able to use the cached version on the local machine.

What this means in practice is an initial, larger download for people using an application with framework caching. However, after this initial download, subsequent downloads will be faster. See Table 15-2 and Table 15-3 for a comparison of the impact of the framework cache for the PhotoGallery application. The total initial download for this application, when using framework caching, is 639KB, which is much larger. However, on every download

NOTE

Also, a Flex feature called modules lets you modularize parts of your application into individually downloaded pieces. This is useful for larger applications that have many views or parts. If you think this is a feature that could help your application, check the documentation for the Module component.

NOTE

Due to the way most browsers work, any Flex application that you view in a web page should be cached by the browser itself. This means, whether you're using framework caching or not, the application will load immediately. Framework caching's real benefit is with multiple applications, or applications which have been cleared from the browser's cache thereafter, the size is only 101KB. Compare this to the application when not using framework caching, where it is 318KB every time.

Table 15-2. PhotoGallery size at initial download

	Framework Cache Used	Framework Cache Not Used
PhotoGallery.swf	101 KB	318KB
External Framework SWF (Downloaded Only Once)	538KB	—
Total Download	**639KB**	**318KB**

Table 15-3. PhotoGallery size on each subsequent download

	Framework Cache Used	Framework Cache Not Used
PhotoGallery.swf	101 KB	318KB
External Framework SWF (Downloaded Only Once)	— (cached)	—
Total Download	**101KB**	**318KB**

If you find the framework cache feature to be a good bet for your application, here's how to enable it: First, select your project in the Flex Navigator, and select Project→Properties. In this Properties dialog box, select the Flex Build Path item in the list at the left (see Figure 15-7). This displays the

Figure 15-7. The Flex Build Path options for PhotoGallery

Flex Build Path dialog box, which has two sections you can switch between using the toggle bar: "Source path," where you can modify the source path and output path locations, and "Library path," where you can specify external libraries to which you want to connect your project.

By default, a Flex application will use the Flex 3 SDK, and this is the first item in the "Build path libraries" list for the "Library path" section. You'll want to change the Framework linkage, which is "Merged into code" by default, meaning the Flex SDK is compiled into your application's final *.swf* file. Change this to "Runtime shared library (RSL)," and the Flex framework components will be exported as separate *.swf* files.

This means your final application *.swf* will be much smaller but will include a couple of larger *.swf* files that will be downloaded in the background separately—but downloaded only once and cached forevermore. In the case of **PhotoGallery**, two extra files are exported to the release version, although they're essentially the same. One is an unsigned version used in older versions of Flash Player, and the other is a more secure, signed version that the current Flash Player version uses. See Figure 15-8 for how the **PhotoGallery** release build looks when using the framework cache feature.

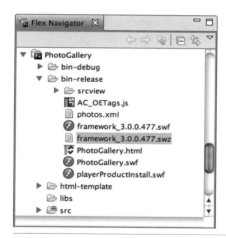

Figure 15-8. The release build folder structure for **PhotoGallery**, *when using framework caching*

Hosting Your Application

Now that you have a release build, you'll want to place it on a server to make it available to the public. If you don't currently have access to a web host, such as one you pay for or one provided by your work or school, you might try signing up for one of the free hosts such as Yahoo! Geocities (*http://geocities.yahoo.com*). If you're serious about your application, however, you'll eventually want to get a web host that you can have full control over. Choosing a host can be an overwhelming process, because you have to consider a number of options to get the best bang for your buck, but luckily they are getting cheaper every day.

NOTE

If you're planning to use a server technology for your Flex application, such as ColdFusion or PHP, you'll want to make sure your host has these capabilities.

NOTE

You can change the name of the exported .html file to create an easier URL for people to point to in their browsers. If you change the name to index.html, most web servers will automatically load the file when navigating to the file's directory. For example, if I change the name of PhotoGallery.html to index.html, you could access the application by going to www.greenlike.com/flex/learning/projects/photogallery/ instead of www.greenlike.com/flex/learning/projects/photogallery/PhotoGallery.html.

Once you have a web server/host, you can copy the contents of the release build into the appropriate directory on your server. Depending upon the domain name and folder structure of your host, the URL to access your application will change. For example, you can see the final version of the **PhotoGallery** application on my site at *www.greenlike.com/flex/learning/projects/photogallery/PhotoGallery.html*, because I placed the contents of the release build into the flex/learning/projects/photogallery directory for my web server, located at *greenlike.com*. You can see the final result in Figure 15-9 or by navigating to that URL in your web browser.

Figure 15-9. The PhotoGallery *deployed as a web application, viewed in a browser*

Tweaking Performance

One of the steps in application development is checking for performance. While you should always be aware of performance as you write code, some feel it's a good idea to wait until core development is finished before you get too concerned with "tweaking" your application.

> *We should forget about small efficiencies, say about 97% of the time: premature optimization is the root of all evil.*
>
> —*Donald Knuth*

If you really want to work on performance, one tool you have at your disposal is Flex Builder's Profiler, included with Flex Builder Professional edition. Accessible by selecting the Run→Profile command or by clicking the Profiler toolbar button (see Figure 15-10), the Profiler checks your application for performance bottlenecks. It does so by taking samples of how long different parts of your application take to finish, such as a method call you've created. This lets you see, at a glance, what methods in your application are most important to performance. You can use this information to take steps to optimize your application.

Figure 15-10. The Profiler toolbar button

Deploying to the Desktop

Flex is more than just a tool to create web applications. Flex is a great framework for creating "traditional" desktop applications as well. Using Adobe AIR, you can easily create applications that people can download and install on their local machines and use any time, whether or not they are connected to the Internet. While this doesn't make sense for all applications, some applications work best on the desktop. Others work great both on the Web and on the desktop. The choice is yours as a Flex developer, because you can easily migrate applications from one platform to the other and even create a code base that can work in either platform.

User (or Friend) Testing

The best way to ensure that your application is usable, or **user-friendly**, is by getting comments from others. Watching how people interact with your application is invaluable in understanding how to streamline and perfect the user experience. Because you may spend so much time with an application as you're developing it, even bad interactions may make perfect sense to you. But a new user, who has never seen your application, may use it entirely differently.

If you don't have a user experience lab or a budget to get one, a few friends will work in a pinch. Just hand your application over to a pal or two, and watch how they use it. Don't explain the application to them or answer questions as they are using it—just sit back and watch them squirm with delight, or frustration. Remember, you won't always be there to help the average user, so don't cheat by giving your buddy privileged information.

Try to listen to their comments and remain patient, even if you don't always agree with them. Chances are, you'll elicit some great feedback that will help you perfect your application.

NOTE

The more diverse the testers of your application, the better. If your testers are from the same background, a lot of potential information could be overlooked.

When you create a new Flex project, you're given the option of deploying to the Web or to the desktop. When beginning a new project, you may not know where the end result will be, or you may want to deploy to both. No big deal, because creating a new project is easy. While it may have been some time since you created a Flex project, try making a new one, this time with a deployment to the desktop. In the next section, you'll be porting the `ContactManager` application to the desktop by creating a new project with its deployment type for the desktop and copying some of the code.

Creating an Adobe AIR Project

Create a new Flex project named `AddressBook` by selecting New→Flex Project. In the New Flex Project dialog box, under the "Application type" section, choose "Desktop application (runs in Adobe AIR)," as shown in Figure 15-11.

Figure 15-11. A new Flex project, using Adobe AIR

Once you click Finish, a new Adobe AIR project will be created. You might notice that the project in the Flex Navigator has a different icon and includes an XML file called *AddressBook-app.xml*. This XML file contains the settings for the desktop application, such as the window title—more on that in a moment.

The main application file that opens also has a small difference: instead of an `<mx:Application/>` tag at the application root, you'll see an `<mx:WindowedApplication/>` tag. The WindowedApplication is just like the Application component but contains additional functionality to help your Flex application work well on the desktop. Your new *AddressBook.mxml* file should look like the following:

```
<mx:WindowedApplication
    xmlns:mx="http://www.adobe.com/2006/mxml"
    layout="absolute">

</mx:WindowedApplication>
```

Now you have a new AIR project, and all you need to do is copy the code from the **ContactManager** application and place it in the **AddressBook** application. To do this, you can copy the files in the **ContactManager**'s source directory and paste them into the **AddressBook**'s source folder. Copy all files except the main application (*ContactManager.mxml*). Doing this makes the supporting style sheet, the external XML file, and the ContactViewer component available to the AIR application.

The next step is to copy the MXML code from *ContactManager.mxml* into *AddressBook.mxml*. One way to accomplish this is to copy all the code between the opening and closing `<mx:Application/>` tags in *ContactManager.mxml* and place that code between the opening and closing `<mx:WindowedApplication/>` tags in *AddressBook.mxml*. Then, in a separate operation, you can copy the attributes from the `<mx:Application/>` tag and paste them into the `<mx:WindowedApplication/>` tag.

Alternatively, you can copy and paste the entire contents of *ContactManager.mxml* into *AddressBook.mxml* and then change the `<mx:Application/>` tag to `<mx:WindowedApplication/>`.

The contents of the *AddressBook.mxml* file should then look like the following:

NOTE

An AIR application requires an `<mx:WindowedApplication/>` at its root in order to run properly.

```xml
<?xml version="1.0" encoding="utf-8"?>
<mx:WindowedApplication
    xmlns:mx="http://www.adobe.com/2006/mxml"
    xmlns:view="com.oreilly.view.*"
    layout="absolute"
    applicationComplete="contactsService.send()"
    viewSourceURL="srcview/index.html">

    <mx:Style source="styles.css"/>

    <mx:HTTPService id="contactsService"
        resultFormat="e4x"
        url="contacts.xml" />

    <mx:Parallel id="fadeAndResize">
        <mx:Dissolve id="dissolve"/>
        <mx:Resize id="fastResize" duration="300"/>
    </mx:Parallel>

    <mx:DataGrid id="contactsDataGrid"
        dataProvider="{contactsService.lastResult.contact}"
        selectedIndex="0"
        left="10"
        top="10"
        bottom="10"
        width="300"
        change="contactViewer.currentState = ''">
        <mx:columns>
            <mx:DataGridColumn headerText="First"
                dataField="firstName"/>
            <mx:DataGridColumn headerText="Last" dataField="lastName"/>
        </mx:columns>
    </mx:DataGrid>

    <view:ContactViewer id="contactViewer"
        contact="{contactsDataGrid.selectedItem}"
        x="318"
        y="10"
        resizeEffect="{fadeAndResize}"
        horizontalScrollPolicy="off"
        verticalScrollPolicy="off">
    </view:ContactViewer>

</mx:WindowedApplication>
```

Once you have that in place, you now have an Adobe AIR application. To see it, you can run it just like any other Flex application in Flex Builder, by selecting Run→Run AddressBook or by clicking the green Run button in the toolbar. The **AddressBook** application will run, and you'll see it in a native operating system window, as displayed in Figure 15-12 and Figure 15-13. Additionally, for Mac OS X you'll see an icon in the Dock, and for Windows you'll see an item in the taskbar.

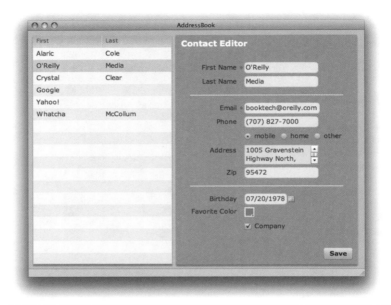

*Figure 15-12. The **AddressBook** application running on the desktop in Mac OS X*

*Figure 15-13. The **AddressBook** application running on the desktop in Windows Vista*

Customizing the Application

The icon that displays in the Dock or taskbar is just an AIR default. To replace this with a custom icon for deployment, you'll want to open the *AddressBook-app.xml* file. This file is the AIR application descriptor file template. Similar to the html-template folder used in Flex web applications, this file is a template for adjusting how your application will look. This file lets you adjust features like the words displayed in the window title bar, the look of the window, and the icon that's displayed in the taskbar or Dock.

You can easily figure out what options are available by reading the comments in the XML file. Many options are also commented out, and you can uncomment these and make changes as needed. For example, you can replace the default icon that your application displays. First, create a PNG graphic with a size of 128 pixels × 128 pixels, or download one I've created at *www.greenlike.com/flex/learning/projects/addressbook/address_icon.png*. Then, replace the following section of the descriptor file:

```
<!-- The icon the system uses for the application. For at least one
    resolution,
     specify the path to a PNG file included in the AIR package.
    Optional. -->
<!-- <icon>
        <image16x16></image16x16>
        <image32x32></image32x32>
        <image48x48></image48x48>
        <image128x128></image128x128>
    </icon> -->
```

with the following:

```
<!-- The icon the system uses for the application. For at least one
    resolution,
     specify the path to a PNG file included in the AIR package.
    Optional. -->
<icon>
    <image128x128>address_icon.png</image128x128>
</icon>
```

This enables (uncomments) the icon property and creates a single 128-pixel × 128-pixel icon that your application will use. Smaller versions of the icon will be automatically created for smaller sizes by scaling this largest image, but for the best results, you can create your own versions in a 48-pixels × 48-pixels size, 32-pixels × 32-pixels size, and 16-pixels × 16-pixels size.

> **NOTE**
>
> *While you can set the height and width of the window for your AIR application in the application descriptor file, you can also set a default height and width using the* **height** *and* **width** *properties of the WindowedApplication.*

Exporting an Installer

To export an installer for your application, you'll use the same command as for a web application, Project→Export Release Build. This opens the Export Release Build dialog box, just like if you were to export a release for a web application (see Figure 15-14).

Figure 15-14. Exporting an AIR application: Step 1

However, unlike the export dialog box for a web application, the AIR export dialog box requires some additional information. Specifically, an AIR application, because it's installed as a desktop application, requires a digital signature. Click Next in the Export Release Build dialog box, and you'll see the Digital Signature page, as shown in Figure 15-15. A digital certificate is a security measure, put in place to make certain that your application comes from you and wasn't modified by anyone else. For the install to work correctly, you'll need to select the first option, "Export and sign an AIR file with a digital certificate." This gives you the option to include a digital certificate you've procured from one of the various certificate sites or gives you the option to create your own. Unless you've gone through the process of obtaining a security certificate, you'll want to create your own by clicking the Create button.

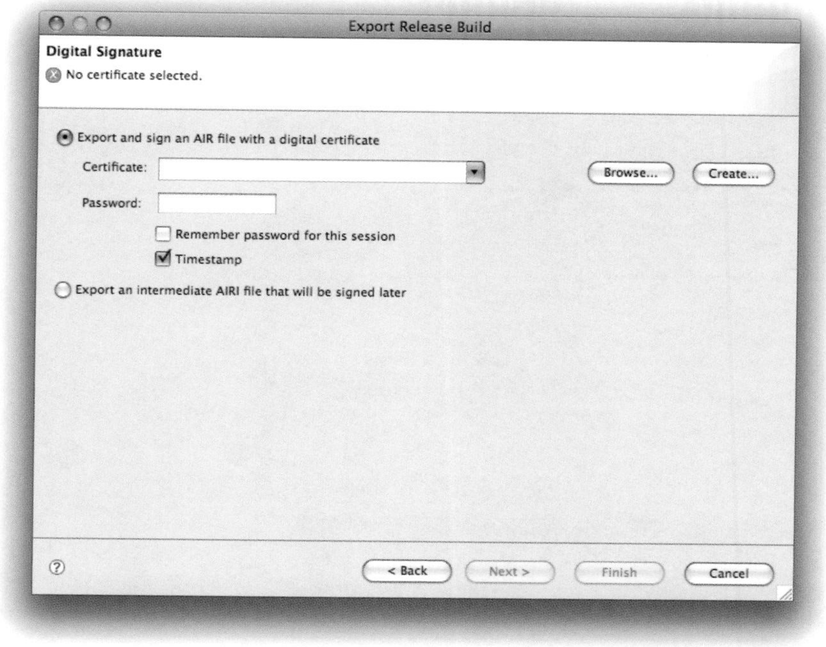

Figure 15-15. Exporting an AIR application: Step 2

About Digital Certificates

A *digital certificate* is a way to verify that a desktop application was not altered since the time it was *signed*. This certificate is in place as a security measure, and it's also used to verify the application publisher's identity.

When an AIR file is signed with a "self-signed" digital certificate, the publisher information can't be verified. Adobe AIR can tell that the installation has not been altered since it was signed, but you have no way to prove the identity of the publisher who signed the file. Because of this, the publisher will be displayed as "UNKNOWN" in the installation dialog box, as shown in Figure 15-21.

To learn about getting a certificate from one of the trusted authorities, check the following websites:

Thawte: *www.thawte.com*

Verisign: *www.verisign.com*

Microsoft Authenticode: *http://msdn2.microsoft.com/en-us/library/ms537364.aspx*

This prompts you with the dialog box shown in Figure 15-16, which lets you create a certificate for your application. All that is required is a publisher name and a password, as well as the certificate name. In this case, I've given the certificate a name of *addressbook.certificate*, though the name doesn't really matter. Be sure to remember this password, because you'll be required to enter it any time you use the certificate you're creating.

Figure 15-16. Exporting an AIR application: Step 3

Once you create your certificate, you'll return to the Export Release Build dialog box, where you'll be prompted to enter the password for your certificate again (see Figure 15-17). Once you've entered it, you'll continue to the last step of the process.

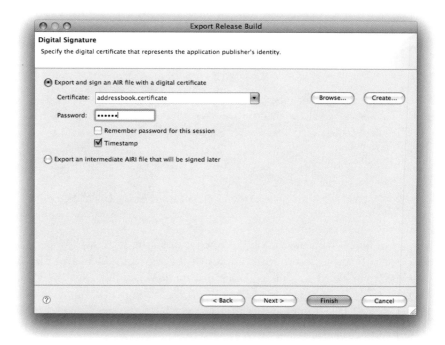

Figure 15-17. Exporting an AIR application: Step 4

The final step in creating an installer for your application is specifying the files you want to include (Figure 15-18). You'll want to ensure that you include all the necessary files for the application to run, but nothing extraneous. The compiled *.swf* file and the application descriptor file are always required, because these two files are necessary for the application to run. For the **AddressBook** application, you'll also need the *contacts.xml* file and the *addressbook_icon.png* file or other custom icon you choose to include. If you've chosen to include the source code, a directory for this code will also be included (typically called srcview).

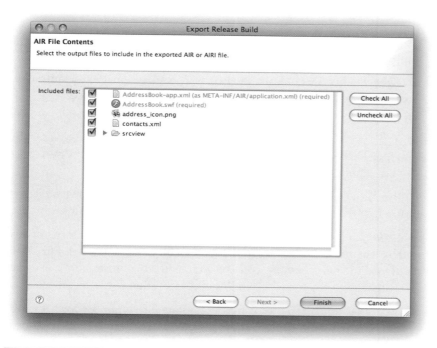

Figure 15-18. Exporting an AIR application: Step 5

Once you click Finish, a file called *AddressBook.air* will be created in the top level of the project. This is your installation file for distributing your application, similar to a *.dmg* file for a Mac or an *.exe* file for Windows.

This installation file will work if the machine has Adobe AIR installed. However, if it doesn't have AIR installed, the file won't do anything useful. Because of this limitation, you'll probably want to provide a more seamless installation process for people using your application. The easiest way to handle this is by using the Adobe AIR *install badge*, which is a convenient way to install your application using a simple, integrated dialog box (called a badge) on a web page. When people don't have Adobe AIR installed, they will be prompted to download and install it right from within the badge, making it a simple solution for people wanting to access your application.

Creating a Seamless Install

To create an installation badge, you'll need to get the necessary files. Luckily, a lot of code needed to enable this badge to work has been written for you. You can access these files at the following locations, assuming you've installed Flex Builder at the default location:

Mac: /Mac/Applications/Adobe Flex Builder 3/sdks/3.0.0/samples/badge

Windows: C:\Program Files\Adobe Flex Builder 3\sdks\3.0.0\samples\badge

The badge directories contain several files, but the ones to concern yourself with are the following:

AC_RunActiveContent.js: This is a JavaScript file that is used for automatically upgrading Flash Player.

badge.swf: This file contains the necessary code to enable the automatic installation of Adobe AIR if the client doesn't have it installed.

default_badge.html: This is a basic *.html* file that displays a badge for a seamless install of Adobe AIR.

test.jpg: This is a graphic that displays as a representation of the application in *default_badge.html*.

Note the instance of the string **My%20 Application**, *which is a URL-encoded string. Replace this with your application name—and if you have an application name that includes spaces, it will need to be URL-encoded as well, replacing any spaces with the characters* **%20**.

The other files included in this directory are for building your own *badge.swf* file, although that isn't typically necessary, and isn't needed for this example.

The *default_badge.html* file is a template you can use to create your own install badge on a website. You can test it by loading it in a browser. This *.html* file will load the image *test.jpg*, creating an Install Now button that a user can click to install the application—and Adobe AIR if that is not installed.

Remember that this set of files is just a template for you to use for your own application. You'll want replace this image with a screenshot of your own application so it gives the user an idea of what they should expect. You'll also want to have the page to install *your .air* file. Because this is just a placeholder, the *default_badge.html* file has a reference to a *myapp.air* file that doesn't actually exist. Just replace every reference of *myapp.air* with your own application's .air file, such as *AddressBook.air*. Also, be sure to replace every instance of the words "My Application" with the name of your application, because this will display in a message under the badge if Adobe AIR is not installed. (By default this message will read "In order to run My Application, this installer will also set up Adobe AIR.")

Ultimately, you'll probably want to integrate this sample badge code into your own website, although you can simply provide a link to the *default_badge.html* file.

NOTE

While this may seem like a lot of trouble to create the installation badge, remember that this is a cross-platform solution. If you were to create a desktop application using other means, you would—at the very least—be required to create a separate installation file for Mac, Windows, and Linux. Creating an installation badge is a comparatively simple process that lets you create one installation for all platforms.

When you've finished editing the *default_badge.html* file, just place these files on your server along with the *AddressBook.air* installation file. When someone loads this *.html* file in a browser, the install badge will display as in Figure 15-19. I've posted this file at *www.greenlike.com/flex/learning/projects/ addressbook/install/default_badge.html*. The process for installation is out-lined in Figure 15-20 through Figure 15-24.

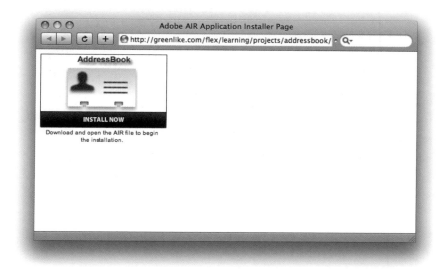

Figure 15-19. The install badge as shown in a web browser

Figure 15-20. Installing an AIR application: Step 1

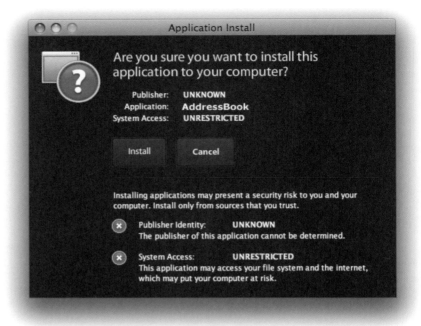

Figure 15-21. Installing an AIR application: Step 2

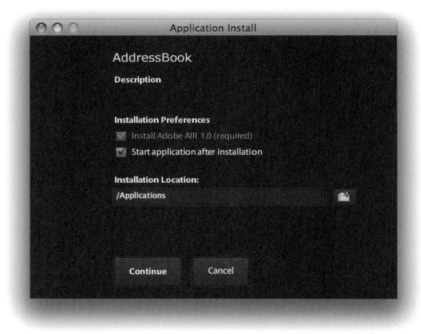

Figure 15-22. Installing an AIR application: Step 3

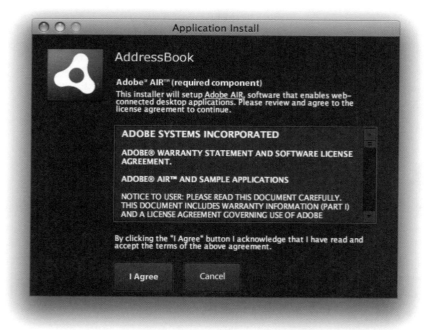

Figure 15-23. Installing an AIR application: Step 4

Figure 15-24. Installing an AIR application: Step 5

Adobe AIR can open up advanced functionality to your RIAs, including drag-and-drop to and from the desktop, local data storage in a database, and so on. The great thing is, all your current knowledge about developing Flex applications for the Web is not lost—you can apply everything you've learned in this book to AIR applications. If you plan to develop primarily for the desktop, I recommend getting a book focused on AIR development using Flex, because the features are too extensive to be covered in this book alone.

NOTE

To see more samples of Adobe AIR applications, point your browser to http://labs. adobe.com/technologies/air/samples.

Now You're Cooking

You've come a long way. Once you start coding your own Flex applications, you may find you need a little help. Need a quick and dirty solution? Try the Flex Cookbook online at *www.adobe.com/go/flex_cookbook*. You don't have to be an expert to get the job done—here you can search for and grab snippets of code to solve your problems (at least those dealing with Flex). You'll also learn a lot along the way.

If you'd like a more tangible reference, grab a copy of the ***Flex 3 Cookbook*** (O'Reilly).

Summary

Congratulations are in order! You've now completed the final step in developing rich Internet applications in Adobe Flex. You've gone from getting acquainted with Flex and Flex Builder to learning about MXML and ActionScript, and you've acquired the skills necessary to develop complete applications such as connecting to data and building a flexible user interface. You've learned to customize your applications using filters, transitions, and CSS. Finally, in this chapter, you gained the skills to deploy your applications on the Web and the desktop. I hope you've enjoyed the book, and I hope to see some of the great applications you'll no doubt create with this powerful—and fun—technology.

INDEX

Design mode, 17, 23
  adding components, 24
  canvas, 23
  controls, 25–26
  CSS files, 228–229
  events, 65
  layout containers, 26–27
  moving components, 24
  MXML code, 37
  navigators, 27–28, 164
  properties, 28–36
  user interface, 35–36
desktop deployment, 6, 239, 251
  creating projects, 251–254
  customizing applications, 255
  exporting installers, 256–259
  seamless installs, 260–263
destinations in data binding, 79
development speed, 6
device fonts, 199
digital certificates, 257–258
disabledSkin property, 233
dispatched events, 63
DisplacementMapFilter, 216
display formatting, 132–136
display lists, 95
  accessing children, 96
  adding and removing children, 96–97
  operation, 95–96
  rearranging children, 98–99
displaying external images, 166–167
displayName property, 85
Dissolve effect, 200, 203–205, 214
divided boxes, 103
documentation, 66
domain property, 124
doSomeMath function, 55
dot notation, 48–49
double quotes (")
  for attributes, 49
  in curly braces, 80

download time issues, 247–249
downSkin property, 233
dragEnabled property, 153
dragging and dropping in lists, 153–154
dragMoveEnabled property, 154
dropEnabled property, 153
dropShadowEnabled property, 217
DropShadowFilter filter, 216
duration property, 202–203, 232

E

E4X technique, 145, 147
Eclipse editor, 13
Eclipse plug-ins, 14–16, 24
ECMAScript language, 145
Edit State Properties dialog box, 184
editable property, 117
effects
  action, 213–214
  common, 197–200
  composite, 203–204
  customizing, 202–203
  effective, 210
  navigator containers, 200–201
  properties, 204–209
  sound, 209–210
  target filters, 214–215
EmailValidators, 122–123
embedding
  assets, 230–233
  fonts, 199–200
Enable integration with browser navigation option, 244
Enable snapping option, 24
Enable view source option, 245–246
enabled property, 33
equal signs (=) for assignment, 49
error messages for validators, 120–126
errorString property, 126
escape characters, 80
Event class, 67
event listeners, 60

projects *(continued)*
    saving, 36
    structure, 21
properties. *See* attributes and properties
Properties panel
    color pickers, 87–88
    skinning, 233–234
    styles, 219–221, 224, 229
    views, 28–29
property attribute
    AnimateProperty, 209
    StringValidator, 120
public modifier, 51
Publish Application Source dialog box, 245
push method, 130
pushing data, 157

Q

query property, 151
&quot character, 80
quotes (")
    for attributes, 42, 49
    in curly braces, 80

R

RadioButton **tag, 118**
RadioButtons, 26
readability, formatting for, 87
rearranging children, 98–99
RegExpValidators, 126
registration state, 179–181
regular expressions, 126
relative positioning, 94–95
relative sizing, 100
relativeTo property, 182
release builds, exporting, 244–246
remote objects, 157
RemoteObject components, 156–157
remove filters, 214

removeChild method, 97–99
RemoveChild tag, 182, 184, 213
RemoveChildAction effect, 213
removedEffect behavior, 198
removing
    children, 96–97
    components, 183–184
required property, 118, 121
requiredFieldError property, 121–122
Resize effect, 207, 215
Resize tag, 202
resizeEffect behavior, 198, 201–204, 211
resizing
    CheckBoxes, 102
    ContactManager, 201–204
    events, 65
restrict property, 131
restricting input, 131–132
result event, 184
return keyword, 54
reusability, functions for, 50
reverse domain naming, 190
rich forms
    creating, 117–120
    formatting display data, 132–136
    restricting input, 131–132
    validating data. *See* validating data
rich Internet applications (RIAs), 1, 5–6
right property, 110, 113
rollOut events, 65
rollOutEffect behavior, 198
rollOver events, 65
rollOverEffect behavior, 198
root tags, 38, 42, 142, 144
Rotate effect, 208
rounding property
    CurrencyFormatter, 132
    NumberFormatter, 135
rowCount property, 139
rows in constraints-based layout, 113–115
rowSpan property, 104

The Authoritative Resource